THE
SIMPLE
TRUTH
BIBLE

ONENESS WITH GOD

SIN & SEPARATION

CONSEQUENCES & CRYING OUT

GOD HEARS & RESTORES

youthministry.com/TOGETHER

THE SIMPLE TRUTH BIBLE
The Best Minute of Your Day

© 2013 Group Publishing, Inc. / 000 0001 0362 4853

group.com
simplyyouthministry.com

Credits
Executive Developer: Nadim Najm
Associate Developer: Tim Levert
Chief Creative Officer: Joani Schultz
Editor: Rob Cunningham
Cover Art and Production: Veronica Preston

ISBN   978-0-7644-9139-9

15 14   20 19 18 17

Printed in the U.S.A.

CONTENTS

We're sure you've noticed, this is a pretty big book. And rather than add a normal table of contents that shows you just how big the book is, we're going to change things up a little. All of the devotionals in this book are numbered...all 366 of them. Rather than list out each passage of Scripture covered in the book, we've decided to provide you with a few articles that will help you get the most out of each devotional. Below, you'll find where each article is located in this book. We encourage you to read these.

We've also included an index of all the verses used in this devotional. We've organized it based on each of the four themes of God's story. You can read more about these themes on p. 1.

This book was put together by a bunch of our friends in the trenches of youth ministry. Men and women, youth pastors, volunteers, designers, business professionals, students, and more contributed to this book. They love Jesus and care enough about you to share a little of their life experience—and a lot about God's truths found in the Bible. Here's a bit about each person involved in bringing you closer to Jesus through this book.

INTRODUCTION

Congratulations! You are holding in your hands a book that can change your life. OK, the book won't change your life, but the God who loves you will use this book to help you become who he created you to be. And that's a pretty big deal.

This book is a little different from other Bibles you may have read. It's written so you can spend a few minutes each day and have a legit experience with God. Here's how we've organized each devotion:

- A Bible passage with a short explanation to read and a thought to ponder
- "Talking With God" — a guide to help you pray
- "A Little Extra" — if you have more than a few minutes to spend, there's an extra activity to help you digest the truth of the passage
- "The Big Picture" — an icon that indicates which stage of the Bible's story the passage reflects

We've also sprinkled some articles throughout the book that may be helpful in your faith journey. Topics include making the Bible smaller, prayer, journaling, sharing your God-story, and a few others. It's a good idea to read "Making the Bible Smaller" (see p. 1) before you dive into the devotions, but you can jump right in if you prefer. As long as you're spending time seeking God, there really isn't a wrong way to do it!

Bottom line, the folks who have written devotions for this book love Jesus and love students, and all of them want you to fall more deeply in love with Jesus. Following Jesus is the best thing you can ever do. It's an adventure that fills the deepest needs of your life. And it's worth it. You'll never regret chasing after Jesus.

And that's the simple truth.

MAKING THE BIBLE SMALLER

THE BIBLE IS PROBABLY THE BIGGEST BOOK YOU'LL EVER READ.

It's so big, you might think you'll never make sense of it. So let's look at a way to break it down into smaller chunks that can help you understand it a little better.

The Bible tells stories in four stages, and you can see them in the story of Adam and Eve in Genesis 1–3:

1. **Oneness with God.** Adam and Eve were in perfect relationship with God, each other, and the rest of creation. They were living the good life in the Garden of Eden.

2. **Sin and separation.** Adam and Eve chose to sin, trusting their way instead of God's way. Sin made them feel shame and pushed them away from God.

3. **Consequences and crying out.** The price of Adam and Eve's sin included having to work the ground to get food (Adam), feeling pain during childbirth (Eve), and getting kicked out of the Garden of Eden (both).

4. **God hears and restores oneness.** God loved Adam and Eve, and even though they chose to reject him, God provided for them and fixed their broken relationships.

The story of the Bible is every person's story. These four stages are repeated over and over throughout the Bible. You can see the stages in the lives of King David, the nation of Israel, the disciples, Paul, and, if we're honest, in our own lives. If we learn to look for these stages as we read the Bible, it will begin to make more sense and feel smaller.

We've added a section in each devotion called "The Big Picture," which includes a small icon that represents one of the four stages. Look for the icon, and think about how you see the specific stage in the passage for the day. If you journal (see pp. 90-91), include the stage icon when you reference a Bible verse.

After you've read for a while, you may notice that the four stages aren't equally represented. There are a lot more passages about stage four—God hears and restores. Guess what the central theme of the entire Bible is? Yep, God loves us, hears our cries, and always takes the initiative to restore us.

SO KEEP READING, AND WATCH THE BIBLE GET SMALLER.

"But forget all that—it is nothing compared to what I am going to do. For I am about to do something new. See, I have already begun! Do you not see it? I will make a pathway through the wilderness. I will create rivers in the dry wasteland." Isaiah 43:18-19

GOD HEARS & RESTORES

"Forget all that." What was God talking about here? The Israelites had been recounting all the garbage going on in their lives—and there had been a lot of it. Life was not going well for them. But that's NOT what God was telling them to forget. God was telling them to forget about all the amazingness he had already done: conquering kings, splitting seas, rescuing them over and over again. God was saying, "Yeah, remember all that? Forget it. It's NOTHING in comparison to what I'm doing next!" Translated into our pop culture, it's as if God was saying, "I've wowed the judges on this reality competition show; I'm a shoe-in to win this whole thing. But I'm gonna kick it up a notch for my next performance!"

TALKING WITH GOD

Think about some of the amazingness God has done in your life so far. Thank God for that. Get specific. Then spend a few minutes expressing your gratefulness for the amazingness that's about to come.

A LITTLE EXTRA

Sometimes journals feel like homework, but they can help us remember what God has done and consider what he might do in the future. Create a photo journal using social media—or just a folder of images on your phone or computer. When God does something cool or amazing, snap a photo of it. Title your album "God Moments" or something else that resonates with you. On days when you are lamenting what's happening in your life, open that journal. Take a look at all God has already done—big and small—and then realize that it pales in comparison to what's next.

GOD HEARS
& RESTORES

VERSE 2:
Acts 1:8

A LITTLE EXTRA

Think of three friends who need to hear about Jesus. Brainstorm ways you can talk about Jesus in your next conversation with them. Start praying for them, and begin the conversations today!

"But you will receive power when the Holy Spirit comes upon you. And you will be my witnesses, telling people about me everywhere—in Jerusalem, throughout Judea, in Samaria, and to the ends of the earth." Acts 1:8

These are the last words Jesus spoke to his disciples, which is a good indication that what he says here is a big deal! These words contain both a promise and a plan.

Jesus promises that as his follower, you have the very Spirit of God living inside you, and the power of the Holy Spirit goes with you through every twist and turn in your day. This means that you are never alone. God is with you *always*. So whether your life is stacked and packed with fun, or you feel like you're drowning in really tough, painful stuff, God's Spirit lives inside you, empowering you to live each day for his glory.

But this verse also contains an amazing plan: Jesus' plan for spreading the good news of his gospel message. And this plan involves YOU! *"You will be my witnesses, telling people about me everywhere."* What an incredible privilege *and* responsibility you have when it comes to sharing Jesus' life-giving message of grace with everyone around you.

TALKING WITH GOD
Notice that Jesus' plan here involves you actively *"telling people"* about him. Who in your life needs to know more about Jesus? Have a conversation with God right now about who you could share your faith with today. Then go do it.

Don't let anyone think less of you because you are young. Be an example to all believers in what you say, in the way you live, in your love, your faith, and your purity. 1 Timothy 4:12

There's only one way to prevent people from thinking less of you because of your age, according to this verse. It's not by debating, arguing, or demanding respect. It's merely by your example. Regardless of their age, people will think more of you when your life exemplifies the way a Christ-follower ought to live.

People look at five areas of your life: how you speak (your language, vocabulary); how you live day to day (your responsibility, work ethic); how you show love and respect for others (parents, siblings, teachers, employers, friends); how you follow (or don't follow) Jesus Christ; and the state of your heart (your dating guidelines, friendship choices, extracurricular choices). When you think about this verse, remember that the way you live reveals what you believe.

TALKING WITH GOD

Spend some time talking with God about the kind of example you are setting. Listen for what God reveals—REALLY listen. Don't just assume you're setting a good example because you are mostly a good person compared with the teenagers around you. Invite God to speak truth into your life, even about the little areas of your example that you might not think much of (such as how you respond to your parents or the quality of your homework).

ONENESS WITH GOD

A LITTLE EXTRA

Make a grid or a digital spreadsheet with four columns and five rows. In the first column, list each example on its own row (speech, life, love, faith, purity). In the next column, list ways you have set a solid example. In the third column, write down ways in which your example falls short. In the final column, write a quick action point for growing in that specific area.

GOD HEARS & RESTORES

A LITTLE EXTRA

Go find something heavy. Try to lift it by yourself. If you can pick it up, go find something heavier; if you can't, go find a friend to help. Why is it easier for two to lift something? Why would Jesus invite you to share life with him? Take the risk to trust Jesus enough to let him into all areas of your life.

Do you ever feel like you're not enough? One of the most significant changes in culture is how much busier teenagers are now compared to 20 years ago. Academics, sports, clubs, volunteering, friendships, family—these things have many students going crazy! And when you try to work church into that list, it often adds guilt and shame instead of offering relief.

Do you want to slow down and rest? Read Jesus' words in today's passage:

Then Jesus said, "Come to me, all of you who are weary and carry heavy burdens, and I will give you rest. Take my yoke upon you. Let me teach you, because I am humble and gentle at heart, and you will find rest for your souls. For my yoke is easy to bear, and the burden I give you is light."
Matthew 11:28-30

A yoke is a big wooden tool that ties two animals together so they can share the workload. Now read Jesus' words again—out loud.

You are invited to share life with Jesus. He wants to help you carry your workload and teach you how to live differently. Interested?

TALKING WITH GOD

Pray this kind of prayer: *Jesus, your words are refreshing. I want to have rest. I want to share all of my life with you; teach me how. Help me grow in my trust in you, so I can live and reveal your kingdom in all areas of my life.*

"Don't be afraid, for I am with you. Don't be discouraged, for I am your God. I will strengthen you and help you. I will hold you up with my victorious right hand." Isaiah 41:10

Think about a time you were really, REALLY scared. It might have been something as simple as a roller coaster you didn't want to ride—or something as serious as the illness of a family member.

What scares us? Usually it's the helpless feeling we have—whether it's being at the mercy of the roller coaster about to plunge over the top of the hill, or knowing that we can do nothing to bring healing to someone we love.

God answers all our feelings of helplessness in this verse. Read the promises in this Scripture again:

- I am with you (you are not alone)
- Don't be discouraged (someone bigger is at work here: God)
- I will strengthen you (in your weakness, God is strong—see 2 Corinthians 12:10)
- I WILL help you (it's not a maybe; it's a promise)
- I will hold you up (you don't have to stand in your own power and strength)
- …with my victorious right hand (victory, success is assured)

TALKING WITH GOD

Pray this passage by naming yourself and inserting your fears into the verses. Picture God talking directly to you about whatever is causing fear in your life right now.

GOD HEARS & RESTORES

VERSE 5:
Isaiah 41:10

A LITTLE EXTRA

Write each promise in this passage on its own sheet of paper, adhesive note, or note card. Decorate your room, car, locker, or bathroom with these promises. Meditate on them and memorize them, and trust God to protect you when you are afraid.

GOD HEARS
& RESTORES

VERSE 6:
John 10:10

A LITTLE EXTRA

There's also a warning in this verse. Who is this thief that wants to rob you of a rich, satisfying life? Satan, the evil one, who spreads deception, destruction, and death.

Make a list of any parts of your life where you are buying the evil one's lies about where to find true, lasting fulfillment. Ask God to help you turn away from those lies and trust him more so you can more fully experience the rich, satisfying life God designed you to live.

"The thief's purpose is to steal and kill and destroy. My purpose is to give them a rich and satisfying life." John 10:10

So what does a rich and satisfying life look like? The accumulation of more and more self-indulgent toys? Having a hot girlfriend or boyfriend? The freedom to do whatever you want? That's the message our culture wants to sell you. But don't be fooled.

According to the Bible, a rich and satisfying life is one that is centered on God. When you trust God, many incredible, life-changing gifts flood into your life. Here are just a few:

- The gift of eternal life with God in heaven (1 John 5:13)
- The right to become God's child, with 24/7 access to the Heavenly Father (Romans 8:38-39)
- Power and strength to get through anything (Isaiah 40:29-31; Acts 1:8)
- The assurance that God will never leave you alone (Hebrews 13:5)
- A future and a hope that is good (Jeremiah 29:11)

Pretty cool, huh? An authentic, intimate relationship with the God of the universe gives you deep, soul-satisfying peace and joy and leaves the temporary thrills of money, sex, and power in the dust.

TALKING WITH GOD

Zero in on one of God's gifts listed above and thank him for it right now.

GOD HEARS
& RESTORES

"For it is my Father's will that all who see his Son and believe in him should have eternal life. I will raise them up at the last day." John 6:40

Have you ever been rejected? Totally not fun. We all need and desire to be loved, respected, and valued. Most times, rejection happens because people want us to be something or someone we're not. The cool thing about God is that he doesn't place unrealistic expectations on us. All God wants us to do is simply come to him. And when we come to God, he promises to never reject us. No matter who you are or what you've done, when you place your trust in Christ, God welcomes you with open arms and promises to never let you go. In him, you have everything you need. So even when friends reject you, let you down, or don't accept you, remember that God loves you no matter what, and God desires for you to spend eternity with him.

TALKING WITH GOD

You may be in a place where you're looking for love, validation, and acceptance. Take a few moments today and talk to God about how you feel. Ask God to help you sense his love for you. Ask God to teach you how to not focus on trying to please the audience of many (friends, classmates, teammates, society), but to focus on the audience of one: God.

VERSE 7:
John 6:40

A LITTLE EXTRA

God has a plan and purpose for your life. You'll fulfill that plan and purpose best when you stay connected to him. God will lead, guide, and direct your path. Read John 15:5—a reminder of what happens when we stay connected to the Father. Talk to a spiritual leader in your life about things you can do to stay connected with God.

ONENESS WITH GOD

A LITTLE EXTRA

Sometimes we believe what we hear. Many of us hear lots of negative words and fewer positive words. Find time today to look in a mirror and say to yourself, *"I am God's dearly loved son/ daughter. God loves me, is proud of me, and is pleased with me."*

After his baptism, as Jesus came up out of the water, the heavens were opened and he saw the Spirit of God descending like a dove and settling on him. And a voice from heaven said, "This is my dearly loved Son, who brings me great joy."
Matthew 3:16–17

Has anyone ever expressed pride in you—maybe a coach, a teacher, a mentor, a youth leader, a parent, family member, or a really close friend? Doesn't it feel really cool to hear someone say words of affirmation, encouragement, and support? God wants to let you know how much he feels that way, too!

This passage is primarily about Jesus getting baptized, but it is also about God delighting in his Son's faithfulness and obedience. God says three distinct things that all of us desire to hear from our loved ones and people who care about us. First, God affirms his relationship with Jesus: *"This is my dearly loved Son."* Second, God affirms his love for Jesus: *"loved Son."* Third, God affirms the joy Jesus brings to him: *"who brings me great joy!"* Jesus received this affirmation from his Father before beginning his ministry and facing Satan's temptations in the wilderness. Bottom line: God knows what we need to hear and when we need to hear it. We simply have to place ourselves in a position to hear God clearly.

TALKING WITH GOD

Reread today's passage. Thank God that he loves you, is proud of you, and is pleased with you. Now allow yourself to believe those words.

ONENESS
WITH GOD

But thank God! He has made us his captives and continues to lead us along in Christ's triumphal procession. Now he uses us to spread the knowledge of Christ everywhere, like a sweet perfume.
2 Corinthians 2:14

Have you ever smelled a sweet perfume or a favorite food that almost pulled you in? Saying that Christ-followers were like *"sweet perfume"* was an attempt to quickly explain what it was like to be around them.

There is something very different about followers of Christ that is hard for people to explain. When we begin this faith adventure, God comes and lives inside of us. Imagine being in the middle of a mall, or your school, or some place with lots of people gathered. If some of those people are Christ-followers and have God's Spirit living inside of them, should you be able to tell? Should it be obvious to everyone?

There IS a difference when God lives in you. Other people can't explain it, but they are drawn to the hope, the love, the peace, the gentleness, the patience—the sweet perfume. That is a perfect way to explain how God uses us to spread the knowledge of Christ everywhere.

A LITTLE EXTRA

Jesus explained in some word pictures what it is like to have God inside of you. You can read these descriptions of his followers in his Sermon on the Mount, found in Matthew 5:13-16.

TALKING WITH GOD

Offer this prayer today: *God, I want to be a sweet perfume that tells people about you everywhere I go. Help me live the kind of life that reveals your kingdom to others. Help me use every opportunity to spread the knowledge of Christ.*

SIN & SEPARATION

A LITTLE EXTRA

Write "In My Place: Isaiah 53" on your bathroom mirror. (Make sure you use washable marker or something that will wash off—or you'll need someone to stand in your place with your mom!) Each day when you look in the mirror and see those words, remember to thank God for the sacrifice he made.

He was despised and rejected—a man of sorrows, acquainted with deepest grief. We turned our backs on him and looked the other way. He was despised, and we did not care. Yet it was our weaknesses he carried; it was our sorrows that weighed him down. And we thought his troubles were a punishment from God, a punishment for his own sins! Isaiah 53:3-4

Have you ever been blamed for something you didn't do? How did that feel? Did anyone commiserate (look it up) with you—tell you how terrible the situation was? Was anyone frustrated on your behalf at the injustice you were enduring? Did anyone take the accusations to heart, believing you really DID do what you were accused of doing? Did people assume you brought it all on yourself?

That's how it was for Jesus—except that he chose to carry those accusations. It's as if Jesus went to the backbiters and said, "Hey, I *want* you to make up these stories about me," knowing that it would take all the bite out of their stories about us.

Have you ever had someone take the blame for you? You have now.

TALKING WITH GOD

As you pray, think about the completeness of how Jesus took your place: the accusations, the lies, the scandal, the loss of friendships, the ridicule of well-respected people, and finally the cross. Thank him, humbly and honestly, for standing in your place.

Andrew went to find his brother, Simon, and told him, "We have found the Messiah" (which means "Christ"). John 1:41

Some Christians don't come from church-going, pew-sitting, hymn-singing families. Some come from families full of beer-drinking, tobacco-chewing, bodybuilding brawlers that even the mafia considers crazy—seriously. When the mafia thinks your family is crazy, you know you're dealing with some serious dysfunction.

But even in the roughest communities, God can change lives. Even the wildest, craziest families can experience new life through Jesus. Even the people least likely to sit in a church pew can find themselves there one day.

People who come from this kind of background usually can't keep their mouth shut about Jesus. This salvation message is such good news, they can't keep it to himself. They tell their brothers, sisters, parents, friends, neighbors, classmates—everyone they know!

If you, too, have met Jesus, then you have a story to tell about your encounter with him as your Savior. Maybe it was dramatic; maybe it was simple. It doesn't matter! Spread the good news!

TALKING WITH GOD

Think back to a time when you had a deep, meaningful time with Jesus. Maybe it was during a worship service, at a retreat, or on a mission trip. What happened? What was the trigger? How did you feel? What did you learn about God? Spend some time right now thanking God for your personal relationship with him. Then go talk to a friend or family member who isn't a Christ-follower.

GOD HEARS & RESTORES

VERSE 11:
John 1:41

A LITTLE EXTRA

Check out the website gospeljourney.com. Consider sending the link to someone who isn't a Christ-follower and asking that person to watch the video. Make sure you ask them later what they thought of it.

GOD HEARS & RESTORES

A LITTLE EXTRA

Make a list of three people that you typically "pass by" on your campus. Find a Christ-following friend and commit to noticing the people on your list this week—and maybe even serving them in some way. Learn how to stop, slow down, and be more aware.

"Now which of these three would you say was a neighbor to the man who was attacked by bandits?" Jesus asked. The man replied, "The one who showed him mercy." Then Jesus said, "Yes, now go and do the same." Luke 10:36–37

Many people know the story of the Good Samaritan, but some people miss the importance of the details. Two very religious people walked right by the man who had been attacked. The one who stopped was probably the last person Jesus' audience expected to stop and offer help. It's important to recognize that Jesus told the parable in response to a question from an expert at religious law who was trying to find a loophole for loving people—and not loving other people.

Experts in the law are sometimes not very merciful, because their lives are guided by rules. Rules aren't always bad, but in typical fashion, Jesus turned the whole conversation upside-down. Whatever the expert in religious law was trying to get away with, Jesus wasn't having any of it! Jesus made it perfectly clear that sometimes rule-followers can miss great opportunities to do ministry—including the two guys who passed by the victim and the guy who asked the question in the first place.

TALKING WITH GOD

Ask God to show you some people in your life that you "pass by." Pray for the boldness to reach out and the wisdom to know how to best meet their needs.

"But when the Father sends the Advocate as my representative—that is, the Holy Spirit—he will teach you everything and will remind you of everything I have told you." John 14:26

Has there ever been a time in your life when you needed someone to look out for you? Or maybe you needed help or comfort, and no one was there for you? That can be a very lonely feeling. In today's verse, Jesus promises an advocate—God's Holy Spirit—who would comfort us, help us, and remind us of everything God promised us. This Advocate also would reassure us that we're never alone—someone to help us, protect us, and care for us.

The Greek meaning of *advocate* is an ancient term used in warfare. Greek warriors went onto the battlefield in pairs, standing back-to-back, covering each other's blind side. The Holy Spirit isn't just our companion; he is our battle partner as we navigate the struggles of life. God sent his Holy Spirit to lead us, guide us, and always have our back.

TALKING WITH GOD

As you spend time in prayer today, be still and listen to your Advocate and Counselor. Ask the Holy Spirit to focus your spirit so you will be able to hear the Father's voice. And remember that as a follower of Jesus, you're never alone.

VERSE 13:
John 14:26

A LITTLE EXTRA

In school you have a guidance counselor to help you make decisions about your personal and educational needs, while providing information about colleges and other life choices. Go say "thank you" to your school guidance counselor today, and every time you pass his or her office, remember that God's Spirit is your greatest counselor. And with the Holy Spirit, you never need a hall pass!

ONENESS WITH GOD

VERSE 14:
1 Timothy 6:12

A LITTLE EXTRA

With your parents' permission, grab a friend who's a Christ-follower and watch the sports movie *Miracle*. In this movie, a team that had every reason to quit continued to fight and came away victorious. As you watch the movie, notice the people who tried to fill the team with doubt. Talk with your friend about the parallels between the movie and the adventure of following Jesus.

Fight the good fight for the true faith. Hold tightly to the eternal life to which God has called you, which you have confessed so well before many witnesses. 1 Timothy 6:12

What are you willing to fight for? What does "fighting a good fight" mean to you? In life, the more passionate you are about something, the harder you're willing to fight for it, and the more committed you are to it. We all fight for things—but is what you're fighting for worth it?

Imagine for a moment what your life would be like if you were passionate about Jesus—or even more passionate than you are today. No matter how hard things got, there would be a determination and motivation to live a life pleasing to God.

When it comes to living a Jesus-centered life, it's a daily fight. However, the fight isn't with God; it's within us. The phrase *"hold tightly"* means holding on to the truth that God has given eternal life and forgiveness for all who trust Jesus. When we allow the Holy Spirit to lead us and live within us, we never lose the fight!

TALKING WITH GOD

Tell God about the things that worry you. Turn them over to God. Resist the urge to try to handle things on your own. Commit to letting God fight your battles with you.

You should clothe yourselves instead with the beauty that comes from within, the unfading beauty of a gentle and quiet spirit, which is so precious to God. 1 Peter 3:4

What does it mean to focus on inner beauty? If that's what God wants us to do, why do we focus so much on our outward appearances?

We sometimes think other people's opinions are more important than God's opinions. We're wrong. Most people judge us on our outward appearance instead of who we are on the inside—the beauty that comes from within. But God doesn't. God loves us for who we are, inside and out. God cares about us, more than we can fully realize. He loved us even before we were born.

So why try to impress other people with outside appearances? Focus on God. Focus more on being beautiful on the inside than on outward appearances.

TALKING WITH GOD

Pray this kind of prayer: *Jesus, thank you for caring about me. But I need your help. Please help me focus on being beautiful on the inside. Help me trust you, and help me care about your opinion, which matters more than other people's opinions. I love you, Jesus—and thank you for loving me.*

VERSE 15:
1 Peter 3:4

A LITTLE EXTRA

Get a blank sheet of paper and write GOD in the middle of it, because God is our center focus. Then, draw a heart around it, because we love him. Next, cut off everything around the heart, because we want to focus on the inside more than the outside. Put that heart somewhere as a reminder of what's most important. And whenever you look at yourself in the mirror, don't just look at your hair or your clothes or your appearance; look into your own eyes and remember that God's opinion is more important than anyone else's. Always remember that.

ONENESS
WITH GOD

A LITTLE EXTRA

Do an online search for "names of God." You'll find "Alpha and Omega" on that list, plus lots of other names. Ask God to reveal himself to you and to remind you of who he is as you continue on your faith journey.

"I am the Alpha and the Omega—the beginning and the end," says the Lord God. "I am the one who is, who always was, and who is still to come—the Almighty One." Revelation 1:8

Imagine receiving this letter from God...

Let me introduce myself! I am the Lord your God. I am everything you will ever need and then some. I am the One who's been in existence from the beginning (the Alpha) of your life until the end (the Omega) of your life. With me, there is no need to worry about one single thing. I am the One who will do just what I said I was going to do. I am God, the Father of the universe, the ruler of your past, present, and future. Without me you have nothing that is eternal, nothing that can change your life, nothing with any true substance, and nothing that can save you from the penalty of sin. Do not fear anything, because I am the Lord your God—the EVERLASTING and the ALMIGHTY. All power is in my hands. So whatever you need today, just ask me and trust me.

TALKING WITH GOD

In Revelation 1:8, God uses alpha and omega—the first and last letters of the Greek alphabet—to express just how much bandwidth he has. Today, make or renew your commitment to give God your entire life. Honor the One who is the beginning and the end of all existence, wisdom, and power.

Think of a time when you went to the doctor because you didn't feel well. And there's that space before you and your parents decide to make the appointment, when you're trying to decide if you need help or not. Maybe you'd had a stomachache for days. Or maybe it was a weird, itchy rash that was mysteriously spreading. Or a deep cough that kept you awake all night long, making you a zombie throughout your waking hours.

At some point, you or your parents had to reach a decision point: *Whatever this is, it's beyond our ability to treat it.* You had to get help from an expert healer.

When Jesus heard this, he told them, "Healthy people don't need a doctor—sick people do. I have come to call not those who think they are righteous, but those who know they are sinners." Mark 2:17

Jesus is the sin-healer, the one who wants to restore you to amazing wholeness. But that healing implies that, well, you're sick. Are you ready to acknowledge that you're a sinner in need of the forgiveness and healing that only Jesus can provide?

TALKING WITH GOD

Take a moment to express to God your need for spiritual healing. This takes some courage, because we often spend so much effort convincing ourselves and everyone else that we're "fine." Admit that you can't fix yourself and you need an expert. Tell God that you know he's the only expert able to provide the healing you need from your sin.

GOD HEARS
& RESTORES

VERSE 17:
Mark 2:17

A LITTLE EXTRA

Make a confidential list of specific sins, attitudes, and patterns for which you need God's healing. Write a sentence or two for each about how that sin, attitude, or pattern developed, and end each with a written request that God would forgive and provide freedom.

VERSE 18:
Mark 8:36

A LITTLE EXTRA

Get a piece of paper and make two lists. Create one list of things that can hurt your soul. Then create a list of things that can nurture your soul. Which list will you choose? Share the lists with a friend or adult you trust, and ask them to hold you accountable.

"And what do you benefit if you gain the whole world but lose your own soul?" Mark 8:36

What do you want out of this life? Money? Fame? Relationships? Popularity? True Love? Success? Relationship with Jesus?

What are you willing to sacrifice to get what you want? Money? Fame? Relationships? Popularity? True Love? Success? Relationship with Jesus?

Is there anything this world has to offer that's worth giving up your own soul? Our culture would say there are many things worth pursuing at all costs, but God disagrees.

Be wise. This world will promise you anything in exchange for everything and leave you with nothing. The amazing thing about a relationship with Jesus is that while we may think we're asked to give up everything, we receive everything that matters, everything that makes a difference in the long run. Hold on to your soul, and seek God's perspective on what is worth pursuing and what can be abandoned because it will pass away.

TALKING WITH GOD

Pray this kind of prayer today: *Lord, make your wants my wants. I want your desires to be my desires. I want your plans to be my plans. The things of this world can look so good and so appealing. Sometimes it's tough for me to trust that your way is the best. Protect my soul, Lord. I can't do this without you.*

Obviously, I'm not trying to win the approval of people, but of God. If pleasing people were my goal, I would not be Christ's servant. Galatians 1:10

You've likely been there. We all have. That awkward moment when you say something about Jesus and suddenly you are very uncool. Whether those you're talking to just roll their eyes before shrugging and changing the subject, or they rudely shut you down cold, either way, you know the feeling. Awkward.

Well, you can shout from the rooftops that AWKWARD IS AWESOME when it comes to being an all-out, fully committed Jesus-follower. And here's why: *Because pleasing God is truly, totally, and eternally far more important than pleasing people!*

Jesus has told us over and over in Scripture that it's our job to tell others about his message of grace and forgiveness. (Check out Romans 10:14, John 20:21, Matthew 28:19-20, and Acts 1:8, to name just a few places.) So get your courage up and talk to your friends about this good news. Embrace the awkward. Jump in with both feet, in love and by the power of the Spirit!

And remember, the benefits to others when you tell them about Jesus are HUGE—starting here and now with a restored relationship with God and lasting for all eternity in heaven.

TALKING WITH GOD

Pray about who you should connect with today about the gospel. Text or call them right away and tell them you want to set up a time to talk to them about God.

GOD HEARS & RESTORES

VERSE 19:
Galatians 1:10

A LITTLE EXTRA

Maybe you have friends who are agnostics, atheists, deists, or followers of specific religions. Go to dare2share.org/worldviews for some insights on how to share your faith with people from a wide range of worldviews. Invite a group of friends with different beliefs to look it over, too, and talk about how you each agree and disagree with what you find.

CONSEQUENCES & CRYING OUT

As you endure this divine discipline, remember that God is treating you as his own children. Who ever heard of a child who is never disciplined by its father?...No discipline is enjoyable while it is happening—it's painful! But afterward there will be a peaceful harvest of right living for those who are trained in this way. Hebrews 12:7,11

VERSE 20:
Hebrews 12:7, 11

A LITTLE EXTRA

Hang out at a gym or a sports team practice for 10 minutes. Watch the different athletes as they train and discipline their bodies. How can you translate that to your spiritual walk? Think about commitments of time, increasing the weight of what you do, or even having a workout buddy for accountability. God disciplines those he loves—and you are deeply loved.

The difference between discipline and punishment is that discipline is designed to help us get better, while punishment is a penalty designed to keep us from doing worse. This passage says nothing of punishment—God exacting a penalty on us because we made a mistake or didn't get it right. It says God disciplines us—he helps us get better. Discipline is uncomfortable and sometimes downright painful. Ask any athlete who has trained for a major event. Discipline hurts, takes work, and requires an all-in mentality. And in the end, it reaps an amazing reward. Embrace that kind of training—that divine discipline from God—so your life can look like the one God has planned for you (see Jeremiah 29:11).

TALKING WITH GOD

Have you ever watched an athlete train hard? Sometimes, in an effort to discipline themselves to run further, lift more, or do better, they'll groan, grunt, scream, cry, yell—they aren't usually meek about discipline. As you approach God today regarding his divine discipline, don't be meek. Cry out about it, if you must—let out the frustration of discipline not being enjoyable at the time. And then feel the rush of relief as the tension of discipline releases.

"So be strong and courageous! Do not be afraid and do not panic before them. For the Lord your God will personally go ahead of you. He will neither fail you nor abandon you." Deuteronomy 31:6

The Israelites—God's chosen people in the Old Testament—had been wandering around in the desert for quite some time after being slaves for generations. They had no GPS and no access to fast-food restaurants. Now the driver of the tour bus, Moses, was near the end of the life and told the people, "Head that way. Bye! Have fun stormin' the castle!"

VERSE 21:
Deuteronomy 31:6

God had done some amazing things in their midst, but the next step was still a terrifying one. And God gave them a hard truth that most of us try to make soft: God was sending them into more problems, more trouble, more people who didn't like them, more places they weren't sure they'd fit in, more hard stuff.

God didn't say "Don't be afraid—everything's gonna be fine!" The hard promise in this passage was that maybe things wouldn't be fine. Maybe it would be hard. Maybe it would be sad. Maybe there would be trouble. The courage God commanded here didn't come from the situation. Courage came from the truth that the Israelites weren't alone. God had waded into the tough spots before. So even though things get rough and you feel forgotten, you can trust that God won't fail or abandon you when times are tough.

A LITTLE EXTRA

Find some images that are brave, courageous, strong reminders for you. Set them as your screen saver—and add Deuteronomy 31:6 as a reminder that God is going before you, wherever you find yourself traveling.

TALKING WITH GOD

Even after that stout promise from God, the Israelites kept messing up. Finding courage and strength of faith in God is a daily struggle. So spend some time today asking God to give you a deep trust in him—a strong and courageous faith—and then ask God for that again tomorrow, and the day after that, and the next day, and every day for the rest of your life.

CONSEQUENCES & CRYING OUT

A LITTLE EXTRA

All day today, keep a little scrap of paper and something to write with in your pocket. Whenever you're feeling any emotion, pull out your paper and jot down a word or two about the feeling. Think of this little list as a prayer journal that God understands better than you do.

Have you ever had a friend step in and provide words for what you were unable to express? Whether it was a private conversation or a more public storytelling, you were stuck and couldn't complete a full sentence. But your friend knew and provided words that expressed your emotion, completed your story, or offered the missing details.

How cool is it that the Holy Spirit does that for us?

And the Holy Spirit helps us in our weakness. For example, we don't know what God wants us to pray for. But the Holy Spirit prays for us with groanings that cannot be expressed in words. Romans 8:26

Sometimes when you're praying—even if that "praying" isn't the sort where you're consciously making your requests known to God—you may struggle with putting words to your feelings, longings, and requests. In those moments, the Holy Spirit expresses (on your behalf!) the deeper knowledge of what you need. And you can rest in the knowledge that your fragments of thought and emotion are fully understood by God, even when you don't fully know them.

TALKING WITH GOD

Quiet yourself for a couple of minutes, and try to shut down your mind's normal train of thought. Then spend a few minutes paying attention to what you're feeling. Is it happiness? frustration? guilt? anxiety? Be aware of that feeling, and offer the feeling itself as a prayer to God, knowing that God is aware of the request you might not be able to formulate into words.

It's funny to imagine people walking around with giant logs sticking out of their eye sockets. It's so silly that the image quickly becomes a two-dimensional cartoon. But that's the ridiculous-sounding comparison Jesus makes to challenge us about our judgmental attitudes:

"And why worry about a speck in your friend's eye when you have a log in your own?" Matthew 7:3

But instead of hearing this instruction as Jesus calling you a jerk for judging others, see if you can frame it in God's massive love for you. What new meaning does it take on?

Could it be that God loves you so much that he doesn't want you to miss out on the best life? (Yes.) Could it be that Jesus knows that focusing on other people's imperfections causes us to miss our own? (Yes.) And might it be that God wants to lovingly help us remove our own "logs," so we can get on with the life God dreams of for us? (Big-time yes.)

TALKING WITH GOD

Ask God to help you identify the logs in your own eyes, those actions and thoughts that deserve God's judgment. Ask God to whittle them down with his love and forgiveness, and to transform you into log-free living!

SIN &
SEPARATION

A LITTLE EXTRA

When we feel angry toward or judgmental about another person, it's really difficult to just stop. But here's a great starting point. Think of someone you have been judging (even if you've never said anything about it), questioning her motives, or even assuming the worst about his intentions. Then pray that this person would experience the love of Jesus. Try to develop the habit of turning your negative thoughts about someone into prayers for them. It's hard to keep judging people when you're praying that they'll experience God's love.

VERSE 24:
Ezekiel 36:26

A LITTLE EXTRA

Get a marker and draw a heart on the inside of your wrist. As you go through the rest of your day, let your little heart remind you that God is in the heart business. God cares about the condition of your heart and the heart of every person you interact with today.

"And I will give you a new heart, and I will put a new spirit in you. I will take out your stony, stubborn heart and give you a tender, responsive heart." Ezekiel 36:26

Did you ever play so hard when you were a little kid that wore out your jeans—or ripped a hole in them? Your mom would take one look at your jeans and decide that instead of buying new clothes for you, she would just sew a patch or two on the jeans. And they probably weren't cool patches. Moms seem to love the fake blue jean-looking patches. No way you're wearing those jeans to school, right?

Like a mom's attitude toward jeans, God knows that our hearts are not disposable. When your heart gets ripped and torn by your choices, God is ready to replace it every time with a new heart. No patches in God's kingdom. God offers a new start every day!

TALKING WITH GOD

Pray this prayer or one with a similar theme: *God, I need a new heart. The heart I have right now is beaten up and bruised. I need a fresh heart that beats for you only. Forgive me for my sins, Lord. I need a do-over. Open my eyes to the broken hearts around me. Give me the courage to live and reveal the kingdom in a world full of broken hearts.*

What are you super passionate about? Maybe you're massively into a particular sport and think about it all the time. Or maybe you love reading and constantly surround yourself with books. It could be gaming, or conversations, or collecting something, or shopping, or even appearing a certain way.

Or your passion could be focused on living like Jesus, loving God, and loving others.

Jesus said this:

"Wherever your treasure is, there the desires of your heart will also be." Luke 12:34

This simple little sentence is a giant challenge. Jesus is saying, "What you value the most is what will get your best attention, your energy, and your love." Jesus isn't telling you to stop loving your sport or video game or books or whatever. He isn't necessarily saying those things are wrong or destructive. But he is challenging you to think about your priorities: Do you love *that thing* more than you love him?

TALKING WITH GOD

Start by thanking God for creating us as people who can experience passion. Then be honest with yourself and with God about the thing or things you're most passionate about. Prayerfully consider where those things stand on your priority list of love, in comparison to your desire to live like Jesus.

SIN &
SEPARATION

VERSE 25:
Luke 12:34

A LITTLE EXTRA

This might be a little scary, but it could produce really helpful results for you: Ask three people to describe your passions. Ask a parent, a friend, and another adult who knows you (such as a youth worker or teacher). Also ask them to suggest ways those passions could be used to bring God's love to the world. You'll probably be amazed at their insight and the helpfulness of their feedback!

ONENESS WITH GOD

VERSE 26:
John 1:1-3

A LITTLE EXTRA

Do an online search of "sayings of Jesus," and see what you find. Pick a couple of the things Jesus said that are challenging to you, and spend some time prayerfully considering how you might respond.

The first three verses of John 1 are three of the coolest verses in the whole Bible. Read them, and then we'll dive in:

In the beginning the Word already existed. The Word was with God, and the Word was God. He existed in the beginning with God. God created everything through him, and nothing was created except through him. John 1:1-3

"The Word" is referring to Jesus. So this passage tells us some really important things about Jesus: that God didn't "create" Jesus, but that Jesus was *with* God and *is* God, and even created the world and everything in it.

That tells us something important: When we get to know the Jesus we see in the Bible, we're really growing in our understanding and knowledge of God—not just of a great teacher or prophet. Jesus reveals God to us.

So if you want to know God, get to know Jesus—and the best place to start that is right here in the Bible.

TALKING WITH GOD

Sometimes when we pray, all we do is list the stuff we need from God. God is OK with that, but it's also great to pray in a way that acknowledges who God is. That sort of prayer builds up your faith. So take a minute to tell God all the cool things you know about him. And tell him how thankful you are that he revealed himself (and still reveals himself) in the person of Jesus.

A guy named Andy Andrews once said, "Each and every one of us—every day—is either in a crisis, coming out of a crisis, or headed into a crisis." Does that describe your life at all?

And we know that God causes everything to work together for the good of those who love God and are called according to his purpose for them.
Romans 8:28

GOD HEARS & RESTORES

Honestly, this can be a hard verse. If you've ever had a tragedy in your life, someone's probably trotted this verse out. You may have asked yourself, *"How can this possible work for the good?!?"* You may not see it now. You may not even see it soon. In fact—and this one can be really hard to swallow—you might not even see the good in this lifetime!

But God says what he means and means what he says. And if God tells us that he works all things for good—well, he's either a liar, or he's telling the truth. You can choose to believe he's telling the truth.

TALKING WITH GOD

Talk to God about this verse and what it means in your life. Maybe you love this verse, and it brings you comfort. Maybe this is a hard verse for you, given the things surrounding you and your life. Maybe it's both at the same time. Share your feelings with God. He's OK with your honesty.

A LITTLE EXTRA

Journal about a time when you saw God use something for good. Write about the experience itself, how you felt at the time, and how God "worked for good" in that experience. If you can't think of an instance, journal about something in your life where you'd love to see how God will work it for good.

29

SIN &
SEPARATION

A LITTLE EXTRA

Make a sacrifice today for someone who doesn't know Jesus. Buy them a latte, help them with their homework, or come up with your own creative idea for being generous to the point of sacrifice. Do an online search for "random acts of kindness" for some ideas.

He himself is the sacrifice that atones for our sins—and not only our sins but the sins of all the world. 1 John 2:2

If a firefighter lost their life in order to save yours, how would you feel? You likely would be deeply grateful. You'd be humbled and inspired. And you'd want to make sure your life counted for something important—that you didn't waste it.

The truth is, someone has sacrificed his life for yours: Jesus. God loved you so much that he sent his Son to die in your place and pay the penalty for your sin. Jesus was *"the sacrifice that atones for our sins."* That's what *atone* means—to make amends for an offense. Jesus died in your place so you could have a restored relationship with God and be with him forever in heaven.

Does knowing that Jesus paid for your life with his make you grateful, humbled, and inspired? Does it motivate you to make sure your life counts for something Jesus told us was truly important—sharing his message with others?

Make your life count today by sharing your faith with someone!

TALKING WITH GOD

Sacrificing for the good of others is a beautiful, noble thing. Talk to God about what it means to you to sacrifice your image and popularity in order to tell others about Jesus. If this is a struggle for you, ask God to help you. Ask him who you should share with. Pray for them, then get on the phone and talk about Jesus today.

Charm is deceptive, and beauty does not last; but a woman who fears the Lord will be greatly praised.
Proverbs 31:30

This world doesn't value what God values. Every day we are told that how we appear on the outside matters and our appearance alone will determine if others love us. We live with this pressure to meet an unrealistic standard of "beauty." This verse is about a woman, but it can be applied to a guy as well. The world says, "Look perfect all of the time." Not only is that impossible, it's shallow and fading.

What is praiseworthy is our ability to understand who God is and to live a life that submits to his ways and his teachings. That is praiseworthy because it is about depth and it can never fade!

When we understand this truth, we experience freedom and joy. We find the freedom to be the person God created us to be and the freedom to stop trying so hard to live up to the culture's definition of beauty. We find the joy that comes from following after Jesus and his ways.

TALKING WITH GOD

Pray this prayer or one that expresses a similar desire: *Jesus, for too long I have believed the lies of the world about what makes me lovable and accepted. Today I want to be a person you consider praiseworthy because of my trust in you and my desire to live and reveal your kingdom. I commit my life to pursuing you and things you call beautiful.*

A LITTLE EXTRA

It's time to redefine beauty. Take a minute to make a list of what beauty is, based on God's standards. Check out the Fruit of the Spirit in Galatians 5:22-23 to help create your list.

GOD HEARS & RESTORES

VERSE 30:
John 8:10-11

A LITTLE EXTRA

Read John 8:1-11. When you get to verse 11, pretend that Jesus is talking to you instead of to the woman, and accept the truth that just as Jesus forgave her, he forgives you.

Then Jesus stood up again and said to the woman, "Where are your accusers? Didn't even one of them condemn you?" "No, Lord," she said. And Jesus said, "Neither do I. Go and sin no more." John 8:10-11

Think about a time that you got caught doing something wrong. How did you feel? Were you embarrassed? Were you ashamed? Were you disgusted with yourself? Did you want to run away and hide? In today's passage, Jesus reveals God's unconditional love and acceptance for us. Jesus reminds us that we all sin and that no one should judge anyone else.

Aren't you glad God isn't like us? People will constantly remind us of the bad things we've done, but God forgives us every time we ask. Like the woman in today's passage, we all get caught up in sins and mistakes and the consequences of our unwise choices. But if we repent—confess our sins and head in a different direction—Jesus tells us, "I forgive you. Go and sin no more."

TALKING WITH GOD

What are you holding on to? What is keeping you from moving forward? Is it guilt? Is it shame? Or do you think you've done something so bad God could never forgive you? Spend time today asking God to forgive you for the sin in your life. Be specific; tell God exactly what you're sorry for. And listen for God's quiet whisper to you: "I forgive you." Because God always forgives you when you ask.

"And when you are brought to trial in the synagogues and before rulers and authorities, don't worry about how to defend yourself or what to say, for the Holy Spirit will teach you at that time what needs to be said." Luke 12:11–12

ONENESS WITH GOD

Question: How many Bible verses and Bible stories do you need to know by memory before you can defend your faith and share the good news of Jesus with people who aren't Christ-followers? Think about it for a minute… OK, what did you come up with? Well, the right answer is "0"!

VERSE 31:
Luke 12:11–12

When it comes to effective ways to share your faith with people who haven't put their trust in Jesus, it's never about your ability to recite your favorite Bible verses. It's always about your ability to allow God's Holy Spirit to speak through you. When you share your God-story with others, simply pray and rely on the Holy Spirit to give you the right, best, most effective words to say.

TALKING WITH GOD

Ask God to give you opportunities today to share your God-story. Maybe there are some friends you can pray for by name. And when God opens the door, ask him to give you the courage to speak and the words to say.

A LITTLE EXTRA

You can always trust God's Holy Spirit to give you the right words to say in every circumstance. And the more time you spend studying God's Word, the more truths and ideas and stories the Holy Spirit can bring to your mind. Spend a few minutes today reading through the "Roman Road"—five passages from Romans that capture the good news of Jesus in a simple and clear way: Romans 3:23, Romans 6:23, Romans 5:8, Romans 10:9-10, and Romans 10:13.

GOD HEARS
& RESTORES

VERSE 32:
Isaiah 45:22

A LITTLE EXTRA

Find a globe, spin it, and then stop it by touching it with your finger. Pray for the people where you landed, that they would turn to God for their salvation. If you landed in water, pray for everyone traveling today—for safety and that they would trust Jesus, if they don't already.

"Let all the world look to me for salvation! For I am God; there is no other." Isaiah 45:22

"I just did something that was so bad that God could never forgive me." Have you ever thought that? Maybe you think, "If God does ever want me back, he will definitely want me to do a lot to make up for the sin before he forgives me."

The people of Israel did a lot of awful things. They ignored God. They worshipped false idols. They lied, cheated, and stole from each other. You'd think that God would have had a long list of things for them to do before he forgave them. However, in today's verse we see that God asked only one thing: that they turn to him for salvation. Turning to God just means saying we're sorry for what we have done, and meaning it. No long rituals. No hard exercises. Just the willingness to say we're sorry, ask for God's forgiveness, and ask for God's strength in living a life that honors him.

TALKING WITH GOD

Pray for God's forgiveness for the times you've done what you wanted and ignored what God wanted. Ask God to help you turn from all of the sin in your life—not just the ones where you get caught—and turn to him. Pray for his strength in living and revealing God's kingdom, so others will look to him as well.

"If you keep quiet at a time like this, deliverance and relief for the Jews will arise from some other place, but you and your relatives will die. Who knows if perhaps you were made queen for just such a time as this?" Esther 4:14

What a bold word from Mordecai! Essentially, he says to his cousin Esther, "Listen, here's the deal. God's gonna get it done one way or the other, but he might be trying to use you—so step up so the shrapnel is minimized. But just know this: Even if you don't step up, God will get the job done." Yes!

Sometimes we shrink from what we think God wants us to do. It's too hard, too bold, too far out of our comfort zones. Can God get it done without us? Sure he can—he's God. But God doesn't WANT to! God wants to use YOU! And when we shrink from God's calling, it's never without consequences. In Esther's case, the consequences of not stepping up would have been disastrous for her and her family. God designed her life and every circumstance to lead to that specific point in time—and God may be doing something similar in your life, too. Do you trust God? Are you ready to step into that calling?

TALKING WITH GOD

When Esther decided to embrace her calling, she rallied people around her—people to pray and fast on her behalf. As you face your God-sized calling, ask God who you can rally to your side as prayer partners.

GOD HEARS & RESTORES

VERSE 33:
Esther 4:14

A LITTLE EXTRA

Esther had a very detailed plan she followed. Think through your understanding of your calling today (it might be different in a year or so, but that's OK). Write out the details of how you understand God's plan for your life. Then share them with your prayer partners.

GOD HEARS & RESTORES

A LITTLE EXTRA

Try something that might feel a little strange: Invite Jesus to have lunch with you, just like he did with Zacchaeus. Whether at home or school, sit by yourself, and imagine Jesus joining you. Think about what Jesus would say to you during that time.

Zacchaeus was a hated little guy. Seriously, *everyone* hated him. He was a tax collector—a traitor to his own (Jewish) people who worked with the Roman oppressors and extorted whatever extra money he pleased because the people were powerless to do anything about it.

The people were starting to wonder if Jesus might be the Messiah, the one sent to rescue them. But their understanding of the Messiah did *not* have room for a Savior who would hang out with a scumbag like Zacchaeus. So when Jesus was being paraded down Main Street, and short Zacchaeus had climbed up a tree to watch, it was a shock to *everyone* when Jesus stopped at that tree:

> *When Jesus came by, he looked up at Zacchaeus and called him by name. "Zacchaeus!" he said. "Quick, come down! I must be a guest in your home today."*
> Luke 19:5

Get this: If Jesus wanted to hang out with Zacchaeus, who did such hated things and had such a horrible reputation, do you think there's anything about you that would keep him away? (The right answer is "no," by the way.)

TALKING WITH GOD

Thank God for loving you and wanting to be close to you. Acknowledge to God that you, like Zacchaeus, are far from perfect and haven't done anything to deserve his loving attention. Ask God to help you trust that he loves you as much as he says he does.

Pure and genuine religion in the sight of God the Father means caring for orphans and widows in their distress and refusing to let the world corrupt you. James 1:27

The book of James is known for being super practical. It's a deep book with lots to think about, but it's very clear what James is calling us to do.

In today's passage, James is wrapping up a paragraph about doing what the Bible says, not just listening to it. James says that once you choose to follow Christ, you need to take the Bible seriously and adjust your life to live it out. One theme in the Old and New testaments is caring for people who are overlooked by culture and possibly can't care for themselves. In this verse, the phrase "orphans and widows" reminds us that there are people in our lives who are hurting and who need help. As Christ-followers who take our relationship with God seriously, we need to reach out to everyone who is in need, giving them both the love of God and a loaf of bread—or whatever else will meet their need.

TALKING WITH GOD

Pray this kind of prayer: *Lord, open my eyes today to see people as you do. Help me recognize the students at my school who are ignored, the families in my neighborhood who are forgotten, and the people in my life who are overlooked. Help me trust you enough to reach out in love to live and reveal your kingdom.*

VERSE 35:
James 1:27

A LITTLE EXTRA

Make a point of looking at every person you encounter today. Look into their eyes to see what they're feeling. When possible, ask them their name and how they're doing. Ask God's Holy Spirit to help you understand their struggles and to respond in love.

GOD HEARS & RESTORES

VERSE 36:
Jeremiah 33:3

A LITTLE EXTRA

What are you asking God for? What questions do you have for God? He knows that sometimes you just want to ask, "Did Adam and Eve have belly buttons?" But we're really talking about legit questions on the things that matter most! Share your questions with a few friends who will ask on your behalf! (Check out Matthew 18:20.)

"Ask me and I will tell you remarkable secrets you do not know about things to come." Jeremiah 33:3

If you're a typical teenager, your head is filled with all kinds of questions about our culture, what a life of faith is all about, your place as a follower of Christ, what the future holds, your purpose in life, and how you can make a difference in this world. You're searching for solid answers to the deepest thoughts inside of you.

Answers only come when questions are asked. You can think about answers, weigh pros and cons, try out different ideas, and measure the outcomes. But if you really want an answer, you just have to ask. And who's the best person to ask? God! Not only does God commit to tell you the obvious things, he also promises to give you secret answers—answers you could never come to on your own. So as you struggle through what to do next, where to go to college, how to talk to your parents, how to help people who've been rejected and ignored, or when to approach your boss, ask God. He already has the answer.

TALKING WITH GOD

Scripture is filled with promises and reminders about what happens when we ask God. He's waiting to hear from you. Check out Isaiah 8:19, Psalm 91:15, Jonah 2:2, Zechariah 13:9, and Matthew 7:7 for more insights.

So the Word became human and made his home among us. He was full of unfailing love and faithfulness. And we have seen his glory, the glory of the Father's one and only Son. John 1:14

Jesus (the Word) invented the whole world. How wild is it, then, that he would insert himself into his own creation? That's like a painter stepping into her own painting, or a chef becoming a soufflé, or a little kid becoming a Lego® Minifigure and walking around his own Lego landscape. (Come to think of it, many little kids have probably wished they could do just that!)

Why did Jesus do this? It's right there in the verse you read: Because Jesus and God the Father are one, we can see God's glory, God's unfailing love, and God's amazing faithfulness when we see Jesus.

Jesus became human in order to make possible God's big story of restoring us, saving us from sin, and reconciling us to God. Jesus' death on the cross and resurrection from death fill out this story. But it all starts with us seeing God, who loves us enough to come to us.

TALKING WITH GOD

Thank Jesus for loving you enough to come to Earth and live as a human, to experience everything you experience, to know your pain and joy. Ask him to help you trust him more today than you did yesterday. And ask him to help you live and reveal his kingdom today.

VERSE 37:
John 1:14

A LITTLE EXTRA

Look up the word *incarnation*. It's possible you've heard that word each year around Christmas. It's the word that describes Jesus becoming human, and understanding it can be really helpful to your faith.

ONENESS WITH GOD

A LITTLE EXTRA

Make a list of three people who you struggle to love. Then think of a way to show kindness to each of them today. Now go do it.

So many things in the kingdom of God seem the opposite of how people normally behave in our world. And this instruction from Jesus is a clear example of that upside-down reality:

"But to you who are willing to listen, I say, love your enemies! Do good to those who hate you. Bless those who curse you. Pray for those who hurt you."
Luke 6:27-28

Here's one way to think of this: God lives out these verses with us. We *should* be God's enemies, because we sin all the time—but God loves us. Our actions often show hatred toward God or become forms of cursing God (when we choose our desires over his)—but God is good to us and blesses us.

Are those verses easy to follow? Not always. You may have people in your life who hate you because of your faith, or mistreat you because you don't fit the mold of the person they think you should be. But when we treat our enemies in the way Jesus described, we're more and more like Jesus. And being like Jesus is the best life!

TALKING WITH GOD

Pray for one of your enemies right now. It's a great way to put this verse into practice. Don't pray that they'll "learn their lesson" or "stop being a jerk." Instead, pray that God would bless them and that God would give you the strength to love them. If you struggle to do this, ask God to help you trust him more, that his way is best.

The Hebrew people were living as slaves in Egypt. Their suffering was horrible, and they wondered if God had forgotten about them. But God hadn't left, and he certainly had a plan. God spoke to Moses, making it clear that he heard the cries of the people and that he had really good stuff waiting for them.

Then the Lord told him, "I have certainly seen the oppression of my people in Egypt. I have heard their cries of distress because of their harsh slave drivers. Yes, I am aware of their suffering. So I have come down to rescue them from the power of the Egyptians and lead them out of Egypt into their own fertile and spacious land. It is a land flowing with milk and honey—the land where the Canaanites, Hittites, Amorites, Perizzites, Hivites, and Jebusites now live." Exodus 3:7-8

This is a real story, with real people (it's not just an illustration)—but there are a couple of super helpful things for us to learn for our own lives. First, in the midst of our own pain and suffering, God is aware and hears our prayers. Second, God has great plans for us—plans to bring us out of difficult places and into new places of wholeness and wonder.

TALKING WITH GOD

Express your pain and fear to God. Ask God for a rescue. And ask him to help you trust that he'll respond to your prayer.

GOD HEARS & RESTORES

VERSE 39:
Exodus 3:7-8

A LITTLE EXTRA

What are the "slave drivers" in your life? Don't just go with the easy answer of a difficult teacher, or a mean boss. Think about the things that hold you captive—temptations and recurring sin, feelings of insecurity or depression, realities where you feel powerless to save yourself. Make a list of them in your journal, and write down what happens as God reveals himself in each situation.

ONENESS WITH GOD

A LITTLE EXTRA

Write a psalm. We don't have to be writers or poets to write a list of the reasons we celebrate God. Try writing five lines of celebration and praise. Start by telling yourself to wake up to God's goodness!

Psalm 103 is a celebration of God and his compassion and love for us. It starts by saying:

Let all that I am praise the Lord; with my whole heart, I will praise his holy name. Psalm 103:1

What are we celebrating? We are celebrating God's generous compassion that offers us life when we deserve death, his compassion that gives us grace at no cost to us, his compassion that sees our brokenness and our weaknesses as unique ways to serve him and others. We celebrate his love that would send his Son to Earth to point us to him, his love that would offer his life in our place, his love that would send his Holy Spirit to live in us.

There is a lot to celebrate. Even if you started now and didn't stop until you died, you still wouldn't be able to finish celebrating all of God and his glorious gifts.

When you look at today's verse, notice that it's a challenge to each of us:

Get ready! Wake up!

All of me—WAKE UP! My heart, my soul, my insides—WAKE UP!

It's time to praise God.

TALKING WITH GOD

Wake yourself up! Right now! Stand up. Stretch. Now go back to the beginning of this devotion and reread each sentence. See how differently it reads when you really are reading it awake and aware inside and out of God's goodness! Take a moment to thank God for his gifts to us. Thank him for the invitation to live and reveal his kingdom as we praise his name.

If you need wisdom, ask our generous God, and he will give it to you. He will not rebuke you for asking. James 1:5

GOD HEARS & RESTORES

This verse comes smack-dab in the middle of a passage about troubles and trials. When we're facing difficult situations, it can be hard to know how God wants us to respond or what he wants us to do. According to James, when we're stuck knowing what to do, God wants us to ask! In the verses that follow, James even tells us *how* to ask: confidently and expectantly.

And here's the deal: God is *generous* with the wisdom! God isn't going to give you bare-bones wisdom; he will be generous and extravagant. And you know how sometimes you have those teachers who talk smack when you ask questions, believing you should already know the answer? God's not like that. God *wants* you to ask him!

TALKING WITH GOD

Think about a difficulty you're facing right now. Tell God all about it, then ask him how you can respond well and wisely. If you're not facing anything difficult right now, pray for a friend who is, and ask God to give your friend wisdom.

A LITTLE EXTRA

In your journal, make two columns. On one side, list the reasons you are sometimes hesitant to approach God with your questions. Next to each reason, in the second column, list what you know to be true about God's nature—those things about God that would remind you it's OK to ask questions. If you have reasons to hesitate but cannot put your finger on a character trait of God that eases your hesitation, ask a trusted friend or youth leader to help you discover those traits.

VERSE 42:
John 14:1-3

A LITTLE EXTRA

A rope is a great illustration of trust. If you're climbing anything that's high off the ground, you're putting your trust in a piece of rope. Find a short piece of rope, and carry it with you as a reminder that you can trust God. And remember that no matter what life throws at you, God will make things right in his time.

"Don't let your hearts be troubled. Trust in God, and trust also in me. There is more than enough room in my Father's home. If this were not so, would I have told you that I am going to prepare a place for you? When everything is ready, I will come and get you, so that you will always be with me where I am." John 14:1-3

If anyone really knew Jesus, it was John. He was one of Jesus' three closest followers, or disciples. John considered being a disciple an honor and privilege, and he saw and heard things that he would never forget.

In today's passage, John isn't sharing something that he *thinks*; he is telling us what he experienced while hanging with Jesus. John reveals that as long as we trust Jesus, we don't have to worry. God doesn't promise a pain-free life, but he does promise that one day he will make it all right—and as Christ-followers, we will be with Jesus forever.

TALKING WITH GOD

If you want to know all of God's love, allow Jesus total access to your heart. Invite God to search your heart and show you areas where you can grow in your trust. God isn't afraid of your doubts, so tell him about them. Ask God to help you trust him more, especially in the areas of life that leave you troubled.

Think about a time when you were really proud of a personal accomplishment. Maybe it was when you made the honor roll, won the big game, or even when your parents let you stay home alone for the first time. Wasn't that such a cool feeling? Now think about the first time you stood up for your relationship with God.

For I am not ashamed of this Good News about Christ. It is the power of God at work, saving everyone who believes—the Jew first and also the Gentile. Romans 1:16

In this verse Paul is letting the world know his pride in the gospel message of Christ! Say what? His pride? Isn't pride something we want to avoid as followers of Christ? Yes, but sometimes pride can be a good thing! It's never a bad thing to be proud of what God has done in your life to bring attention to his kingdom.

What are you proud of that God has done in your life?

TALKING WITH GOD

In a few sentences tell God what you are proud of that he has done in your life. Then read the passage again and let God know how unashamed you are of the work he has done in your life.

ONENESS WITH GOD

VERSE 43:
Romans 1:16

A LITTLE EXTRA

Write today's passage on three adhesive notes. Put one on your mirror in your bathroom, one in your locker at school, and one where you might see it every day, such as your car, your phone, or your computer.

DOING THE RIGHT THINGS

Your relationship with God is not about how much you know or how much you do; it's about how much you trust God. Growing in your relationship with God takes time, but there are six THINGS you can do to help:

IME WITH GOD DAILY (SEE P. 1, PP. 90-91, PP. 136-137)

Spending time with God every day is the most important thing you can do to grow in your trust in God, because relationships grow as you spend time together. If you're reading your *Simple Truth Bible* every day, that's an amazing start—keep it up!

⒣ONEST FRIENDSHIPS

Finding a few friends who share your trust in God will be a huge help to your spiritual growth. We all need friends who love us enough to tell us the truth, even when we might not want to hear it.

⒤NVOLVEMENT WITH THE CHURCH

You may already be plugged into your youth group—and that's awesome—but deepening your connection with the larger church will help you grow in your trust in God. Seeing Christ-followers of all ages and all stages of relationship with God is encouraging and inspiring. And they need you, too!

⒩OTICE AND SERVE OTHERS (SEE PP. 270-271)

People are hurting all around us, but sometimes we're so busy that we don't see them. If you get in the habit of noticing the people around you, God will invite you to serve them in ways that will strengthen your trust in him.

(G) IVE TO GOD

Unselfishness is one mark of a growing trust in God. You may not have lots of money to give, but do you have time to volunteer, or energy to work, or patience to help, or other resources to invest? As you give to others, you trust God more to give you everything you need.

(S) HARE YOUR GOD-STORY (SEE PP. 316-317)

Every Christ-follower has a story to tell, including you. It's scary to put yourself "out there," but when God nudges you and you respond, God's Holy Spirit uses your words to help others trust God more. And you learn to trust God more as well.

Just like a tree that needs the right environment to grow, these six THINGS put you in a place to grow in your trust in God. Commit to doing the right THINGS today.

GOD HEARS & RESTORES

A LITTLE EXTRA

Write a short apology note to God. Then, as a prayerful symbol of accepting God's perfect love and forgiveness, wad it up and throw it away—or, if you can do this in a safe way, burn it!

If you're not familiar with Jesus' parable of the prodigal son, here's a quick version: Selfish son takes his inheritance early and blows it all on wild living. Then he decides to go home and beg his way into becoming one of his dad's servants, thinking it would be better than the ruin his life had become. But while he's walking home and rehearsing his apology speech, this happens:

"So he returned home to his father. And while he was still a long way off, his father saw him coming. Filled with love and compassion, he ran to his son, embraced him, and kissed him." Luke 15:20

Jesus told this story to teach us about God's love. We might expect an angry God, one who makes us pay for our mistakes. We might expect a God who waits for us to come and grovel at his feet. But that's not the God we see in this story. This Father runs to us, throws his arms around us—not even waiting for the apology!—and shows us love and compassion.

You're the prodigal, and that's the kind of relentless love God has for you.

TALKING WITH GOD

Quiet yourself for a minute, freeing your mind of other thoughts. Then prayerfully imagine yourself as the prodigal, walking down the road toward home, expecting a not-so-warm welcome, but ready to accept anything your dad offers you. Now picture God, the loving Father, running out to meet you and embracing you with love and acceptance and restoration.

Then he said to the disciples, "Anyone who accepts your message is also accepting me. And anyone who rejects you is rejecting me. And anyone who rejects me is rejecting God, who sent me." Luke 10:16

This passage is part of a set of instructions that Jesus gave to 72 of his followers as they went out to tell others about Jesus. He knew some people would welcome these disciples, while others wouldn't want anything to do with them, and Jesus wanted to prepare them for both responses.

As Jesus' followers, we represent him today. If people accept our message, they're accepting Jesus, so we can't take credit. And if people reject our message, they're rejecting Jesus, so we can't take it personally. Just as Jesus was taking all the pressure off the disciples when he sent them out, he wants to take the pressure off of us as we live and reveal God's kingdom.

TALKING WITH GOD

Pray this prayer or one with a similar theme: *God, I want to tell your story with my life and my words. Help me trust you today to speak out when you give me the opportunity. Use my life to reveal your kingdom.*

VERSE 45:
Luke 10:16

A LITTLE EXTRA

Go back and take a look at Luke 10:1-18. The encouragement is that there are people who can't wait to hear about him and what he does. Practice telling your God-story in three minutes or less. (Check out page pp. 316-317 for all the details.) Talk about life before you trusted Jesus. Explain how you trusted Jesus. And describe your life since you trusted Christ. Write out your story, practice telling it to yourself in the mirror, then tell it to a trusted friend, and then share it with someone God nudges you about.

GOD HEARS
& RESTORES

Then God said to Noah, "Yes, this rainbow is the sign of the covenant I am confirming with all the creatures on earth." Genesis 9:17

Did you know that wherever there is water in the air or sunlight in the sky, a rainbow appears? Most often, we can only see the rainbows in perfect conditions after a rainstorm, but they are always there!

God created the rainbow as a promise to us that he would never flood the Earth again like he did during the time of Noah and the ark. Think about it: Whenever we see a rainbow, it is God's voice projecting across the sky saying, "Don't worry, I will keep you safe. I gave you just the amount of rain that you needed, and I will never flood the Earth again." God is always giving us little reminders of his promises to us, and a rainbow in the sky is exactly that!

TALKING WITH GOD

You have probably spilled secrets a few times in your life and broken promises you made. Even if it was a pinky promise that you broke, it still counts! Can you imagine never breaking a promise? God is the only one in all of history who has never sinned, never gone back on his word, and never broken a promise. Thank God for his wonderful promises to keep you safe and walk with you through every situation in life.

VERSE 46:
Genesis 9:17

A LITTLE EXTRA

A rainbow is a sign of one of God's promise to us. What are some other promises God has made to us, and what are some things you can identify as signs of these promises? Make your own list of "signs from God" to remind you of his promises. Then share your list with some friends to help them remember God's promises, too.

How do you know what your life will be like tomorrow? Your life is like the morning fog—it's here a little while, then it's gone. James 4:14

Take a moment to imagine the picture James paints for us: morning fog slowly disappearing as the brilliant light of sun begins to blaze through. Can you see it? This is James' illustration for us as we think about the shortness (and uncertainty) of our time here on earth.

James was writing to Christ-followers who made plans based on their comfort, not on their conviction of God's purposes for their lives. James was challenging them to give up control and gain wisdom from God. After all, none of them really knew what the next day would hold.

What about you? Are your everyday decisions focused on seeking the light of God's plans, or does the fog of comfort and control consume your plans?

TALKING WITH GOD

Take a few minutes to pray and talk with God about your plans and decisions. Ask God for direction and clarity in your decisions for today. Ask God for a long-term vision for your life. Don't expect an instant answer; this likely will take time as God reveals one piece at a time. The key is to seek God for a long-term plan.

VERSE 47:
James 4:14

A LITTLE EXTRA

Write down the following: "If I had one month to live, God would want me to...." Think about what God would call you to do, including the following:

- Which relationships would need forgiveness and healing?

- What work or service would God call you to do?

- Which people would you need to spend the most time with?

Consider how you could begin living your one-month-to-live plan. What steps could you take today?

GOD HEARS
& RESTORES

A LITTLE EXTRA

Buy a roll of Life Savers® candy. Savor them one by one, remembering Jesus' sacrifice on your behalf. Share a candy with a friend, and use it as an opportunity to tell the story of Jesus.

Even so, he saved them—to defend the honor of his name and to demonstrate his mighty power.
Psalm 106:8

Did you hear the story about a lifeguard who lost his job after saving someone? From the tower, the lifeguard witnessed a man drowning, so he jumped in and rescued him. But the lifeguard was fired. Why? The man was swimming in an area marked "unguarded beach." The lifeguard dragged the man to shore because he needed saving, not because he deserved it. Fortunately for us, God saves and rescues those who don't "deserve" it!

God knows we will drown in this life without a relationship with him. He brings us back to life, not because we ever have or ever will do anything to "get it right." But God allows people to know that he is who he says he.

Today's verse is actually talking about the Israelites when God brought them out of slavery in Egypt. They could have been drowned in the Red Sea, but instead he took them to the Promised Land. God wants nothing less for us.

TALKING WITH GOD

Draw a life-preserver doughnut on a piece of paper. Around the life preserver, write words that represent what Jesus has saved or rescued you from. As you think about what God has done for you, thank him as you write each word or phrase down. Yes, God has saved you from your sin, but are other things going on that still leave you feeling like you might sink? Talk to God about those, too.

We can all be a bit blind at times, clueless about our imperfections and the ways we're in need of a Savior. That's why the psalmist wrote:

Search me, O God, and know my heart; test me and know my anxious thoughts. Point out anything in me that offends you, and lead me along the path of everlasting life. Psalm 139:23-24

Most of us are pretty good at asking God for help when we're aware of our need. "Help me pass this test!" "I don't know how to forgive her, God." "Should I go to this college or that college?"

But there's stuff in our hearts that we miss. God, of course, is completely aware of all that junk (and loves us in spite of it). So if we really want to live the best life, the one God dreamed up for each of us, it makes sense that we would humbly ask God to help us see into those shadows.

TALKING WITH GOD

These verses are a prayer! So pray the verses (really—read them out loud as a prayer to God). Pray it a few more times. Ask God to help you trust him as he leads you.

CONSEQUENCES & CRYING OUT

VERSE 49:
Psalm 139:23-24

A LITTLE EXTRA

Sometimes God speaks to us most clearly through other Christ-followers. So if you really want to dig into the spirit of the prayer in these verses, ask someone who loves Jesus and loves you if they see some blind spots in your life that you should be addressing. (Try not to be defensive, even if you're not thrilled with the answer—remember that God wants to do a work in your life!)

CONSEQUENCES & CRYING OUT

Don't worry about anything; instead, pray about everything. Tell God what you need, and thank him for all he has done. Then you will experience God's peace, which exceeds anything we can understand. His peace will guard your hearts and minds as you live in Christ Jesus. Philippians 4:6-7

VERSE 50:
Philippians 4:6-7

A LITTLE EXTRA

Copy and paste this verse as a calendar reminder on your computer or phone so it will pop up two days away. Then copy and paste it for two weeks away. Do it again for three months away. Use these reminders to turn your worries into prayers.

Worry is a common part of life for most people. The specific worries might change, but there will always be something attempting to consume our minds. The good news: The Apostle Paul teaches us how to deal with anxiety. Paul himself had every reason to be anxious: When he wrote these words, he was in prison for his faith, and his future was anything but clear. But Paul chose to trust God in the midst of difficult times, and you can, too.

What are the biggest things that are worrying you today? Whether it's friendships, future, failures, or struggling with who you are, God is bigger than any of your anxieties, fears, or worries.

TALKING WITH GOD

Write down your list of worries—the biggest things consuming you today. Tell God why you are worried and what you need. Thank God for how he is going to take care of each worry. As you pray, cross through each item on your list as a sign that you are trusting God to help. Then pray for God's peace to replace your anxiety. Sit quietly and allow God's peace to guard your heart and your mind.

Some days we wake up and wish we could just stay in bed. We might be able to pretend like everything is all right, but really we are falling apart on the inside. Whenever you're feeling low, remember today's passage, as it tells us one of God's promises to his followers.

"He will wipe every tear from their eyes, and there will be no more death or sorrow or crying or pain. All these things are gone forever." Revelation 21:4

One day, God will make all things right. When we get to be with Jesus in heaven for eternity, all of that junk we have to deal with in this life will be totally gone. Today might not be easy, and other hard things may come, but we can handle it knowing one day it will all be gone.

TALKING WITH GOD

God is good and just, which means he always does the right thing and fixes what's broken. Thank God that one day, everything that is wrong will be made right—in your life and in the lives of all Christ-followers. Ask God to help you trust him and to give you opportunities to live and reveal his kingdom when life is going great—and when life is especially tough.

GOD HEARS & RESTORES

VERSE 51:
Revelation 21:4

A LITTLE EXTRA

Write a list of your top five hurts. Talk to God about them, and ask him for his peace and hope. Then rip up the paper into a million pieces. When you are done, throw those little pieces into the air like confetti. Thank God for the day when you will be with him for eternity, when all of the bad will be done once and for all. Now clean up the confetti—and remember God's promises throughout your day.

GOD HEARS
& RESTORES

A LITTLE EXTRA

Conduct a small investigation on a couple of past struggles. Think about (or write about) each struggle, what you learned from it, and where God was in the midst of it. This could also be a cool activity to do with a friend.

Most of us naturally avoid pain. Tough times aren't fun, and we all refine our skills at dodging them. But if you think of the times in your life when your faith grew, they often have some sort of challenge or difficulty associated with them. Even something like a mission trip causes growth in the midst of us being uncomfortable with the gap between what *we* have and what *others* have.

James has some great insight for us on this reality:

Dear brothers and sisters, when troubles come your way, consider it an opportunity for great joy. For you know that when your faith is tested, your endurance has a chance to grow. So let it grow, for when your endurance is fully developed, you will be perfect and complete, needing nothing. James 1:2-4

Notice that James *doesn't* say that we should constantly seek out pain and suffering. He's realistic, though, and knows that troubles come to everyone's life at some point. The question, then, is how you will respond *during* times of trouble. Will you gripe and whine, or will you take hold of the opportunity to grow in faith and endurance?

TALKING WITH GOD

Think of a trouble you're facing right now. It might be a huge thing you've dealt with for a long time, or a short-term issue that will likely resolve in the near future. Ask God to help you to endure and to grow in faith during this struggle. Ask him to help you trust him in the midst of the pain.

Stop and think about a love song that you have heard recently. Maybe you heard it on the radio, online, your MP3 player, or even when you gathered with people as a church. Who was the artist describing or talking about in the song? How did the song define the word *love*? Was it selfish, adoring, sad, or happy?

Dear friends, let us continue to love one another, for love comes from God. Anyone who loves is a child of God and knows God. But anyone who does not love does not know God, for God is love.
1 John 4:7–8

VERSE 53:
1 John 4:7–8

Our world is filled with hundreds of thousands of songs that sing about love. Most of them talk about being in love, falling in love, or being hurt by love. This Scripture tells us that we only can know what love is when we know God and who God is. If we love God with all of our heart, mind, and soul, we are compelled to express our love to him and for him. We express our love to others by our behavior and our actions, in addition to our words. The same is true regarding our love for God.

A LITTLE EXTRA

Take a few minutes and write a short love song or poem to God and tell him how much you love him. If music isn't your thing, draw God a picture; maybe he'll hang it on his heavenly fridge!

TALKING WITH GOD

Ask yourself: Do I love God? Do I tell God I love him? Do I show God I love him every day by keeping his commands? Does my love for God move me to take time to study Scripture and learn more about him and his commands? Take time today to tell God how much you love him.

GOD HEARS & RESTORES

VERSE 54:
James 2:17

There's a difference between belief and faith. People believe all sorts of things they won't act on. Maybe you have some beliefs that fall into that category. Faith, on the other hand, requires some action. Faith is belief put into motion.

That's why James writes this:

So you see, faith by itself isn't enough. Unless it produces good deeds, it is dead and useless.
James 2:17

A LITTLE EXTRA

Ideally, good deeds will naturally flow out of our lives as a result of our faith. But sometimes we need a little practice, a little jump-start. So take a moment to plan a "random act of kindness" that you can carry out in the next 24 hours. Then carry it out without telling anyone. Do an online search for "random acts of kindness" if you're struggling to think of something to do.

You've probably met someone at some point who surprised you when you found out he or she was a Christian. You thought, "There's nothing in the way you live that would have given me that idea!"

But what about you? Do the things you believe about following Jesus and living for him actually show up in practical ways in your daily life? Do your beliefs "produce good deeds"? If not, you might have a nifty collection of beliefs, but not an active faith. And a life of faith—well, that's what we were made for, and it's the very best life.

TALKING WITH GOD

Prayerfully think through the past 24 hours of your life. Where do you see evidence of your faith in action? Ask God to give you the strength and courage to move beyond belief alone and live an active life of faith, one that shows up in good deeds of love and kindness.

For you have been called to live in freedom, my brothers and sisters. But don't use your freedom to satisfy your sinful nature. Instead, use your freedom to serve one another in love.
Galatians 5:13

When you were a little kid, did you ever ride your bike really fast? So fast that you could feel the wind blowing in your hair almost like you were flying? Sometimes that feeling made you think that you were going so fast that you could just let go of the handle bars and close your eyes and you would continue going in a perfectly straight line on the sidewalk. But then, when you opened your eyes, you realized it was way too late to slop yourself from crashing into a bush and flying over the top of your handle bars into a metal garden gate or your neighbor's fence.

Just because you can act on every desire you have doesn't mean you should. Christ sets us free to live the life he's called us to live, but we sometimes use our freedom in selfish ways. The Apostle Paul, who wrote this letter to the Galatians, says that instead of using our freedom in self-centered ways, we can use our freedom in others-centered ways—serving others, meeting people's needs, and demonstrating God's love.

TALKING WITH GOD

Ask God to help you stop living for yourself and live in his kind of freedom. Commit to setting aside your own desires and living the life God calls us to live every day.

VERSE 55:
Galatians 5:13

A LITTLE EXTRA

Read 1 Corinthians 10:23-24. What reasons does the Bible give us for limiting our freedoms? If you had to explain this concept to someone else, what would you say?

GOD HEARS
& RESTORES

A LITTLE EXTRA

Each time you have to make a choice today—especially if you have a choice about which piece of chocolate to eat—remember this verse. Remember that God's way is always best and that when you choose God's way, you are choosing life and blessing.

"Today I have given you the choice between life and death, between blessings and curses. Now I call on heaven and earth to witness the choice you make. Oh, that you would choose life, so that you and your descendants might live!"
Deuteronomy 30:19

At first glance, today's verse can feel pretty scary. But look carefully and you'll see that God simply gives us a choice between two very different paths. The choice is ours. We can choose life. Better yet, we can choose a life of blessings.

Here's the challenge: Sometimes what we *think* will be blessings turn out to be curses. It's like diving into a box of assorted chocolates: creamy, smooth chocolate on the outside, but when you bite into it, you find coconut inside. (If you like coconut, picture something else gross on the inside—maybe a gooey center, or a piece of fruit.)

In our broken world, some things look good from the outside, but once we experience them, they aren't. God offers us a life of blessing, a life centered on him and his will for our lives.

TALKING WITH GOD

Ask God what his plan for your life looks like. Talk to him about things you desire, and why you desire them. Ask God if they're consistent with his plan. Thank God for the blessings in your life, and welcome anything that brings you back to a blessed life with him.

Have you ever been hanging out with friends enjoying small talk when suddenly someone says something that totally changes the mood of the conversation? That is what seems to happen in our passage from Mark. The disciples are with Jesus, eating a meal—and Jesus changes the mood and the atmosphere of the conversation as he broke bread and shared a cup of wine.

GOD HEARS
& RESTORES

VERSE 57:
Mark 14:22-24

As they were eating, Jesus took some bread and blessed it. Then he broke it in pieces and gave it to the disciples, saying, "Take it, for this is my body." And he took a cup of wine and gave thanks to God for it. He gave it to them, and they all drank from it. And he said to them, "This is my blood, which confirms the covenant between God and his people. It is poured out as a sacrifice for many."
Mark 14:22-24

We practice communion as an act of remembering the Last Supper and ultimately Jesus' sacrifice of body and blood. The purpose of remembering is reflection and thankfulness. Communion should cause us to pause and reflect on why we follow Jesus and why we give our lives to bring his kingdom to earth. We remember together and we offer thankfulness together.

TALKING WITH GOD

Offer a prayer to Jesus, thanking him for the sacrifice he made on the cross. Ask him to help you remember his love for you and for others every day.

A LITTLE EXTRA

The next time you share communion, imagine that you are sitting at the table with the disciples and hearing Jesus say these words to you. Allow it to be fresh and new in your mind. Let the beauty of his promise and his sacrifice fill you with thankfulness that impacts how you live each day.

ONENESS
WITH GOD

VERSE 58:
Mark 1:35

A LITTLE EXTRA

If you haven't already, add several entries to your calendar this week for "meeting with God." Instead of just reading a daily devotion, consider spending extended time in prayer, or fasting, or singing along with worship music on your phone or digital music player.

Do you ever get overwhelmed and stressed by your schedule and the decisions you have to make on a regular basis? Do you spend lots of time thinking about classes, homework, practices, friends, youth group, chores, work, and time for yourself? And what about the bigger decisions coming up in the next year? Maybe you have to choose classes, try out for a sports team, apply for college, or even change your friendships. Are you stressed just thinking about some of these things? OK, if you weren't stressed a moment ago, you probably are now!

Jesus understands the pressure you face on a regular basis. He walked this earth as both fully God and fully man, and he faced pressures of all kinds. There were always more people to heal, more messages to speak, and too many "fires" to put out. As someone who experienced the pressures, what did Jesus do in times like this?

Before daybreak the next morning, Jesus got up and went out to an isolated place to pray. Mark 1:35

TALKING WITH GOD

Take some time to talk with God about your schedule, and spend time being quiet and letting God share his priorities for you. Ask God for peace and for wisdom as you plan your week and look ahead to the rest of this year. Ask God to help you say no when you need to, so you'll be able to say yes to the right things.

Then I heard the Lord asking, "Whom should I send as a messenger to this people? Who will go for us?" I said, "Here I am. Send me." Isaiah 6:8

Isaiah had a pretty intense encounter with God. He had a vision—something that you might describe as an "extreme daydream" in which he heard the Lord's booming voice and saw his awe-striking angels. Isaiah is shown how sinful he is in the presence of the God, and in a miraculous turn of events his sin is taken away. God then asks a question meant directly for him. "My people need to be reminded of who I am; do you think there is someone who could tell them?" Isaiah doesn't even pause: "PICK ME!" he screams without hesitation.

This is an example for all of us today. For those of us who have been changed by knowing and following Jesus, the Lord asks a question: "Will you live and reveal God's kingdom?" We can choose to be like Isaiah and say, "Yes!" or we can wait for someone else to come along. But which one is the greater decision, the choice that will have the most amazing impact on our lives?

TALKING WITH GOD

Pray this kind of prayer today: *Thank you, God, for loving me enough to send someone to tell me about your love. Help me have the courage to tell someone today.*

GOD HEARS & RESTORES

VERSE 59:
Isaiah 6:8

A LITTLE EXTRA

Call or send a message to the person (or people) who told you about God's love. Thank them for having the courage to live and reveal God's kingdom. Ask them to pray for you to follow in their footsteps and to share God's love with someone today.

GOD HEARS & RESTORES

VERSE 60:
James 5:16

A LITTLE EXTRA

Make a list of trusted friends. Assess which people on the list you believe to be solid in their faith. Consider asking a few of those friends to enter an accountability friendship with you— one where you confess to one another, pray for one another, learn to trust God together, and celebrate the results. Not only will this help you grow in your journey with Christ, but it'll also help you build stronger, deeper bonds with your accountability friends!

Confess your sins to each other and pray for each other so that you may be healed. The earnest prayer of a righteous person has great power and produces wonderful results. James 5:16

Telling other people your struggles can be one of the hardest things to do! After all, how do you just wade into a conversation where you throw all your cards on the table about viewing porn, hating your classmate, fighting with your parents, getting revenge on your back-stabbing friend, or cheating on a test? It's not easy, but it's worth it.

Here are a few key components of your times of confession:

- Don't expect it to be easy. Confession is difficult and humbling.
- Be selective, and choose wisely. Know which individuals you can trust with your confessions.
- Make prayer the point. Don't get so focused on the details of the confession that you forget to pray.
- Expect results—wonderful ones.

TALKING WITH GOD

Confessing to a good friend is key—but also remember to confess your sins and struggles to God. Anything you share in accountability with another person is something that God also wants you to share with him, your Abba Daddy Father.

ONENESS
WITH GOD

"Study this Book of Instruction continually. Meditate on it day and night so you will be sure to obey everything written in it. Only then will you prosper and succeed in all you do." Joshua 1:8

This verse can be challenging. We see people around us living their lives according to God's Word, yet their lives don't seem successful. But God's Word is truth, right?

The mistake likely starts with the reality that we don't fully understand God's ideas about success. Our thoughts and perspective have been tampered by sin and by the world's view of success. Money, fame, and fortune tend to be part of our definition of success.

If we meditate on God's Word to the point that we live it out daily but then use the culture's standards to evaluate ourselves, we will probably find ourselves to be "failures" because God's definition of success is not the same as the world's!

If you read the verses before and after Joshua 1:8, you'll find a phrase repeated: *"Be strong and courageous."* Is it success when we are strong enough to follow God's Word? Is it success to choose the courage to follow God's way rather than the world's way? Definitely!

TALKING WITH GOD

Invite God to rewrite your definition of success. Put your hands on your head and ask him to change your thinking. Put your hands on your eyes and ask him to change the way you see things. Put your hands on your mouth and ask him to change your words.

VERSE 61:
Joshua 1:8

A LITTLE EXTRA

Sit silently for 60 seconds and reflect on what your life would look like if you followed God's words with strength and courage. Write down one thing you can do today. And when you do it, celebrate your success!

ONENESS WITH GOD

A LITTLE EXTRA

There is probably someone in your life that you don't understand or don't get along with very well. The next opportunity you get, instead of judging that person, reach out and try to engage them in a conversation. Try to understand them from their point of view. Be genuinely interested in them, their story, and what makes them who they are.

Those who feel free to eat anything must not look down on those who don't. And those who don't eat certain foods must not condemn those who do, for God has accepted them. Romans 14:3

You might read this verse and think that it's talking about a special diet or vegetarians during biblical times who looked down on people that ate meat. This verse actually speaks to something much bigger than just what we eat and how we look at what other people eat. Paul wrote this letter to Christ-followers to help them understand to live for Jesus every day.

In today's verse, Paul is talking about how we look at what other people do and how we judge them. God loves all people, and although he doesn't like all the things we do, he still loves us. Instead of worrying about what other people do, we ought to spend our time loving people, and we ought to focus more on our relationships with other people and with God than on what people are wearing, eating, or doing.

TALKING WITH GOD

God loves all people. Ask God to open your heart and show you how he is able to love no matter the circumstances. Write out ways in which you haven't shown love to some of your friends or classmates over the past week, and how you can be different this week.

" 'You have seen what I did to the Egyptians. You know how I carried you on eagles' wings and brought you to myself. Now if you will obey me and keep my covenant, you will be my own special treasure from among all the peoples on earth; for all the earth belongs to me. And you will be my kingdom of priests, my holy nation.' This is the message you must give to the people of Israel."
Exodus 19:4-6

In today's passage, God was telling Moses what to say to the Israelites. After being delivered from slavery in Egypt, getting bread and meat from heaven, and drinking water from a rock, the Israelites were still grumpy. They wanted more. They wanted the Promised Land, and they wanted it now.

Even in the darkest day or in the grumpiest mood, you can find reasons to be thankful. God has provided for you in the past and is providing for you today. You can become more aware of what God is doing when you take the time to be thankful. As you're thankful, you begin to trust God and his plan more and more. Then you can follow God more closely as his cherished treasure.

TALKING WITH GOD

Ask God to open your eyes to see clearly his provision for your life: food, shelter, clothing, friends, and family—and even many of your wants.

GOD HEARS & RESTORES

VERSE 63:
Exodus 19:4-6

A LITTLE EXTRA

Take out a sheet of paper, or turn to a fresh page in your journal. Write down five things for which you're thankful—from today, from this week, from this month, from this year, and from a long time ago. Read the list out loud, and after each phrase say, "God did this because he loves me."

GOD HEARS & RESTORES

A LITTLE EXTRA

Draw a small cross on your hand. Every time you see it, say a quick prayer of commitment to God. If you can get in the habit of praying throughout the day, you will be more likely to follow God's plan—and experience the blessings and rewards of that plan!

"Why are you sleeping?" he asked them. "Get up and pray, so that you will not give in to temptation."
Luke 22:46

Most parents who are Christ-followers teach their children to say prayers before meals and before bedtime. Jesus never says that we have to pray before we eat dinner or before we go to sleep, but he does tell us that is important to be in constant prayer with him. Throughout the day, a simple "thank you for getting me through that class" or "please help me focus on my homework tonight" prayer can help us remain in constant communication with our Father. If we are continually thanking God for all he does for us throughout the day or asking him to help us through whatever situations come our way, it will be easier to avoid temptation.

When faced with a difficult choice, ask God to guide you! All it takes is a conversation with him to have clearer judgment and be focused on what God wants for you, rather than ignoring him and doing what you want for yourself.

TALKING WITH GOD

Start each day with a prayer. Ask God to give you wisdom as you face the day and help you through any tempting situations. Satan will do whatever it takes to hurt you and tempt you to choose his path rather than God's path. Ask God to remind you how important it is to call on him when you feel you may give in to temptation.

Then, turning to his disciples, Jesus said, "That is why I tell you not to worry about everyday life— whether you have enough food to eat or enough clothes to wear. For life is more than food, and your body more than clothing." Luke 12:22-23

Why do we worry? Often it's because it provides a sense of comfort. We think that if we worry, then that attention will somehow make it all end up all right. It's a way of trying to exert control over something. But here's the truth: You have no more control over a situation if you worry about it than if you don't.

When we worry, we're not trusting that God is our Heavenly Father who cares about us. Of course, we aren't supposed to just sit back and "let God take care of everything." We still have to follow through and go where God leads us. But if we've done that, we can trust, have faith, and stop worrying.

TALKING WITH GOD

In the passage containing today's verse, Jesus talked about a field of wildflowers. Find a flower (or if you're able, a field of flowers), look at it, and think about how God loves you more. Thank God for caring about you more than birds and flowers. Confess the things you worry about, and ask him to forgive you for not trusting him more. Ask him to show you ways you can trust him more.

VERSE 65:
Luke 12:22-23

A LITTLE EXTRA

Write down all the things you worry about. Then go over the list, and honestly evaluate whether you've done everything in your power as it relates to that thing. For the things where you have work to do, do it. And then take comfort in doing your part and trusting God to do his part.

GOD HEARS & RESTORES

VERSE 66:
Revelation 3:20

A LITTLE EXTRA

Draw a picture of the "perfect" friend. Write down some descriptions and characteristics. How many of those things describe Jesus? What are some things Jesus can bring to a friendship that no one else can? With your parents' permission, do an online search for Israel Houghton's song "Friend of God" and listen to it (or read the lyrics).

"Look! I stand at the door and knock. If you hear my voice and open the door, I will come in, and we will share a meal together as friends."
Revelation 3:20

You're sitting in your room with the door closed, and someone knocks. "Who is it?" "It's me, Jesus!" you hear. Now you have a choice. You can ignore it. You can tell him to go away. Or you can open it and invite him in.

Jesus wants us to know that he comes to us and wants into our lives. He makes it clear that he's there. (You can't miss it when someone is knocking and calling your name.) However, Christ is not a bully who will beat down the door and force his way inside.

Few things symbolize friendship more than hanging out over a meal. That is when you laugh, share stories, and talk about life. This is the promise Christ gives if/when we open the door and invite him inside.

TALKING WITH GOD

Have you heard God knocking and calling, and you haven't wanted to let him in? Many people have felt this way because of misunderstandings about who Jesus is. Talk to God about your struggles and concerns. Ask him to give you a clear understanding of who he really is and what he's really like. Thank him for wanting to be your friend. Ask him to help you understand what that means and be a good friend to him.

But he was pierced for our rebellion, crushed for our sins. He was beaten so we could be whole. He was whipped so we could be healed. All of us, like sheep, have strayed away. We have left God's paths to follow our own. Yet the Lord laid on him the sins of us all. Isaiah 53:5-6

Most days it's easy to think about our shortcomings and failures. We aren't perfect. We mess up every day in big and small ways. We even make the same mistakes multiple times and struggle to learn from them. We are like sheep—forgetful and not that smart.

That can leave us feeling hopeless, right? It is true but it's only part of the truth.

The other part...*Whole.* This passage says that we can be whole. It's done because Jesus' act of being broken is done. Our wholeness is done *and* it's still happening.

Healed. This passage says that we can be healed. It's done because Jesus was whipped. Our healing is done *and* it's still happening.

So, yes we are broken and a mess, but we are also whole and healed. Each day we get to live out our wholeness and healing. We get to be living, walking examples of Jesus' work on the cross.

VERSE 67:
Isaiah 53:5-6

A LITTLE EXTRA

Watch this to get an idea of how smart sheep can be: http://www.youtube.com/watch?v=ZMOCA66O_dU. What can we learn from this silly and fun video about ourselves?

TALKING WITH GOD

Read and speak this prayer or one similar to it: *Jesus, thank you that your work is done and being done in my life. I fail and I make mistakes, but you have already healed me and forgiven me. Teach me to live and reveal your kingdom, and use me to point others to your work of wholeness and healing.*

71

ONENESS
WITH GOD

A LITTLE EXTRA

Find a permanent marker. Then take a walk, pick up some rocks, and on each rock write something that is weighing you down right now. You may need three rocks. You may need 30 rocks. Keep one final rock blank. Take the rocks you've written on and throw them in a pond, lake, river, ditch, or trashcan. (Just be smart: Don't throw them at cars, people, animals, or windows.) As you release each rock, say out loud to God, "I will not give up." Once you're finished, write "Don't quit!" on the final rock. Keep your "Don't quit!" rock in a place where you can see it often.

So let's not get tired of doing what is good. At just the right time we will reap a harvest of blessing if we don't give up. Galatians 6:9

Doing what is good doesn't guarantee that everything in life will go perfectly. Relatives still get cancer. Homecoming court still gets chosen, and you may not be on it. People may say you're crazy for believing in a guy named Jesus. But there is something amazing about knowing that you are living with a heart that's open to Jesus. Things around you may be falling apart, but there is hope in knowing that one day we will reap a harvest of blessing if we don't give up.

Satan wants you to give up. He wants you to believe the lie that it's just not worth it—but it is. Don't give up. Jesus will never fail you.

TALKING WITH GOD

Talk to Jesus about everything that is weighing you down. Tell him how you're trying to stay focused on doing what is good in his name, but sometimes life gets difficult. Ask him to give you the courage to not give up.

ONENESS
WITH GOD

"However, no one knows the day or hour when these things will happen, not even the angels in heaven or the Son himself. Only the Father knows."
Mark 13:32

For most people, celebrating a birthday is something you look forward to every year, especially when you hit important milestones along the way. When you turn 10 years old—double digits! When you're 13 years old—you're a teenager! At 16 years old, you can drive, and at 18 years old, you can vote and you're almost out of the house! Each year, like clockwork, your birthday falls on the same day. You can easily predict it and prepare for your birthday.

But no one can predict when Jesus' promised return will occur. It's a 100 percent certainty, but only God the Father knows when it will be. So what do we do?

We can trust that God's timing is perfect, and we can live the life God has invited us to live. Nothing to worry about, or stress over, or argue about. Trust God, and live and reveal his kingdom.

TALKING WITH GOD

If you're someone who worries about End Times stuff, ask God to help you with your worry. Don't be ashamed of it; just ask God for help. Then recommit yourself to loving God with everything you are and loving your neighbor as yourself.

VERSE 69:
Mark 13:32

A LITTLE EXTRA

If you don't already have one, find an analog watch to wear for the day. Don't use your phone, and don't use a digital wristwatch. Now pull the pin so the watch hands stop moving. Every time you look down at the watch today, remember that God knows all things, and recommit yourself to trust him and live the life God has called you to live.

SIN & SEPARATION

A LITTLE EXTRA

On a separate sheet of paper, write out what type of person you want to be seen as. How do you want people to view you? Then ask yourself, "What changes do I need to make so people would believe I am this person I'm trying to be?"

And he was amazed at their unbelief. Mark 6:6

In today's passage, Jesus returned to his hometown of Nazareth with his disciples. When he got there, he began to teach and share the gospel with the local people, his friends, and his family members. He had a great word to share, full of wisdom and power, but people wouldn't listen to him because they only remembered him as the little carpenter guy! First they were amazed by what he said, but then they were offended. Jesus' response basically was, "Everywhere I go, people respect me, love me, and believe in me—except here in my hometown." If Jesus could have texted his feelings about the situation to the disciples, he probably would have just written "SMH!!!"

Jesus could have done greater miracles in Nazareth, but he chose not to because the people were too prideful and didn't believe. The miracles he did perform had little power, because the people had little belief. Therefore, Jesus had to look elsewhere and find people who would respond to his miracles.

TALKING WITH GOD

Are you like the people in Jesus' hometown? Or are you the kind of person who's experienced a changed life but the people closest to you don't believe you've really changed? Depending on which category you fall in, pray today that God will either forgive you for your unbelief and help you to trust him more, or open the hearts of others to receive the blessings he has for them.

But the wisdom from above is first of all pure. It is also peace loving, gentle at all times, and willing to yield to others. It is full of mercy and good deeds. It shows no favoritism and is always sincere.
James 3:17

Do you want to be a leader who others follow? Do you want to have influence on your team or become someone that others listen to at your school? Today's verse provides a clear picture of how you can become a leader who has influence.

First, seek God and his Word for truth and wisdom. God's truth is pure and faultless and will help you become a person of strong confidence and character. Confidence and character will help people wonder, "What does that person have?"

Second, have the right attitude to go along with God-given wisdom. Being peace loving, gentle, teachable, and sincere will help others to trust you. After all, who wants to follow someone who is arrogant, harsh, stubborn, and insincere?

Where do your wisdom and confidence come from? How are you filling your life with God's wisdom? How do others truly see you?

TALKING WITH GOD

God promises to generously give wisdom to all who ask him. Ask God for wisdom daily, so you can point others to him and live in a way that reveals God's kingdom. Ask God to show you the areas of your life that limit your influence. Ask God to help you trust him enough to make the changes he desires in your life.

ONENESS
WITH GOD

VERSE 71:
James 3:17

A LITTLE EXTRA

Create a list of qualities from this verse in James, and ask two trustworthy friends how you match up to these qualities. It's risky, but it's a great reality check to see how others view your wisdom and leadership.

ONENESS
WITH GOD

A LITTLE EXTRA

Read the whole story
of this man in John 9,
and each time you read
forms of the words *blind*
or *see*, underline them.
Then, with your parents'
permission, go online
and listen to the song
"Open the Eyes of My
Heart."

"Yes, Lord, I believe!" the man said. And he worshiped Jesus. John 9:38

Have you ever heard of a "blind spot"? If you drive or have taken a driver's training class, you've definitely heard that phrase. It's when we can't see another car that's near us on the road—but the phrase can apply to other areas, too. It might mean that we can see something on the road of life, but we choose to ignore it. But it also might mean we really can't see it.

The man in today's verse was physically blind. If you read all of John 9, you'll learn that after the man was healed, he didn't "see" who had given him sight. For this reason, Jesus came back around and asked the man, "You can see with your eyes now, but do you want to understand who I am?" Jesus' question was not about the man's physical sight, but about the man's heart and his spiritual sight.

Do you have a "blind spot" in your own life when it comes to the Lord? Can you "see" him for who he is?

TALKING WITH GOD

Ask God to help you see him clearly and to understand who he is. Ask God to help you trust him like the man in today's passage trusted Jesus. End your prayer time today by worshipping God through a song, a psalm, or a time of celebrating who God is.

We are imperfect human beings—every single one of us. We aren't capable of living perfect lives, and our sins hurt us and hurt others. Can you think of a time when this has been true in your life? Is it true right now?

Our sins separate us from our loving God, who wants to be in relationship with us. When sin rules, we are without hope, joy, and meaning. God created us for so much more! God created us to be in relationship with him for eternity, but first, we have to be saved from our sinful nature.

Jesus told him, "I am the way, the truth, and the life. No one can come to the Father except through me." John 14:6

God sent his Son, Jesus Christ, to this earth to be our Savior. Jesus lived a perfect life and chose to die for us. He was hung on a cross to pay the price for all of our sins. He was raised from the dead and now will live in us!

Without Jesus, we cannot be with God for eternity. When we trust Jesus as our Savior, we accept the gift of true life and surrender our sinful lives to God.

TALKING WITH GOD

Where are you on your faith journey? Ask God to meet you right where you are. Ask God to show you next steps to take with him. Ask God to help you trust him more and live a life that reveals his kingdom to others.

GOD HEARS
& RESTORES

VERSE 73:
John 14:6

A LITTLE EXTRA

Read Philippians 1:20-21. Record five ways that you can show courage in your faith in God, such as confessing your sin, sharing your reason for joy when someone asks, or standing up for your beliefs when they are challenged.

GOD HEARS & RESTORES

A LITTLE EXTRA

Write five things that Jesus did that were acts of love for others. (Look through Matthew, Mark, Luke, and John if you can't think of five.) Next to each one write something you could do today that would be an act of following his lead.

Either way, Christ's love controls us. Since we believe that Christ died for all, we also believe that we have all died to our old life. 2 Corinthians 5:14

Following Jesus is about death. Oh wow, this got deep really fast!

Being a follower of Jesus provides salvation from eternal death and separation from God. But it's not just about eternity. Following him also is about death to self and our own desires.

The death of death is love. That sentence is both weird and powerful, isn't it? Our salvation and our willingness to die to our own desire and self start with love. Not our love. Never our love. Christ's radical love. A love that will take control of our lives and lead us to death—a good death. We can do it because we know it is what Jesus did for us and for all.

How do you die to self and to your own desires? There are no easy steps to fully embracing this spiritual death, but we can start by allowing Christ's love to control us.

Warning: It won't always feel great or be the fun thing to do. But it will be an adventure that goes beyond your wildest dreams.

TALKING WITH GOD

Take a minute and ask God's Spirit to fill you with love. Tell God that you want to die to yourself so he can control your life. Ask God to control you with his love so you can live and reveal his kingdom.

"So fear the Lord and serve him wholeheartedly. Put away forever the idols your ancestors worshiped when they lived beyond the Euphrates River and in Egypt. Serve the Lord alone. But if you refuse to serve the Lord, then choose today whom you will serve. Would you prefer the gods your ancestors served beyond the Euphrates? Or will it be the gods of the Amorites in whose land you now live? But as for me and my family, we will serve the Lord." Joshua 24:14–15

VERSE 75:
Joshua 24:14-15

Joshua was the guy who took over for Moses in leading the people of Israel, and after 40 years of wandering around the desert, he's the one who led them into the Promised Land. However, once there, they half-heartedly worshipped God. Joshua told them they had to choose— and made it clear that he would follow God.

We face the same choice as Joshua. Today people worship status, fame, money, and power. Anything we put in front of our relationship with God is an "idol." Many people attempt to give some of themselves to the Lord while still doing what they want. But Christ wants all of us.

A LITTLE EXTRA

Grab a friend who's a Christ-follower and commit to meeting before school weekly or monthly to pray for your friends. Invite other followers of Jesus to meet with you. Show your friends that you serve Jesus by living and revealing the kingdom of God every day.

TALKING WITH GOD

Ask God to give you the courage of Joshua, so you will be willing to make a clear statement to your friends that you're a follower of Jesus. Ask God to help you trust him enough to take the risk of making your faith public.

GOD HEARS & RESTORES

VERSE 76:
Mark 4:39–40

A LITTLE EXTRA

Read the whole story of Jesus calming the storm in Mark 4:35-41. On a piece of paper, draw a picture of a large cloud. In the middle, write the words that describe any "storms" going on in your life. Now write "JESUS" in big letters over everything. Do you believe that he can take care of all of these things?

When Jesus woke up, he rebuked the wind and said to the waves, "Silence! Be still!" Suddenly the wind stopped, and there was a great calm. Then he asked them, "Why are you afraid? Do you still have no faith?" Mark 4:39-40

Have you ever gotten caught in an unexpected storm? The skies appear sunny and clear. Suddenly the wind picks up, and clouds as dark as night roll in. Before you can even get ready, a wall of rain follows one raindrop. You can't see your hand in front of your face. You can't find shelter. You feel stuck, alone, and afraid.

That is what happened to Jesus' disciples, on a boat. Jesus was there, but he was asleep. Wasn't he supposed to keep the storm away in the first place? He used this actual rainstorm to remind his disciples (and us) that trusting him was not about having faith in circumstances. It is about trusting in who Jesus is.

When things happen in your life that seem really horrible, what will your reaction be? Will you panic and think that Jesus doesn't care? Or will you trust that Jesus is always with you and has control over all things?

TALHING WITH GOD

Pray for God's help in focusing less on your circumstances and more on him. Pray that you will trust in him, even during the biggest "storms" of life.

You must warn each other every day, while it is still "today," so that none of you will be deceived by sin and hardened against God. Hebrews 3:13

The buddy system is always encouraged when swimming. It keeps both swimmers safe as they look out for each other. In today's verse, we are encouraged to help one another keep away from the dangers of sin so we can keep focused on God. It sounds easy, but we must be always alert and warn each other when something we are about to do will hurt our relationship with God. We also have to be receptive to our friend who is trying to warn us! Notice how urgent this Scripture is by talking about today! Do not wait until tomorrow to warn a friend that he or she is doing something bad or headed in the wrong direction—do it today.

TALKING WITH GOD

Who is someone in your life that tells you the truth, even when it's hard to hear? Offer thanks to God for those kinds of friends. Ask God to help you be that kind of friend to others.

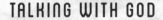

VERSE 77:
Hebrews 3:13

A LITTLE EXTRA

Reach out to the person who tells you the truth, and give them permission to keep doing it! Make a list of the things you struggle with, and give it to them, so they know what questions to ask you to help you stay focused on God.

ONENESS
WITH GOD

A LITTLE EXTRA

These three verses are some of the most important in the entire Bible, particularly if you want to live the best life. So take a few moments to try to commit them to memory. Just go with this part: " 'Love the Lord your God with all your heart, all your soul, and all your mind.' This is the first and greatest commandment. A second is equally important: 'Love your neighbor as yourself.' " Write it on a piece of paper and review it until you've got it nailed.

So many people think that following Jesus is primarily about a big list of things you have to do, and another big list of things you can't do. Lots of people view the Bible this way, too—as if it's page after page of rules and regulations.

But Jesus boils it all down for us. He says there are just two essential rules:

Jesus replied, " 'You must love the Lord your God with all your heart, all your soul, and all your mind.' This is the first and greatest commandment. A second is equally important: 'Love your neighbor as yourself.' " Matthew 22:37-39

Love God, love others. That's it. That's the entire "way to live like Jesus" in four words. That's the entire Bible summarized in two tiny statements.

And here's the cool part: If you give yourself to a "love God, love others" life completely, you will experience the very best life—better than *any other* possible way of living.

TALKING WITH GOD

Take a moment to examine your life. Do you live a "love God, love others" life? Pray that God would help you understand what this looks like and would give you the courage to put it into action. Ask God to help you trust him enough to live and reveal his kingdom.

And he said, "Yes, it was written long ago that the Messiah would suffer and die and rise from the dead on the third day. It was also written that this message would be proclaimed in the authority of his name to all the nations, beginning in Jerusalem: 'There is forgiveness of sins for all who repent.' You are witnesses of all these things." Luke 24:46–48

Do ever feel that you're just not good enough? Maybe your boyfriend/girlfriend just broke up with you, or you did something with them you really didn't plan on doing. Maybe you got into a fight with your friends or parents, or you said something really cruel to them. Maybe you got a bad grade on a test, or you cheated on a test.

No matter what, remember that God sent his Son for you. God loves you so much that before you were born he sent Jesus to die for your sin. God will forgive everything and anything you have ever done. God loves you no matter what the circumstances are in your life, whether you caused them or not. How awesome is that?

TALKING WITH GOD

Pray this kind of prayer: *God, I know things won't be perfect all of the time, but I thank you for sending Jesus to pay for my sins. Thank you for loving me, no matter how I may feel. Even though it's sometimes hard to admit that I'm hurt or that I've messed up, help me remember how much you love me, and remind me that you sent Jesus for me.*

A LITTLE EXTRA

Make a list of all the ways you can think that God has blessed you in your life. We've given you one to get started.

1. God sent his Son to pay the price for my sins

2.

3.

83

GOD HEARS & RESTORES

A LITTLE EXTRA

Try your own Opposite Day. If you usually sit in the front of the class, sit in the back. Instead of a latte in the morning, try a smoothie. Throughout the day, remember that Jesus keeps people guessing so they'll think differently. It's vital to listen closely to him constantly, and he'll speak in surprising ways.

Do you remember Opposite Day in elementary school? Up was down, left was right, in was out, and even siblings switched identities for a day. Kids kept the adults guessing all day.

Jesus focused on many opposites while here on Earth. The last will be first...whoever tries to save his life will lose it...faith like a tiny mustard seed can move mountains. Here's one more:

Jesus told her, "I am the resurrection and the life. Anyone who believes in me will live, even after dying." John 11:25

Jesus' disciples and the community had to listen to him closely because he was causing them to rethink nearly every aspect of their lives. He wasn't keeping everyone guessing to get on their nerves; Jesus knew people needed to be challenged to think differently. Death was final; there was no question about it. Yet Jesus promised life after death. His beautiful plan of salvation, to bring people back to him, allows for an eternal life of unfathomable bliss in heaven with him after death here on Earth.

TALKING WITH GOD

Thank God for his plan of salvation and the opportunity to spend eternity with him. Identify the major challenges in your life today, the ones where you need God to work. As you commit these challenges to God, joyfully trade them for something you're looking forward to in heaven: "Today I'm dealing with _____, but in heaven I'll be able to _____."

Surely your goodness and unfailing love will pursue me all the days of my life, and I will live in the house of the Lord forever. Psalm 23:6

There aren't many absolutes in life. Material things come and go, and people seemingly change like the weather. But in Christ, there are at least two absolute guarantees: God loves us, and God is good to us. We often look at our situations and circumstances to determine how God feels about us. When things are going great, we may think, "Wow! God really loves me!" But when get bad, we may wonder, "Why does God hate me?" or "God isn't good to me at all!"

So what do we trust when our feelings about our circumstances contradict what the Bible says about God? We must allow our trust in God to change our perspective. When we have a bad day, our perspective changes from thinking God hates us to understanding that our world is broken, but God still works to bring beauty form ashes. Choose to trust God today. God's love never fails.

TALHING WITH GOD

Confess to God your struggles with trust. Don't be ashamed—God is amazingly patient with us when we're open and honest. Tell him when you struggle, and ask God to help you trust him more. God is good enough to answer your prayers.

VERSE 81:
Psalm 23:6

A LITTLE EXTRA

Take a few minutes and make a list of as many good things God has done for you as you can remember. You can be as detailed as you want—include big and little things. When you struggle with something that makes you doubt God's goodness, pull out your list and remind yourself that God is good and his love never fails.

GOD HEARS
& RESTORES

A LITTLE EXTRA

Take a moment to see the big picture. Be creative. Drive to the foothills and look over your city. Or go to the top floor of a building and look out over the campus or landscape. Reflect on the fact that day to day, you may not see the big picture; you can only see your small portion. Thank God that he is in control of the big picture, from beginning to end, and every small detail in between.

Yet God has made everything beautiful for its own time. He has planted eternity in the human heart, but even so, people cannot see the whole scope of God's work from beginning to end. Ecclesiastes 3:11

Have you read a book—starting in the middle? (And we're not talking about when you start reading a book because the report is due the next day.) What would happen if you played a video game working on the final level first? Or baked a cake following only half the steps?

It just wouldn't make sense. You need the whole picture. Each chapter, each step, each level has a purpose and works together for an incredible result. And the only one who knows how it all fits together is the author, the chef, the creator.

You can trust God's design of your own life just like you would trust the story, the recipe, and the adventure. God plans for things to fit together perfectly for an incredible result—even though people may not understand in the moment. You can trust God with the outcome.

TALKING WITH GOD

As you talk with God today, think about how he brought you to where you are today. Be honest on this journey, and allow the past to give you confidence and trust in your Creator.

Have you ever been on a mission trip and built something that would help people, such as a porch or wheelchair ramp? Do you remember building a sandcastle at the beach? Have you ever created something out of building blocks? When you build something, what is the most important part of the structure?

And now, just as you accepted Christ Jesus as your Lord, you must continue to follow him. Let your roots grow down into him, and let your lives be built on him. Then your faith will grow strong in the truth you were taught, and you will overflow with thankfulness. Colossians 2:6–7

VERSE 83:
Colossians 2:6–7

The foundation is the most important part of a structure. When you build something, its foundation needs to be strong enough to support the weight of your creation. Similarly, you need to have a strong foundation to your faith. To let your roots grow deep and build a foundation to support you in life, you must follow God. As you learn to pray, study, and listen to God, your roots will grow deeper and give you a strong foundation.

TALKING WITH GOD

Spend the next few minutes asking God to build in you a stronger foundation of trust in him. Commit to spending a little more time with God every day.

A LITTLE EXTRA

Grab a pen and a piece of paper and draw a tree. It doesn't have to be a perfect tree; it could just be a tree that inhabits a world of stick-figure people. Now draw roots out from the tree. Write these words at the end of three of those roots: *Pray, Study,* and *Listen.* Below each of these words, write down a time that you can do it each day. Put your creation in a place where you'll see it when you get ready every morning.

GOD HEARS & RESTORES

A LITTLE EXTRA

Read Matthew 5:43-45 and reflect on these questions. Take an extra moment to journal your answers.

- How does loving our neighbors and loving our enemies look the same? different?

- In what ways has God allowed the "sunlight" to shine on both you and your enemies? How about the ways God has allowed the "rain" for both you and your enemies?

Jesus said, "Father, forgive them, for they don't know what they are doing." And the soldiers gambled for his clothes by throwing dice.
Luke 23:34

Even while Jesus was hanging on the cross, he continued to display amazing love and kindness toward people. He saw everyone as brothers and sisters and wanted them to know him personally, to be forgiven, and to follow God's plan for their life. You'd think they would've had a better reaction to him, but they just continued their plans.

Throughout his life (and especially at the end), Christ was persecuted, treated terribly. Scorned. Publicly ridiculed. Manipulated. Falsely accused. Doubted.

Sound familiar?

You might have people in your life who are just plain mean. But you don't have to live in their shadow and allow them to ruin your life.

See Jesus as the true example that he is, and continue to love and pray for your enemies. You don't need to trust them or pretend to be best friends. But there is such sweet freedom in praying for your enemies and allowing God to work in you as he works in them.

TALKING WITH GOD

Make a list of the people who persecute you. Name them one by one, and pray for them. Be careful to not pray for justice, but pray for each person as an individual. Pray that God blesses the ups and downs of life and that he will make himself known to them.

Close your eyes for a moment and envision a clear night full of stars. Then read this verse from the Old Testament:

"You alone are the Lord. You made the skies and the heavens and all the stars. You made the earth and the seas and everything in them. You preserve them all, and the angels of heaven worship you."
Nehemiah 9:6

When you look at the stars in the sky, or the mountains, or the ocean, you can see how BIG God truly is! This Scripture is another reminder that God set the world in motion and created everything that we see. We sometimes need a reminder to slow down and see how great and powerful God is—and to take time to worship him as the creator of the universe.

TALKING WITH GOD

Spend some time in prayer, and thank God for the awesome creation that he has made. Do an online search for the song "God of Wonders," and read the lyrics as a prayer.

ONENESS
WITH GOD

VERSE 85:
Nehemiah 9:6

A LITTLE EXTRA

Tonight, take a blanket outside; lie down and look at the star-filled sky. Take a picture, and upload it, and put today's Scripture as the caption.

SPIRITUAL JOURNALING

JOURNALING IS TELLING YOUR LIFE STORY. Spiritual journaling is telling your spiritual story; it's a way to record and remember what God has done in your life. Whether you're new to journaling or a veteran, here are a few suggestions to help you out:

1. **Include dates in every entry.** Think of it as God's history in your life. You might look at your spiritual journal in 20 days or 20 years. How cool will it be when you're a college senior to look back and see what God was doing in your life as a high school freshman?

2. **Don't worry about writing in complete sentences.** Write things down as they pop into your mind. Make sure you write enough so that when you read your journal later, you'll remember what you were talking about. As long as it makes sense to you, it makes enough sense.

3. **Write Bible verses that speak to you.** If you want to add some details about why the verse was significant, go for it!

4. **Write down things your pastor says that speak to you.** Include the sermon title and/or Bible verse.

5. **Write down song lyrics that speak to you.** You don't have to write the whole song—just the part that's meaningful to you.

6. Write down prayers during significant times—good or bad. If you feel like writing a lot, do it. If you can only manage one sentence, that's fine, too. Add as much detail as you want.

7. Spend time writing about important spiritual events: camps, retreats, baptism, leading someone to Christ, and other big moments. You may not forget the feeling, but you'll lose the details if you don't write them down.

REMEMBERING IS A BIG DEAL IN THE BIBLE. Your spiritual journal is a way to remember God's faithfulness in your life. It might not be something you do every day, but it could be a cool way to record how you've grown in your trust in Jesus.

GOD HEARS & RESTORES

A LITTLE EXTRA

Pick one setting you will be in this week, such as your home, school, youth group, or sports team. Spend the entire week looking for ways you can serve the people in that setting. As you go out of your way to "wash people's feet," think about how Jesus serves you. It might change the way you view Christ's love.

"You call me 'Teacher' and 'Lord,' and you are right, because that's what I am. And since I, your Lord and Teacher, have washed your feet, you ought to wash each other's feet." John 13:13-14

In today's passage, Jesus has just finished washing his disciples' feet. This was no pleasant task. In that time, people wore sandals, streets weren't paved, and feet got really dirty. Jesus was performing a true act of service. It was an act fit for a slave, not a king. It was an act of humility that demonstrated the depth of Jesus' love for his disciples and for us.

The story does not end here, however. When he is finished, he told his followers that they should wash each other's feet. If they were going to be his followers, they needed to perform similar acts of selfless service toward others, and expect nothing in return.

As Christ-followers we are called to be servants. Serving others is not easy, especially when they treat you like a servant. Are you ready to embrace Jesus' invitation to live a life of service?

TALKING WITH GOD

Thank God for the ways he blesses you each day. Ask God to show you one thing you could do to serve someone today that would bless that person. Ask God to lead you to someone who really needs to see God's kingdom lived out.

Sometimes it praises our Lord and Father, and sometimes it curses those who have been made in the image of God. And so blessing and cursing come pouring out of the same mouth. Surely, my brothers and sisters, this is not right! James 3:9-10

This week, as the church gathers all around the world, teenagers will use their voices to worship God and sing songs of praise to him. In the following days, some students may use these same voices to throw junk at someone they dislike or don't agree with. You might say, "How hypocritical is that?"

But let's get really honest for a moment—don't we all do the same thing at some point? It's important that we guard our words, because God wants us to use our voices to share his story. If we speak with no self-control, we could lose an opportunity to share our faith with our friends.

TALKING WITH GOD

Take a few moments to be quiet and think about the way your words can be used for good or bad. Ask God to help you develop greater self-control, so you can guard your language and use it to live and reveal his kingdom. This is one of those areas where God's work in your life may be gradual or seemingly absent—but a month from now or a year from now, you'll see how God has helped you change.

VERSE 87:
James 3:9-10

A LITTLE EXTRA

Read the rest of James 3, as James continues his comments on language following today's verse. He argues that fresh water and salt water should not come out of the same spring. Each time you drink water today, remember that God wants to use your words to bring fresh, healthy truth into people's lives.

ONENESS WITH GOD

A LITTLE EXTRA

How do we really follow the words of this verse? Think about what it means to love mercy— and then send a text or social media message to a friend explaining your thoughts.

No, O people, the Lord has told you what is good, and this is what he requires of you: to do what is right, to love mercy, and to walk humbly with your God. Micah 6:8

"Everyone tells me I am supposed to live for God. What does that mean?" Have you ever thought this? What does it mean to have a relationship with Jesus and be totally his?

Well, there are several places in the Bible where God makes it clear for us, and today's verse is one of them. God invites us to trust him. The way we demonstrate our trust is by doing what we know to be right. Be in love with mercy. This means that we are called to have compassion for those around us—it must be a priority.

What does it mean to walk humbly with our God? Someone who's humble is willing to put others first, be selfless, and live a life of a servant. In other words, walk with God in a way where we are always his. It may not be easy, but it reveals our trust in God and his way of living. Put God first always, do what is right, and stand up for the hurting no matter what.

TALKING WITH GOD

Even when the Bible tells us exactly how to live, we can still wonder what it means for our lives. Do you struggle having compassion for some people in your life? Do you put God first in everything? Ask God to show you today what each part of this verse means for you.

Then the Lord God said, "It is not good for the man to be alone. I will make a helper who is just right for him." Genesis 2:18

If someone asked you to say what's most important to God in one word, you might suggest *love*. And that would be a great answer. But another word that could fit is *relationships*. God is really into relationships, and we see that in this verse from the opening pages of the Bible.

VERSE 89:
Genesis 2:18

God didn't want Adam to be alone. In fact, God said, "It's not good." In other words, it was bad!

Couldn't God have just made Adam to be completely happy being alone in the world? Wouldn't it have been totally possible for God to invent Adam so he would be happiest all by himself in his man-cave, with the football game on, and no one to distract him?

Get this: It's not just that God noticed Adam was lonely. God *made* Adam to have a need for relationship. And the reason for that is that we're made in the image of God, and God is all about relationship (the Trinity: Father, Son, and Holy Spirit). You are *like* God when you pursue relationships of love, respect, humility, and trust.

A LITTLE EXTRA

Spend a minute prayerfully considering if you know someone who's lonely, someone in need of a caring friend. Would you be willing to reach out to that person and start to establish a friendship? You'd be acting "in the image of God" if you're willing to do so.

TALKING WITH GOD

Thank God for wiring you for relationships. Name each person you really care about (really—say their names as a prayer of thanks).

GOD HEARS & RESTORES

But now you are free from the power of sin and have become slaves of God. Now you do those things that lead to holiness and result in eternal life. For the wages of sin is death, but the free gift of God is eternal life through Christ Jesus our Lord.
Romans 6:22–23

VERSE 90:
Romans 6:22-23

A LITTLE EXTRA

Look up Ephesians 2:8-10 and Titus 3:3-7. What do you read in these passages that is similar to Romans 6:22-23?

Life is all about choices. What clothes will you wear? What food will you eat? Which friends will you hang out with this weekend? Will you do homework, or watch TV? Each day represents a series of choices—some minor, some major, but all with consequences of some kind.

This idea carries over into our faith journey, too. God didn't create us as robots or puppets. Instead, God gives us the freedom to choose, and he makes it clear that we basically have two choices: life with Christ or life without Christ.

In today's passage, the Apostle Paul shares the results of those two choices. The consequence of choosing to stay in sin is death, but the result of choosing to trust Christ is eternal life. As you read over today's passage, the question for you is simple: What choice will you make? It's a choice we can't avoid—it's a decision each of us must make.

TALKING WITH GOD

Spend some time today thanking God for the free gift of salvation and eternal life with him, made available through your faith in Jesus. Recommit yourself to living a life where your choice to live for Jesus is visible and evident to God and to people around you.

Think about all of the voices that are speaking into your life right now: friends, bullies, teachers, parents, your own inner voice. Are they mostly bad? Good? Are you able to drown out the negative ones, or do they overtake your every thought?

But even as he spoke, a bright cloud overshadowed them, and a voice from the cloud said, "This is my dearly loved Son, who brings me great joy. Listen to him." Matthew 17:5

If I heard a voice from a cloud telling me to listen to someone, I imagine that's just what I'd do. God's voice is the most important sound among the many noises competing for our attention.

How can we concentrate on his voice? What you're doing right now (reading Scripture) is one way. Prayer is another. We're also obeying his voice when we do what he's commanded us to do—feed the hungry and clothe the naked, for instance.

TALKING WITH GOD

Ask God to help you concentrate on the voices that matter in your life. Ask him to help you listen closely so you're able to focus on and take strength from the positive voices in your life. God's voice may be the only one left after that filter, but it will always be there to encourage you.

GOD HEARS & RESTORES

A LITTLE EXTRA

A pastor named Charles Stanley once said, "God's voice is still and quiet and easily buried under an avalanche of clamor" (look up that word if you don't know it). Sometime in the next few days, find 30 minutes to shut out the clamor and just *listen*. No music. Turn off your phone. Walk away from the distractions. Go someplace where you won't be interrupted. And listen. Sometimes the clamor that buries God's voice is our own.

After your 30 clamor-free minutes, write down what you sense God telling you.

GOD HEARS & RESTORES

A LITTLE EXTRA

Go stand in front of a mirror. Make a face that communicates determination. (Don't worry if this feels a little awkward; no one else is watching.) Remember that true determination flows from your relationship with God. The deeper that relationship, the stronger your determination will be.

As the time drew near for him to ascend to heaven, Jesus resolutely set out for Jerusalem. Luke 9:51

We easily think of the highlights of Jesus' earthly ministry: healed bodies, miraculous meals, transformed lives, and countless other amazing moments. But sometimes we forget that Jesus also faced opposition. Not everyone was happy with the truth he spoke and the message he delivered.

What kept him going? In part, it was his dedication to following God's plan and revealing God's kingdom to this world. He knew that God's plan was best. He knew that God was with him each step of the way. He knew that his life mission was to bring people forgiveness and salvation and restored relationship with God.

Your life has purpose, too. God has a plan for you and will never leave you alone as you lead a Jesus-centered life. The sacrifices you'll make, the service you'll display, the choices that will stun some of the people around you— it's all part of your process of maturing as you continue your faith journey.

So when you face challenges or tough times, allow your God-based resolution and determination and commitment to carry you through—and know that you're in good company. Jesus has walked this path before you!

TALKING WITH GOD

Pray for God's strength when you face obstacles or opposition. Pray for resolve, determination, and commitment to follow God's path, even when people around you ridicule you or head in a completely different direction.

Therefore, let us offer through Jesus a continual sacrifice of praise to God, proclaiming our allegiance to his name. And don't forget to do good and to share with those in need. These are the sacrifices that please God. Hebrews 13:15–16

Do good. Seems easy enough, right? Or maybe not. Doing good and sharing with others aren't always easy. If they were, the writer of Hebrews wouldn't have called it a sacrifice.

Why we would choose something that is going to cost us? After all, that's what a sacrifice is—it's costly.

For starters, it pleases God. One of the greatest joys we can experience as Christ-followers is to know that God is pleased with us.

If we sing praise and worship with our mouths, then we must follow it by doing good and helping others. They are both acts of worship.

People who've been following Jesus for years know that they won't always get it right, but when they do, they are aware of unspeakable joy and peace. It's always worth the sacrifice.

TALK WITH GOD

Take a minute and dedicate your life to following Jesus and pleasing him. Ask him to show you what is good, and ask for wisdom to see the needs in others. Commit to living and revealing God's kingdom today.

A LITTLE EXTRA

Want to try something radical? Get your parents' permission, and then look around your home—maybe even your own bedroom. Is there something in there that could help another person in need? Don't pick something you don't like anymore, and don't just look at things your parents paid for. Consider giving something away that you'll miss having. And every time you miss it, say a prayer of thanks for the opportunity to bless someone in Jesus' name.

GOD HEARS & RESTORES

A LITTLE EXTRA

Write out a list of the sins you struggle with. Confess them to God and realize you are forgiven! Then in big, bold, capital letters, write the words PAID IN FULL across your list. As a reminder that Jesus has paid the penalty for your sin, rip your paper up into tiny pieces and **throw it away**! If your parents are Christ-followers, ask them to do this with you, and then you can all tear up your lists together.

But God showed his great love for us by sending Christ to die for us while we were still sinners.
Romans 5:8

Did you know that the word *gospel* means "good news"? The really good news at the core of the gospel is that even though we are all sinners who have fallen short of God's holy and perfect standard, God the Father loved us so much that he made a way for our relationship with him to be restored—by sending his Son, Jesus, to die on the cross in our place.

Jesus—who was fully God and fully man—lived a perfect life, died a horrible death, and rose from the grave for one reason: to pay the price for our sin and redeem us. Because of his sacrifice, we can be declared "not guilty" in the eyes of God.

When we accept this free gift of forgiveness and salvation, our penalty is paid, and we are set free to pursue God with all our hearts—to trust him, know him, love him, and serve him.

Have you shared this good news with your friends who don't know and follow Jesus? Jesus' gift of grace is the best news on the planet. Share it today!

TALKING WITH GOD

Think of a friend who needs to hear that Jesus paid the price for their sin by dying on the cross and rising from the dead. Talk to Jesus about your friend. Then talk to your friend about Jesus today!

As you read through the biblical accounts, you'll find there are many attributes of God that are highlighted throughout the pages of Scripture. The Gospels show him as our loving Father. Genesis shows him as the creative designer of the heavens and earth, and Revelation reveals God as the righteous judge of humanity. But in the writings of the prophets we see his holiness, as even the angels cover their faces and declare the awesomeness of God.

They were calling out to each other, "Holy, holy, holy is the Lord of Heaven's Armies! The whole earth is filled with his glory!" Isaiah 6:3

Holiness. What does that mean? It's not a word we use every day, so the weight of it can get lost. It means being set apart for God's purposes. It means that sin and evil do not have a place in our lives, because we trust that God's way is best.

TALKING WITH GOD

It's really hard to live a life of holiness. There are a lot of distractions, and to be honest, sin can really feel good (though the consequences of sin don't feel so good!). That's what makes it so tempting. Take a moment to thank God for being holy and ask him to help you trust him enough so that your life reveals his kingdom.

SIN &
SEPARATION

VERSE 95:
Isaiah 6:3

A LITTLE EXTRA

First Peter 1:16 reminds us of God's call to be holy because he is holy. Think about the areas of your life that you struggle with, and list them out. Then write a letter to yourself based on the impact those decisions are having on your walk with God. Be honest, and then ask someone you can trust for help in addressing the issues.

CONSEQUENCES & CRYING OUT

A LITTLE EXTRA

Do an online search for "names of Jesus." If there are any you don't understand, spend some time researching them. Pick a few that you like the most, and spend one day reflecting on each name. Doodle about it on your notebook, post it on social media, or share it with a friend.

Then he asked them, "But who do you say I am?"
Matthew 16:15

If you had to convince a friend that Jesus Christ is the Son of the Most High God and the Savior, who died on the cross for the sins of all humanity, could you do it? What would you say—especially if your friend had been taught something totally different or had never been taught anything about God at all? For you to convince someone of who Jesus is, you must be completely convinced yourself! You can't teach what you don't know.

Right after Jesus asked this question, Peter gave a simple yet profound answer: *"You are the Messiah, the Son of the living God."* Peter declared that Jesus was the Savior that God had promised throughout the Old Testament.

Salvation depends on us fully trusting Jesus as our Lord and Savior. There is no one else on whom it can depend. The major issue in our lives then becomes whether or not we truly believe that Jesus is the Son of God and whether or not we live our lives differently because of that faith.

So, who do you say Jesus is?

TALKING WITH GOD

Talk to God today about what he means to you, and acknowledge his role in your life. Allow God to have full ownership of your life, access to your heart, and to be your Savior and Lord.

"Those who accept my commandments and obey them are the ones who love me. And because they love me, my father will love them. And I will love them and reveal myself to each of them." John 14:21

Jesus gives you the choice to do your own thing or to follow and live by his commandments. When you choose to live a Jesus-centered life, you show respect to Jesus. It shows you choose Jesus over the world. It demonstrates your love for him. As you trust God a little, he will reveal himself more and more to you as your trust in him grows. God doesn't want you to obey out of guilt or because you feel like you're forced to obey; God wants your obedience to be rooted in your love for Jesus.

TALKING WITH GOD

Do you have problems following the rules? Or maybe you have trouble living by the rules because other people in your life don't follow them either? It's important and worthwhile to obey God's instructions for life, but God knows you're not perfect. Let God know you accept his commandments and want to obey them. Be completely honest with yourself and God, and tell him what you struggle with and why. Ask God to help you. Then sit quietly in peace for a few moments, knowing that God's plan for you is best.

VERSE 97:
John 14:21

A LITTLE EXTRA

As you trust God and obey his commandments, God reveals himself to you. Make a list of three things God has revealed to you since you began your faith journey. Write down a few sentences of detail, so you'll remember the story. Continue to follow and obey God, and add to your list as God continues to reveal himself to you.

GOD HEARS & RESTORES

A LITTLE EXTRA

Spend some time sketching out your life goals and plans—be as detailed or as vague as you want. Take your plan, and share it with God. Let God challenge things, if needed. When what you want to do contradicts what God wants you to do, ask God to help you trust that his plan is always best.

People may be pure in their own eyes, but the Lord examines their motives. Commit your actions to the Lord, and your plans will succeed. Proverbs 16:2–3

Have you met people who are convinced they are good at something, but they really aren't? You've likely seen them on TV reality competition shows where they are judged for abilities. In their eyes, they're destined for stardom, but everyone else is covering their eyes and ears as they perform. How can someone not get it? It's simple: They are self-deceived.

In our own way, we can each become self-deceived. It's easy to go through life and think that everything is going well. It's not always easy to be completely self-aware of potential issues in the undercurrent of our lives. We must acknowledge that only God can expose our real heart and motives.

Ultimately, God is the one we need to seek out to get an honest account of our motives and our current direction in life. How in tune are you with God? How well are you listening as God exposes your heart and points you forward in life?

TALKING WITH GOD

Ask God to help you do an honest evaluation of your motives—why you do the things you do. As you discover these motives, ask God to help you make whatever adjustments are necessary to have pure motives that honor him.

For his Spirit joins with our spirit to affirm that we are God's children. Romans 8:16

We are God's children. Chosen royalty. Wow! God loves you so much that he wants you to be a part of his family. God wants this so badly that he sent his Son, Jesus, to die for your sins. He wants to be by your side forever. God wants you to trade the emptiness of this world for him, his salvation, and his life for you.

It's similar to the story *Annie*, a musical that was made into a movie in 1982. Annie was an orphan adopted by billionaire Oliver Warbucks. It's a classic rags-to-riches story. More than the money and grandeur, Annie found a place to belong and a family to love her.

You might have a great relationship with your parents, specifically your father. This connection to God the Father is an easy and logical one for you to make. Unfortunately, you might struggle to see and accept God as your Heavenly Father because of a broken relationship with your own earthly father. Either way, God does not change. He is a solid, dependable, and loving Father who wants nothing but the best for you.

TALKING WITH GOD

Share with God what your relationship was and is like with your earthly father. Wrestle with how this is similar to or different from your relationship with God. Thank God for being your heavenly Father, taking you into his family, and providing for you.

GOD HEARS & RESTORES

VERSE 99:
Romans 8:16

A LITTLE EXTRA

Watch the movie *Annie*. Reflect on how this relates to your own life, your earthly father, and your Heavenly Father.

- Describe your life before you met Christ.

- How is your life different now that you know Christ and are a part of God's family?

SIN & SEPARATION

VERSE 100:
Matthew 21:45

A LITTLE EXTRA

Read the entire parable (Matthew 21:33-46) and answer these questions.

- Stop at verse 40. What would you do with the tenants if you were the landlord?

- Jesus became the capstone (look up the meaning), or cornerstone (look it up, too), of Christianity. Why was this necessary?

When the leading priests and Pharisees heard this parable, they realized he was telling the story against them—they were the wicked farmers.
Matthew 21:45

Jesus was telling a crowd—including religious leaders called Pharisees—a parable about a landowner that rented his land to tenants. The landowner sent his servants to collect rent when it was harvest time. The tenants killed the servants. After the landowner sent a second group of servants, the tenants killed them as well. Finally, the landowner sent his own son. The tenants killed him, too. While debriefing the parable, the crowd guessed the landowner would bring the tenants, or wicked farmers, to justice and rent the land to someone else. Jesus affirmed them and drew the parallel to how it is with the news of salvation.

The Pharisees were listening, despising what Jesus was doing with "their" religion. For them, it was all about keeping rules, not a true relationship. In that moment of realization, they must have gasped. Jesus was calling them the wicked farmers?

How do you react when you know you're wrong, you've made a bad choice, or you just plain blew it?

TALKING WITH GOD

God loves you and wants you to live according to his plan. It's not about rules. It's about an ongoing relationship with him. God knows you're not perfect—and doesn't expect you to be perfect. Look back at the last week and confess to God the wrongs you've done. Commit to making better choices in line with his story for your life.

Run from anything that stimulates youthful lusts. Instead, pursue righteous living, faithfulness, love, and peace. Enjoy the companionship of those who call on the Lord with pure hearts. 2 Timothy 2:22

Running away from things can make you feel like a coward, but it takes a wise and mature person to recognize that there are things in this world that need to be avoided so your heart can remain pure.

Some temptations are easy to walk away from, but others seem so amazing that making a good choice is crazy difficult. Temptation is different for everyone, and it won't let up once you graduate from high school.

Knowing when to stand firm and when to run is crucial to living a life that is fully devoted to Christ. Put on your running shoes and run from anything that will drag you down. Running from sin is rarely easy, but it's worth it—it's good for your heart. Your heart needs you to set yourself up to succeed, so sprint when temptation draws near. And your friends need you to do this as well.

Do you have a temptation that is difficult for you to resist? If so, are you ready to run?

TALK WITH GOD

Spend some time talking to God about the sin and temptation that is difficult for you resist. Ask God to give you the strength and wisdom to run from anything that causes you to struggle spiritually.

VERSE 101:
2 Timothy 2:22

A LITTLE EXTRA

Even if you're not a runner, lace up your shoes and go out for a jog. Notice how focused you need to be to keep your pace. You have to pay attention to your breathing, your footing, your direction, your distance. Running is difficult, but it's worth it—good for your heart.

ONENESS
WITH GOD

VERSE 102:
John 20:21

A LITTLE EXTRA

Check out the video by Lecrae for his song "Send Me" (youtube.com/watch?v=Fv6sQKHdgOA). As you listen to the lyrics, think about how he feels called to be sent into the world with the message of Jesus. What are some of the reasons he gives? How do you relate to any of those reasons?

Again he said, "Peace be with you. As the Father has sent me, so I am sending you." John 20:21

Jesus sends us out as his followers just as the Father sent Jesus out. Jesus was sent to bring the message of forgiveness and restoration to all who would hear. He came to bring healing to the broken, hope to the hopeless, and comfort to the hurting. In a similar way, Jesus is sending you out into the world to share this same good news.

Today, keep an eye out for ways you can share his message. Maybe a friend at school has never heard the message of Jesus, and God nudges you to witness to them. Perhaps a family member or friend is hurting, and God nudges you to show compassion. As a Christ-follower, you have been sent into the world to live and reveal the kingdom of God. Let's get going!

TALKING WITH GOD

In Isaiah 6:8, God asks, *"Whom should I send as a messenger to this people?"* Isaiah cries out, *"Send me!"* As you talk to God today, tell him that you are ready to be sent into your world as his messenger. Ask God to show you people who need to hear about the hope he offers, and to give you the right words to share. Ask God to help you trust him more as you live and reveal his kingdom.

Embarrassed. Fearful. Doubtful. Scared. Ignorant.

Have you experienced any of these feelings when someone asks you about God? What do they believe? What will they think of you? What if they ask you questions you just can't answer? How will this affect your friendship? It might just be easier to not talk about it.

"Everyone who acknowledges me publicly here on earth, I will also acknowledge before my Father in heaven. But everyone who denies me here on earth, I will also deny before my Father in heaven."
Matthew 10:32-33

Think of this a bit differently. Just because someone asks you about God doesn't mean you have to start reciting Scripture or take them through the steps to salvation. Try having a casual conversation. Answer their questions the best you can. This might be your chance to share with them how genuine and real a life lived for God can be. This is where the journey begins. Give them time to absorb what you're saying as you're earning the right to share Christ with them.

Be strong! You can stand up for Jesus in the small things and big things alike. He'll bless you and stand before God on your behalf.

TALKING WITH GOD

Review the past week. Celebrate with God the times you acknowledged him. Confess to him the times you denied him. Ask God to remind you this week to stand up for him and commit to making some changes.

GOD HEARS & RESTORES

VERSE 103:
Matthew 10:32-33

A LITTLE EXTRA

Read the passage where Peter denies Jesus three times, in Matthew 26:69-75. When have you acknowledged Jesus this week? When have you denied him? Jesus predicted that Peter would deny him earlier that evening. Do you think God knows beforehand if you choose to acknowledge him or deny him?

GOD HEARS & RESTORES

A LITTLE EXTRA

You probably won't be asked to lay down your life for one of your friends today. But be creative on how you can encourage them and make their day. Pay for their coffee in the morning, take them flowers, say something kind, wash their car, or even bring them an energy bar for a late-night study session.

"There is no greater love than to lay down one's life for one's friends." John 15:13

Christ is the ultimate example of a friend, and he literally laid down his life for us. Jesus died on the cross when he had done nothing wrong, so we wouldn't to pay the price for our sins. To be free from sin, we acknowledge Christ and what he's done, confess our own sins, ask for Christ to forgive us, and live according to his plan. Beautifully set free.

How do you treat your own friends? You may have experienced a one-way friendship, where one friend is always bailing out the other friend. Or a competition friendship, where friends are constantly trying to one-up the other. How about the friend who's always there, but you don't know anything about him?

You can be intentional with your friendships. Take time to get to know your friends—their goals, their struggles, their celebrations. You can talk about Jesus, study God's Word together, and grow together. Yes, friends add so much to your life. God is also using you to bless your friends.

TALKING WITH GOD

Thank God for your friends. You know, your true friends—not just those who wave as you pass and want to borrow your dad's truck when they move. God has blessed you with these incredible people in your life. He hand-selected your friends to make your life better.

"Keep on asking, and you will receive what you ask for. Keep on seeking, and you will find. Keep on knocking, and the door will be opened to you."
Matthew 7:7

Many of us are eager to ask God for things: "Help me on this test—even though I didn't study." "Make that guy like me." "Keep me from getting caught doing that dumb thing I chose to do." But as you grow closer to Jesus, you may begin to ask less for yourself and more for others—more for the important things in life. Spend time with God in prayer and read his Word, and you may be surprised as you see his heart and act more like him.

And don't forget the other parts of that verse. Seek and you will find. If you are earnestly seeking God and his will and his way, you will find it. God isn't a cosmic pirate, hiding his treasure behind cryptic clues and under secret palm trees. God *wants* you to find, but you must seek first.

TALKING WITH GOD

Ask God to show you the things he has a heart for. Make sure you're aware and open to his leadings, because if you ask to follow God's heart, he will lead you to people's needs.

VERSE 105:
Matthew 7:7

A LITTLE EXTRA

You can influence the people around you. People who hang out with you will start to take up some of your habits—make sure they have Christ-like habits to emulate. Take an honest inventory of things you do that you wish you didn't—or ask a close friend to do that for you, but be prepared for them to be honest. Then pray over that list and ask God to help you overcome those bad habits and reveal a picture of Christ for others.

GOD HEARS & RESTORES

A LITTLE EXTRA

Read Philippians 2 and create a list of all the ways Jesus humbled himself. In what ways can you humble yourself, too? What actions or habits can help you think less about yourself and more about God?

Humble yourselves before the Lord, and he will lift you up in honor. James 4:10

British author and theologian C.S Lewis is credited with saying, "Humility is not thinking less of yourself but thinking of yourself less." Along those same lines, for us to be able to think of ourselves less, we must ensure that we are thinking about God more. If we truly want to see how we need to live, it's essential that we don't compare ourselves to our fallen world. Instead, we ought to compare ourselves to God's holy standards. As we make this comparison, we see our true need for God and understand that we are helpless without him.

When we meet God in humility, he promises to meet us there and lift us up in honor. God will not only bring us honor in eternity, he also will give us favor for today as we humbly live out our lives depending on him. And that honor helps us point the attention right back toward God—where it belongs.

TALKING WITH GOD

Spend a few minutes thanking God for as many amazing characteristics about him as you can think of. Take the focus off yourself, and place it on God. Confess to God any areas of your life where you have failed or are struggling. Ask God to give you a humble heart and dependence on him in the plans of your day and throughout this week.

Are you going through a time where life seems a bit unclear, or a situation that just doesn't make sense? In all times, but especially times like these, it's vital to call on God. All Scripture is useful and applicable to your life. As you read, listen to what God is saying.

Begin by asking God for a clear mind and for wisdom. God freely gives wisdom to anyone who asks.

And the Spirit of the Lord will rest on him—the Spirit of wisdom and understanding, the Spirit of counsel and might, the Spirit of knowledge and the fear of the Lord. Isaiah 11:2

Read today's passage aloud. Then read the passage aloud a second time. What word or phrase stands out to you?

Take a deep breath and even take a quick walk around the room. As you come back, read the passage a third time. What stands out to you?

Using the word or phrase that stood out to you, take an extended quiet time to listen to what God is saying to you. It might not be an audible voice answering all your big questions. But God is here. God is listening to you and wants to talk with you. Commit to seeking God's wisdom on a regular basis—and to act on what he says.

TALKING WITH GOD

Thank God for speaking. Your situation may still seem a bit unclear. Some say God rarely reveals his entire plan in full detail. Others say God opens the way before you—one step at a time. Trust God and his plan, and take that next step with him today.

ONENESS
WITH GOD

VERSE 107:
Isaiah 11:2

A LITTLE EXTRA

Look up Proverbs 3:5-6 and journal the answers to these questions.

- How do these verses complement each other?

- In what areas of your life do you need God's wisdom and understanding?

GOD HEARS & RESTORES

A LITTLE EXTRA

Think about a food that's not good for you, and give it up for one full month—not because it will help make you spiritually clean, but because it will help make you healthier. When people ask you why, tell them God is teaching you discipline.

"For from within, out of a person's heart, come evil thoughts, sexual immorality, theft, murder, adultery, greed, wickedness, deceit, lustful desires, envy, slander, pride, and foolishness."
Mark 7:21-22

One of the catch phrases of our culture is that people should go away to "find themselves." But if we actually do that, we might not like what we find.

Just prior to this passage, Jesus talked with people who thought that not eating certain things (such as pork) would keep them clean. Jesus came right out and said that what goes into you doesn't make you unclean—what comes out from inside does.

So does that mean we can use Jesus to excuse behavior that's harmful or unhealthy? Not at all. There are lots of good, biblical reasons not to indulge in those things—keeping yourself "clean" just isn't one of them.

But back to Jesus' point. He's saying there's something deep down that needs fixing—a foundational part of us that is just, well, bad. What's the cure? Only a relationship with Jesus.

TALKING WITH GOD

Maybe you've never admitted that there's something not right within you. Ask God to help you come to a place of seeing that you are a broken person and you need to be healed. Thank God for his plan to heal us, and thank him for sacrificing his Son to make us right with him.

Think of a time you were really, really, really hungry but couldn't find anything in the house that you wanted to eat. Did you settle for something else, or did you try to put random things together to satisfy your hunger?

Jesus took the five loaves and two fish, looked up toward heaven, and blessed them. Then, breaking the loaves into pieces, he kept giving the bread to the disciples so they could distribute it to the people. He also divided the fish for everyone to share. They all ate as much as they wanted, and afterward, the disciples picked up twelve baskets of leftover bread and fish. Mark 6:41-43

In today's passage, Jesus took a few food items, fed thousands of people, and still had 12 baskets of food left over. The disciples gave away fragments of five loaves and two fishes, and received back a basketful each—that's more than they started with! This is crazy to think about when you notice that the crowds were hungry and that the disciples fed the crowds before they received their miraculous increase. Sometimes we can look at our lives and think we have nothing to offer the kingdom of God, but when we give the little we have to God, big things will happen.

TALKING WITH GOD

Make a list of five things you know that you do pretty well. Ask God to take these gifts and talents in your life and turn them into big things to help grow his kingdom.

SIN & SEPARATION

VERSE 109:
Mark 6:41-43

A LITTLE EXTRA

Go to your kitchen. Option 1: Bake some cookies, put them in small plastic bags, and hand them out at school. Option 2: Get some candy, put it in small plastic bags, and hand it out at school. Use the opportunity to talk with your classmates about what you learned from today's Scripture.

CONSEQUENCES & CRYING OUT

A LITTLE EXTRA

Take some time to think a little. What allows you to give thanks in all circumstances? Why would God want you to give thanks in all circumstances? How can you remain joyful when things aren't going well? How does prayer relate to joy? How can you share your joy with others?

Have you ever had a bad day? Of course you have. Have you experienced one recently? Did you stop during your bad day to pray?

Always be joyful. Never stop praying. Be thankful in all circumstances, for this is God's will for you who belong to Christ Jesus.
1 Thessalonians 5:16–18

Paul is telling us to be joyful always? Is that even possible? Even during a bad day when nothing seems to be going the way we planned? That sounds like a big task to tackle. It can be very hard to be joyful during tough circumstances, but when you pray during these times, you can be comforted by God and you can be thankful. God may not take the tough situation away, but he will be there to help you through the good and the bad times. As you practice being joyful and continue to pray, those bad days won't seem as bad anymore!

TALKING WITH GOD

Consider these three ideas that are shared in today's passage:

1. Be joyful

2. Pray

3. Give thanks

For each of those, write a couple of things that come to your mind when you think about God being a part of your life.

Take a good look at your feet. If you have shoes and socks on, take them off so that you can see the skin and toenails and crusty stuff between your toes. (Gross!) What is one word you would use to describe them? Did the word *beautiful* come to mind? That's not a word we use to describe our feet? Or is it?

How beautiful on the mountains are the feet of the messenger who brings good news, the good news of peace and salvation, the news that the God of Israel reigns! Isaiah 52:7

This passage talks less about what our feet look like and more about what we do with them. It creates a picture of someone who is constantly moving to tell people about Christ. No matter what we think our feet look like, when we use them to bring hope to others, they become our most attractive feature. Will you take those first steps to having "beautiful feet" today?

TALKING WITH GOD

Do you struggle to have those gorgeous feet this passage talks about? Check out the song "Beautiful Feet" by Lecrae. Share your feelings with God about telling others about him. Ask God to give you courage to develop beautiful feet. Ask God to help you trust him enough to take the risk to share his love with someone today.

GOD HEARS & RESTORES

VERSE 111:
Isaiah 52:7

A LITTLE EXTRA

Trace your foot on a sheet of paper. (If your feet are really big, tape two sheets together.) Write Isaiah 52:7 and Romans 10:15 in the center of it. Place the paper somewhere that you can be reminded that as followers of Christ, we all can have beautiful feet.

GOD HEARS & RESTORES

A LITTLE EXTRA

For the next week, whenever you see a cross—at the top of a light pole, in a window frame, the crossroads of two streets—make a conscious effort to reflect on what the cross is: what it means and what actually happened on a cross so long ago. It was a torture device, but Jesus turned it into something both terrible and beautiful.

Think about a time you got away with something—a time you were supposed to get in trouble or get caught but you didn't. Maybe someone else involved did get caught. Or maybe blame fell on someone who had nothing to do with the incident in the first place. How did that make you feel?

So to pacify the crowd, Pilate released Barabbas to them. He ordered Jesus flogged with a lead-tipped whip, then turned him over to the Roman soldiers to be crucified. Mark 15:15

Jesus' "trial" was anything but fair. In his attempt to please the crowd, Pilate let Barabbas go and ordered that Jesus be crucified. Barabbas actually was guilty, and Jesus was innocent. But Jesus died just the same.

Just like Barabbas, we all are guilty. We have a death sentence upon us, and we will face the penalty. Unless someone takes our place. Unless someone who is totally innocent goes ahead of us. Jesus has already done that—we have only to accept it.

TALKING WITH GOD

If you haven't yet accepted Jesus' free offering of forgiveness, maybe you're ready to do that right now. If you have accepted that gift, maybe there's someone close to you who hasn't. Ask God to help you see opportunities to minister to the person who comes to mind. You might be afraid you won't know what to say, but all you have to do is tell your own story.

Create in me a clean heart, O God. Renew a loyal spirit within me. Psalm 51:10

We all sin. Oftentimes when we sin, we feel tons of guilt, conviction, and criticism. Too often when we sin, we withdraw from God in an attempt to hide in our shame. Rather than run from God, we ought to run to him. Even as we remember that God hates sin, we also need to remember that Jesus shed his blood on the cross, and he spoke the sweet words "It is finished."

In this Scripture, David is asking God for help: *"Renew a loyal spirit in me"*—and that's exactly what God does for David! Sometimes it's hard for us to believe that God responds to our prayers quickly. We feel that we have to wait for God to forgive us, and in our minds it takes a long time. Remember that God has said you are forgiven. Do not wait for a feeling; trust that God has forgiven you. As you believe God (and that's what faith is), you can accept God's forgiveness and do what God wants you to do.

TALKING WITH GOD

Think about the word *grace*—receiving something you don't deserve. God offers us forgiveness through Christ—not because we deserve it, but because he loves us. Let God's grace take hold of your heart. What a loving Father we have.

SIN &
SEPARATION

A LITTLE EXTRA

Get a pencil, an eraser, and a piece of paper. On the paper, write sins that you want to give over to God. Then pray over all that is listed. Now use the eraser to erase all the sin. It's a messy exercise, but it reflects something that's 100 percent true: God erases our confessed sin.

CONSEQUENCES & CRYING OUT

A LITTLE EXTRA

Write or print Matthew 11:28-30 on a card and place it in your backpack, purse, or wallet. Every time you see it, remember Jesus' invitation to give him all of your worries. Every time you see someone carrying a heavy bag, remember Jesus' promises to carry your struggles if you let him.

Give all your worries and cares to God, for he cares about you. 1 Peter 5:7

Do you ever have days where all of the things you worry about feel like a huge weight on your back? It's almost like your life is an enormous backpack. At the start of every day it's empty. However, as you go through the day, you "pick up" things like worry, fear, anger, sin, bitterness, and disappointment that weigh you down.

Did you know that not only does Jesus want you to empty all of that out, he also wants you to give it to him? Try an experiment. Picture yourself taking your pack off. Inside that pack is every struggle you have right now. Look at every fear, anxiety, concern, or care inside your pack. Can you feel how the bag is heavy? Jesus wants you go to him every time things get too heavy. He wants you to do this because he loves you that much.

TALKING WITH GOD

Close your eyes. Think about the concerns and worries that are filling that "backpack" you carry around every day. Now open the pack, take out your worries, hold them up and name them, and then open your hands and say, "Lord, I release these things to you." When you are done, thank God that he wants to take all of your cares.

Jesus had told the disciples that he was going to come back to life after being put to death, but they didn't get it. And even after a bunch of them had seen him, Thomas—who wasn't there when Jesus first returned—didn't believe. He said that he wouldn't believe the news until he put his finger in the nail holes in Jesus' hands, and his hand into the sword wound in Jesus' side. Ew. Ick.

But then Jesus shows up again:

Then he said to Thomas, "Put your finger here, and look at my hands. Put your hand into the wound in my side. Don't be faithless any longer. Believe!"
John 20:27

What tone of voice did Jesus use here? Was Jesus angry? Or did he shame Thomas, like we might talk to a disobedient puppy? But what if Jesus had a smile on his face and a wink in his eye?

Expressing (and thinking about) doubts is a massively important part of being a teenager (especially if you grew up around Christianity) and growing in your faith! Jesus isn't freaked out by your doubts. In fact, Jesus *wants* to hear your doubts and help you with them.

TALKING WITH GOD

Here's a wild idea (and a really good one): Pray your doubts! That's right—just tell God your doubts, and don't use pretty church-y words, or apologize, or soften it. Be honest with God!

GOD HEARS
& RESTORES

VERSE 115:
John 20:27

A LITTLE EXTRA

Wrestling with doubts is such an awesome thing. So take it a step further and make a written (or typed!) list of your spiritual questions and doubts—and then, take it to an adult you trust and ask if they'd help you dig into a couple of them. Doubts are normal and good, but not if we just ignore them or let them lie there forever!

ONENESS WITH GOD

VERSE 116:
Deuteronomy 7:9

A LITTLE EXTRA

Look up the word *faithful* in a dictionary, and write the definition on a piece of paper. Now take five minutes and write down all the ways that God has been faithful to you in your life. Make the list as long as you can because remembering God's faithfulness yesterday helps us trust him more today and tomorrow.

"Understand, therefore, that the Lord your God is indeed God. He is the faithful God who keeps his covenant for a thousand generations and lavishes his unfailing love on those who love him and obey his commands." Deuteronomy 7:9

Take a close look at today's verse. What does it tell us about our Lord? First, he is faithful. That means that God is loyal, reliable, trustworthy, and believable. He will never let you down. Next, God lavishes his unfailing love on you. This means he does not just love you a little bit; he gives you his love in the greatest amount imaginable. God holds nothing back. This is the God who calls you his child!

The next time you feel like God doesn't care about you, or you can't trust God to come through, or you don't know if God is actively involved in your life, just remember that you serve a faithful and loving God who gave everything, including his only Son, for your sake. God will always come through because you are precious to him.

TALKING WITH GOD

Thank God that he loves you lavishly. Think about what that truly means, and ask God to help you trust him more. Thank God that he is always there for you when times are hard. Ask God to help you live and reveal his kingdom to others who are going through difficult times.

So now there is no condemnation for those who belong to Christ Jesus. Romans 8:1

To condemn someone is to pronounce that person guilty and sentence him or her to a harsh punishment for crimes committed. In today's verse, the Apostle Paul tells us if we belong to Jesus, there is no condemnation, even though we are guilty of sin and deserve to be punished. But we don't avoid punishment because the judge was in a good mood and dismissed all charges. We escape because someone else was punished for us.

Jesus, who never sinned, took our guilty verdict and endured our punishment, so we wouldn't have to. And to receive this amazing gift, we simply need to respond to God's grace and trust that Jesus paid our price. When we do that, we are allowed to walk out of God's courtroom as one who has been set free. That's a reason to celebrate and give thanks!

TALKING WITH GOD

Pray this prayer, or one with a similar theme: *Jesus, thank you for forgiving me and loving me. I'm a sinner; you're sinless. I deserve death; you died so I wouldn't have to spend eternity separated from God. Everything I have comes from you. Let everything I say and do point to you. And help me trust you enough to share the truth of today's verse with my family and friends.*

GOD HEARS & RESTORES

VERSE 117:
Romans 8:1

A LITTLE EXTRA

With your parents' permission, go online and listen to the song "Live Like That" by Sidewalk Prophets. The song shares a compelling challenge to live and reveal God's kingdom. After listening, make your own list of things that describe the kind of life you want to live.

GOD HEARS
& RESTORES

A LITTLE EXTRA

In addition to your quiet time with God, dive into some deeper books on Christianity. These books wrestle with tough topics that often aren't discussed when the church gathers together. For starters, try books by such authors as Mike Yaconelli, David Nassar, Brennan Manning, or C.S. Lewis.

Have you ever participated in (or just watched) a baby food-eating contest? The lucky contestants are given jars of baby food. Of course, the most disgusting meat and vegetable combinations are chosen. No sweet bananas and pears here. Whoever can eat the most—without throwing up—wins. The contest is nauseating and therefore a great show.

Solid food is for those who are mature, who through training have the skill to recognize the difference between right and wrong. Hebrews 5:14

You wouldn't go on a date to a nice restaurant and order puréed mixed vegetables and beef; you're beyond that. In the same way, you can move on from the basics of Christianity and dive into deeper truths of what it means to follow Jesus.

It is fascinating to see what's going on behind the scenes in the Bible. Here, you'll find how Jesus broke many of society's rules. No wonder some people saw him as a troublemaker. You can also experience how your life is transformed when you embrace next-step truths.

- How does your life reflect your true priorities, and how can you change them?
- Does being a Christ-follower mean being compliant and boring?
- How do you hear God's voice?

Begin the journey of diving deeper with God.

TALKING WITH GOD

Talk to God about things that are tough to understand. (Don't worry; many people see truths as confusing and complex.) Ask God to help you deepen your understanding through deeper Bible study, a conversation with a trusted mentor, or personal research.

A third time he asked him, "Simon son of John, do you love me?" Peter was hurt that Jesus asked the question a third time. He said, "Lord, you know everything. You know that I love you." Jesus said, "Then feed my sheep." John 21:17

The Apostle Peter was an incredible guy, and this is one of his most memorable scenes in the New Testament. Jesus has risen from the dead, and Peter—who felt great shame because he had denied knowing Jesus three times—is "reinstated."

Why did Jesus say, "Feed my sheep" three times? Was it to match the number of times Peter denied Jesus? Maybe. Did Peter seem distracted, so Jesus felt he had to say it three times to make sure he had Peter's attention? Perhaps. We do know that Jesus felt this was *really* important. Was he talking about feeding people physical food or spiritual food? Or both?

TALKING WITH GOD

Ask God to show you the sheep he wants you to "feed." He might show you a hurting friend who needs a shoulder to cry on. Or someone questioning her faith, who needs a friend to offer some encouragement. Or maybe your parents think your faith is ridiculous, and you need to feed them a little of God's kindness every day, so one day they'll start asking questions about God.

VERSE 119:
John 21:17

A LITTLE EXTRA

Grab a friend and commit to volunteering at a soup kitchen or homeless shelter this weekend. (Ask your youth leader if you need help.) When people's most basic needs aren't being met, it's very difficult to be receptive to the good news of Jesus. This can be a great opportunity to give people both physical food and spiritual food.

GOD HEARS & RESTORES

A LITTLE EXTRA

In the spaces below, write the names of three people who you want to be ready.

1.

2.

3.

Need help in finding the right words to help those individuals know about Jesus? Check out dare2share.org for more information.

Have you ever missed out on something because you didn't know about it? Usually you're hearing about it after the fact from your friends, who said it was the best thing ever!

Just as bad, have you ever been unprepared for something? You had heard about the test; you remember the teacher talking about it. In the back of your mind you knew it was coming, but it didn't cross your mind that it was today.

But how can they call on him to save them unless they believe in him? And how can they believe in him if they have never heard about him? And how can they hear about him unless someone tells them? And how will anyone go and tell them without being sent? That is why the Scriptures say, "How beautiful are the feet of messengers who bring good news!" Romans 10:14-15

God is a gift to all of us. God is someone we can trust. God is the only one who provides eternal life. In today's passage, Paul clearly tells us that people won't know about God unless we tell them. When we do, it will be so powerful it will take our breath away.

TALKING WITH GOD

If sharing your God-story is difficult or feels uncomfortable, ask God to give you the courage to do it anyway. Ask God to open the door and provide an opportunity for you to share what you believe and why. Just be ready—because if you ask, God will give you the opportunity sooner than you think.

" 'Yes,' the king replied, 'and to those who use well what they are given, even more will be given. But from those who do nothing, even what little they have will be taken away.' " Luke 19:26

In today's passage Jesus is telling the parable of the talents (also known as the parable of the minas or the parable of the 10 servants). A wealthy man gives different servants a small amount of money (one mina) and returns shortly after to see how they have used what he gave them. He discovers that one servant has made 10 minas, one has made five, and one servant has done nothing with his single mina. The man becomes so angry with the servant who has done nothing with his mina, that he makes him give it up to the servant who earned 10.

The talents in this parable can represent our abilities, opportunities, responsibilities, or even the gospel. Jesus gives to each of us, and he expects us to use whatever it is wisely. Jesus trusts us, and we have the opportunity to honor him by everything we do until he returns for us.

TALKING WITH GOD

Ask God to reveal to you what your "talents" are. Ask God to show you how to use them. Ask him to give you an opportunity to use them to share the good news of Jesus with others.

VERSE 121:
Luke 19:26

A LITTLE EXTRA

Make a list of a few things that you believe you're great at! How can you use these talents to share Christ and love others? Share your list with a friend, and help each other be creative. Look for ways that your talents can be used for God's glory!

SIN & SEPARATION

Understand this, my dear brothers and sisters: You must all be quick to listen, slow to speak, and slow to get angry. James 1:19

The truth hurts sometimes, doesn't it? Have you had those times when a friend has spoken truth to you and it hurt to the core? Even so, hard truth from someone who cares about us can often be the very thing that gets us to see the need to change for the better.

And when those words come, it's often easier to respond with words—rebuttals and defenses to justify our actions or attitudes. It's more difficult to follow the wisdom in this verse to eagerly listen but be cautious to speak or get angry.

But this isn't just true when it comes to the words of our friends. In challenging times it's easy to become angry at God's words to us. James challenges us to pause and to listen to God's truth during the hard situations in life. If we trust God, he promises to redeem our pain and turn it into something good. Are you spending your life being bitter at God, or are you willing to listen to him to discover valuable life lessons?

A LITTLE EXTRA

Draw a smiley face in the margins of this book. Include all of the appropriate facial features (make sure you draw one mouth and two ears). Anytime someone offers you feedback today, listen twice as much as you speak.

TALKING WITH GOD

As you pray today, consider some of the challenges you are facing in your life. Take time to talk about them with God and to thank him for the ways he is going to strengthen your faith through these tough times.

You've seen adorable toddlers imitating their parents. It's cute to see them walking a silly way just like their mom or dad. It can also be embarrassing if the child says something the parent doesn't want repeated. The child can't help it; she's just copying what she sees and hears.

So Jesus explained, "I tell you the truth, the Son can do nothing by himself. He does only what he sees the Father doing. Whatever the Father does, the Son also does." John 5:19

Jesus was completely dependent on the Father. Similarly, we're to mimic Jesus, a perfect example of what to do—and he has no examples of what not to do. In what ways is it hard to mimic Jesus? Are there ways it's easy?

Stay close to Jesus, and learn as much as you can about him. Watch what he did on Earth and what he's doing today. He's alive and showing you the way.

TALKING WITH GOD

Thank God that he provided an example for you to follow: Jesus. Honestly talk with God about ways it's hard or easy for you to follow Jesus' example.

GOD HEARS
& RESTORES

VERSE 123:
John 5:19

A LITTLE EXTRA

Take out a piece of paper or turn to a fresh page in your journal. Draw a line down the middle of the paper. On the left-hand side, write "Ways I'm like Jesus." On the right-hand side, write "Ways I'm not like Jesus." There's absolutely no shame in this exercise. It's simply a way to take a genuine look at your own life. Thank God for the work he's done and is doing in you—in each area you're like Jesus. Pray that he helps you continue. In the same way, pray for God to continue his work in you for the things on the right-hand side. God is committed to complete his good work in you.

GOD HEARS & RESTORES

A LITTLE EXTRA

Share the goodness of God. It's easy to use social media to let people know. When you see the goodness of God today, take the extra moment to share him. You'll encourage others in their walk.

Have you found the most perfect coffee shop? Did you hit a sale at your favorite store? When you've seen the most incredible blockbuster movie, what did you do? Did you keep it to yourself? (OK. In all honestly, you might keep the coffee shop to yourself. If you tell too many people, they might show up and ruin the experience. But follow the point here.) Did you hide it? Did you think others wouldn't care or wouldn't listen? Of course not! You were so excited about these things that you shared them with your friends.

But you are not like that, for you are a chosen people. You are royal priests, a holy nation, God's very own possession. As a result, you can show others the goodness of God, for he called you out of the darkness into his wonderful light. 1 Peter 2:9

Like any amazing discovery, tell others about the treasure you've found in Christ. He has produced and is continuing to produce life-change in you. It's cool. It's exciting. It is for everyone.

It's an honor to show others the goodness of God. Now, this often isn't the sit-down-with-a-friend-and-go-through-the-five-steps-of-salvation experience. In fact, you can preach the gospel always—if necessary, use words. Let God's love and your excitement flow into your conversations naturally.

TALKING WITH GOD

Thank God for how he called you out of the darkness into his wonderful light. Thank God for blessing you with salvation through Jesus, encouraging friends and family, and ways to meet your needs. Pray for those in your life who need to know his salvation.

"This is my command—be strong and courageous! Do not be afraid or discouraged. For the Lord your God is with you wherever you go." Joshua 1:9

What's the difference between a suggestion and a command? One gives a choice; the other requires action. Joshua is feeling pretty shaky about leading God's people into the Promised Land. But God loves him so much that he gives a command: "I am with you, so don't be afraid or discouraged. Be strong and have courage!"

Armed with this directive and the knowledge that God is with him, Joshua watches river waters part in two and the people walk across dry ground.

Wouldn't it be awesome if the feeling of fear could be gone in a word? Most of the time, like Joshua, we have to step out in the action of being strong *while* we are still afraid. But when God asks us to do something for him, he doesn't leave us—and we know we can be strong *and* courageous!

TALKING WITH GOD

Confess to God the things you fear about your faith journey. As you share these things with God, make fists with each hand. As you talk, clinch your fists tighter. Tell God about all of the fears you are holding on to. Then look up to the heavens, hold up your arms, and open your fists. Ask God to give you the strength and courage to live and reveal his kingdom in your life today.

VERSE 125:
Joshua 1:9

A LITTLE EXTRA

Find a place where you can see your shadow. Watch as it responds to everything you do. Even in dark places, your shadow is with you wherever you go. And so is God. Every time you see your shadow today, remember that God is with you as you strive to live and reveal his kingdom.

GOD HEARS & RESTORES

A LITTLE EXTRA

With a parent's permission, do an online search for videos of modern-day lepers. (You might want to watch the videos with your parent.) Consider watching one, and you'll get an idea of just what this devastating disease is—and what it took for Jesus to throw aside all "common sense" and tradition and heal this man.

Jesus reached out and touched him. "I am willing," he said. "Be healed!" And instantly the leprosy disappeared. Luke 5:13

In Jesus' day, lepers were the lowest of the low. They were so feared and rejected that when they approached a group of people or a town, the lepers had to yell, "Unclean!" so people would know to stay clear. The man in today's verse likely hadn't been touched by another person for years. But here came the rabbi everyone was talking about, and Jesus didn't stand 30 feet away and yell for the man to be healed. He touched the leper.

Like so many things that Jesus did, this was scandalous, unexpected, surprising—and life-changing.

You might feel that you're an outcast, untouchable, unclean—a social "leper." Maybe some people at school seem to do everything they can to avoid you. But the same Jesus who healed this man is reaching out to you. He doesn't care what the world thinks; he made you, and he loves you.

TALKING WITH GOD

Think about a time this week when you felt as though you weren't seen. Share it with God. Tell him how you felt. Ask him to work through your heart in this. You can't go back and be seen, but you can be aware that whatever your situation, God knows you and sees you!

For everyone has sinned; we all fall short of God's glorious standard. Yet God, with undeserved kindness, declares that we are righteous. He did this through Christ Jesus when he freed us from the penalty for our sins. Romans 3:23–24

Have you ever messed up and sinned? Of course.

We've all missed the mark and fallen short of God's just, holy, and perfect standard—whether our struggle is gossip, lying, cheating, lust, pride, or something else.

The result: Our sins separate us from God, and they lead us to a life of discouragement, guilt, suffering, and shame.

But God hasn't left us all alone to deal with the consequences of sin! God sent his Son, Jesus, to pay the penalty for our sin and to restore us into a deep, intimate, personal relationship with him. And as followers of Christ, our past, present, and future sins are all forgiven—all because of what Jesus did on the cross for us.

But perhaps you have friends who are struggling with sin's effects in their lives and don't know this freedom found in Christ. Maybe they're innocent bystanders, impacted by the sin of others, or perhaps they're experiencing the consequences of their own choices. Either way, they need to hear about the amazing gift of forgiveness and freedom that God extends to anyone who trusts in Christ.

It's time to tell them the good news!

TALKING WITH GOD

Spend some time praying for your friends who need to hear about Jesus. Then step out today and share your faith with at least one of them!

VERSE 127:
Romans 3:23–24

A LITTLE EXTRA

You have 100 times more influence on your friends than a stranger does! Check out dare2share. org/thecause/the-cause-circle for a simple tool that will help you get serious about sharing your faith with them. Grab a friend from your youth group and do THE Cause Circle together!

133

GOD HEARS & RESTORES

A LITTLE EXTRA

Read this entire passage (Luke 12:22-34) for context, and answer these questions.

- Reflect on a time when you were stressed about a situation. Did stress help you in the end? Was the stress necessary?

- If people were looking into your life (for example, how you spent your money and time), where would they think your treasure and heart are?

"So don't be afraid, little flock. For it gives your Father great happiness to give you the Kingdom."
Luke 12:32

The fear Jesus is talking about isn't the same fear you face while watching a scary movie. It's not even the fear people experience during a natural disaster. It's the paralysis-inducing fear from anxiety.

The modern world is built on anxiety. Our culture feeds off of people setting super high goals for themselves and stressing out every day about whether or not they've done enough to reach their goals. When the goals are reached (often at the expense of family, friends, or quality of life), even higher goals take their place. It's a vicious cycle that leads to exhaustion and loneliness.

Jesus came to redeem life and to save everyone from it. Rather than setting your own goals and taking on too much, look to God for priorities and goals. You will face circumstances beyond your control, but these circumstances give space for your dependence on God to grow. God wants you to truly relax and know that he alone is in control.

What is causing stress for you today? Take a deep breath and trust that God is in control and wants only what's best for you.

TALKING WITH GOD

Talk with God about the things stressing you out today. Thank God that he's in control, and tell him how you're going to trust him with each item.

Then Peter came to him and asked, "Lord, how often should I forgive someone who sins against me? Seven times?" "No, not seven times," Jesus replied, "but seventy times seven!"
Matthew 18:21-22

GOD HEARS & RESTORES

Jesus must have been out of his mind. He mentioned exceptions to this statement, right? What if the person lies to you—again? What if your friend steals something from you that she knew was valuable to you? Or what about the friend you've forgiven over and over for the same thing? Certainly, in these circumstances, Jesus couldn't have meant to forgive again, and again, and again.

Or could he?

It's important to understand that there's a huge difference between forgiving someone, and forgiving them *and* trusting again. Forgiveness means no longer resenting someone and choosing to pardon an offense. There's no more punishment within forgiveness. Trust is reliance or confidence in the integrity, strength, and ability of someone.

With God's help, you can be the one to forgive. It's your responsibility, but God wants to help. Forgiveness is freedom for you. It's up to the other person to earn your trust back. You can be open to having the trust restored.

TALKING WITH GOD

Tell God about a person you need to forgive. Take your time. Feel free to tell God the whole story—how you feel, and how it was wrong. Without judgment, pray for that person. Ask God to soften your heart and help you forgive. While you're at it, thank God for forgiving you again, and again, and again.

A LITTLE EXTRA

Is there someone who you need to ask for forgiveness? Take a moment to write out an apology—mentioning specifically that you're sorry and what you're sorry for. Pick up the phone (not to text, but to actually dial the number) and begin the conversation.

PRAYER

When you think about prayer, does your mind get filled with happy thoughts or bored thoughts? Are you excited to pray, or do you dread it? It's OK; everyone struggles. But what if God hoped prayer would be an important part of our relationship with him? And what if Satan wanted us to be confused about prayer, so that we never really figured it out?

PRAYER is a two-way conversation with the person who knows us best and loves us most. It's talking and listening. Prayer isn't God lecturing us—though sometimes God teaches us difficult things in prayer—and it's not us telling God our "wish list"—though sometimes we ask God for things in prayer. Prayer is all about God giving us his perspective on whatever we're going through in life. Here are some suggestions on getting started.

1. **USE NORMAL WORDS.** God speaks your language, so be yourself. Don't try to impress God—he already thinks you're pretty awesome. Pray just like you talk.

2. **PRAY ALL DAY.** Maybe not "heads bowed and eyes closed" praying—especially if you're driving or operating heavy machinery—but you can be in a constant conversation with God as you live your day. When you're in a tempting situation, whisper a silent prayer asking God for help. When you're sharing your God-story with someone, quietly ask God to give you the right words. When you see someone who's hurting, silently ask God to bless that person.

3. **SET ASIDE SPECIFIC TIME TO PRAY.** Take some time, block out everything that distracts you, and give your total attention to God. This is a great time to practice spiritual journaling (see pp. 90-91).

4. **PRAY WHEN YOU DON'T HAVE WORDS.** Even when you don't know what to say, set aside some time to be with God in prayer, and let his Holy Spirit pray for you (Romans 8:26-28).

God wants to sit with you, the real you. God wants to hear everything you have to say, he's never too busy, and he has an amazing attention span. God isn't looking for flowery words or poetic phrases; he wants to have a real conversation with you. Give it a try and see what happens.

GOD HEARS & RESTORES

A LITTLE EXTRA

Do you have a friend or two with whom you can be gut-level honest? Share your fears (this is best done in person, rather than online or by text), and ask if they're willing to share theirs. Then pray for each other. You can actually be a part of God's comfort to your friends.

If you started listing the benefits of following Jesus, you could have a very long list! But right there near the top of most people's lists would be God's protection and comfort. That's why this verse is a favorite for so many people:

Even when I walk through the darkest valley,
I will not be afraid, for you are close beside me.
Your rod and your staff protect and comfort me.
Psalm 23:4

Ah… just reading that is comforting!

Here are a couple of really cool things to think about:

First, God's willingness to provide protection and comfort when we're afraid means God is near and God is aware. That's pretty amazing—God isn't a distant, disconnected idea; God is a person, one who knows what you're going through.

Second, God's willingness to provide protection and comfort is an obvious sign of his love for you. If God didn't love you, he wouldn't protect and comfort, but God *does* love you!

TALKING WITH GOD

The verse describes fear as a valley, which means we're not always in it—it's something we go through from time to time. But whether you're in "the valley of fear" at this moment or not, you can probably identify some of the things you are afraid of. There's no reason to pretend you can keep those a secret from God (even if you've never told anyone else). Share your fears with God, and trust him to protect and comfort you.

If you are reading this, then you are somebody's son or daughter. And at one time every one of us was a child. So we know what it means to be children. We know what it means to belong to a parent.

John uses words and a picture in today's passage that we can all understand. You know what's not easy to understand and what is a complete mystery to many people? How is it possible that we could be children of God?

VERSE 131:
John 1:11–12

He came to his own people, and even they rejected him. But to all who believed him and accepted him, he gave the right to become children of God.
John 1:11–12

How can it be that by simply believing and accepting Jesus, we can become children of God? That's right, children—not servants or slaves but children. It's a mystery and it's a miracle—and it's true.

God is not just a Father; he is our Father. We are his children when we believe Jesus. That is one powerful truth that can transform your heart and mind today!

TALK WITH GOD

Embrace your role as a child with our Heavenly Father as you pray right now. Admit your belief and acceptance of Jesus. Thank God for being a good and faithful Father to you and to all who believe. Ask him to help you trust him more today so you can live and reveal his kingdom.

A LITTLE EXTRA

Get out a piece of paper and write three things that parents typically do for their children as demonstrations of their love and concern. Now read Matthew 7:7-11. Write a quick prayer of thankfulness for God as a Father.

CONSEQUENCES & CRYING OUT

A LITTLE EXTRA

Ask your parents if you can have some aluminum foil. Snag a huge sheet of the foil and mold it into an idol/statue that represents an achievement that might affect your relationship with Jesus. Once you've finished, take a long look at your handiwork, place it on the floor, and smash it with your foot. Then place your crushed idol on a shelf in your room to remind you that our idols are nothing compared to what we can have in Jesus.

I once thought these things were valuable, but now I consider them worthless because of what Christ has done. Philippians 3:7

Have you ever put your achievements above your relationship with Jesus? Paul did. Before he became a Christ-follower, he worked hard to become a powerful political leader in his city. Once he began following Jesus, however, he realized that all of his accomplishments, honors, and successes were worthless compared to what he had with Jesus.

Is Paul saying it's wrong to want to be successful? No—he's warning us to not let our desire to do something great become more important to us than our relationship with Jesus. Is there an achievement in your life that is more important to you than your relationship with Jesus?

TALKING TO GOD

If something has become more important to you than your relationship with Jesus, pray this kind of prayer: *Jesus, forgive me for putting my sport, my grades, my music, my art, my dream, my hobby, my _____ in front of you. I want to be successful, but I want a relationship with you more. Help me see my dream as a way to live out your plan. Forgive me for turning my achievements into an idol. You are my God, and I love you.*

Have you ever been in a group when a joke was told and you where the only one who didn't get it? It's a strange feeling watching everybody laughing—and you wondering what was so funny. Usually someone explains it and moments later you suddenly "get it."

The message of the cross is foolish to those who are headed for destruction! But we who are being saved know it is the very power of God. 1 Corinthians 1:18

To some people, the cross is a joke. It's foolishness. It's powerless. And to those people, watching Christ-followers give their lives and their dreams to following the Savior who died on the cross seems ridiculous!

But to those who "get it" and to those who have experienced its saving power, we understand that what happened on the cross 2,000 years ago was nothing short of the greatest day of all times.

On the cross, Jesus died and took along with him our sin and our shame—and our death. And on the third day, Jesus came back from death to offer us the same: life after death.

There is nothing foolish in that message. There is nothing foolish in giving your whole life for that message!

TALK WITH GOD

Read and speak this prayer or one with a similar theme: *Jesus, I thank you for the message of the cross. The message that says I can experience your life and your grace. Thank you for the power of God in my life. Today I dedicate myself to living and revealing your kingdom.*

GOD HEARS & RESTORES

A LITTLE EXTRA

Draw a small cross on your hand as a reminder of who you are and your goal of living and revealing God's kingdom.

CONSEQUENCES & CRYING OUT

A LITTLE EXTRA

Search for the song "All I Am" by Phil Wickham, and listen to the chorus a couple of times. On a blank sheet of paper, make a list of the things you have been holding on to; be as detailed as you want. When you're done, find a big marker and write over your list in huge letters, "I TRUST GOD." And the next time you're being tempted, sing the line "All I am is yours" from that song a few times to remind you that God's way is always best.

I want to do what is good, but I don't. I don't want to do what is wrong, but I do it anyway.
Romans 7:19

Remember when you were a little kid and your mom always told you not to touch the hot stove? Well, there is always that one curious child who decides to touch it anyway just to see if it is actually as hot as Mom says. Surprise! She was right.

It is in our human nature, ever since we came into this world, to follow our own path and want to make our own choices. Sometimes, no matter how much we have learned from our parents or pastors or friends, we still choose to sin. We so badly want to do the right thing, but it is just too tempting to avoid it.

TALKING WITH GOD

Ask God to help you be honest with yourself about your sin. It's normal to struggle, and pretending that you don't struggle won't make it go away. Confess your sin and your struggles to God, and ask him to help you trust him more than you trust yourself. And the next time you're being tempted, remember that God's way is always best.

Where do you feel most comfortable? Maybe it's at home during the holidays. Maybe it's at your best friend's house for a sleepover. It's that place where you have that warm, secure, feeling where you are totally protected. Totally safe. Totally at ease. Totally cared for.

Now, shift gears, and think of a place where you feel a bit more exposed. You're just not quite comfortable. Things seem to stack up and weigh you down.

And this same God who takes care of me will supply all your needs from his glorious riches, which have been given to us in Christ Jesus. Philippians 4:19

God will take care of everything you need. Read this next sentence a couple of times: "God will take care of everything I need." Let that sink in; maybe even read it out loud. You don't have to worry. You don't have to live in that place where you feel exposed and burdened. By trusting God to care for you and your needs, that safe, secure place begins to expand and push everything else out of its way. The place where you feel comfortable becomes the majority instead of the minority, and regardless of whom you are with or where you are, you feel the presence of God comforting you and protecting you.

TALKING WITH GOD

Thank God for the things he has already provided you. Ask God to help you to use those things for whatever he desires. Confess to God the things you are worried about. Listen for him whispering, "I'll take care of everything you need."

ONENESS
WITH GOD

A LITTLE EXTRA

Read Hebrews 4 in several different translations of the Bible. If you don't have different translations, check out BibleGateway.com. Part of Hebrews 4 is about rest. Think about what the author might mean when he writes about the promise of entering God's rest.

ONENESS
WITH GOD

A LITTLE EXTRA

Explain the word of truth by your actions. Go and serve someone today. Provide them with something as simple as speaking words of encouragement or buying a meal. Give some of your time, your strength to someone else today. Show them the freedom that is in you through Jesus.

Work hard so you can present yourself to God and receive his approval. Be a good worker, one who does not need to be ashamed and who correctly explains the word of truth. 2 Timothy 2:15

Today's verse can make it seem like following Jesus is an assignment or task, but that's not the case. God doesn't accept you more if you study the Bible more, and he doesn't accept you less if you study less. Spending time in the Bible makes you more aware that he already accepts you, and you can soak in more joy and more understanding the more you're in God's Word.

When this verse talks about "hard work," it means more than just reading. The words imply effort, or toil. The root word in Greek means to make haste—to exert oneself or endeavor, which is way more than just taking in knowledge. It's actually *doing* something. We're called to put effort into being doers of the Word, not just studiers of it.

TALKING WITH GOD

Pray this kind of prayer: *Lord, thank you for your words of truth and hope that bring new meaning to my relationship with you every time I read them and learn from them. Please provide the energy and motivation to hear you clearly and be equipped to do your Word and not just read it. Please guide and protect me and speak your truth into my life.*

The temptations in your life are no different from what others experience. And God is faithful. He will not allow the temptation to be more than you can stand. When you are tempted, he will show you a way out so that you can endure.
1 Corinthians 10:13

GOD HEARS & RESTORES

Today's passage reveals a few things. First, everyone is tempted. Even Jesus. And if Jesus was tempted, yet never sinned (Hebrews 4:15 explains this), then temptation is not sin.

Second, you are not alone in your temptation. You're not alone because others are or have been tempted in the same way. And you're not alone because God is always with you, helping you.

That leads us to the third thing: God always provides you a way out of sin. It may not be easy, and it may not be immediately obvious. But your temptation does not have to lead to sin.

Pretty cool, huh?

TALK WITH GOD

Spend time on each of the things we learned from today's passage. First, tell God all the things you know are temptations and ask God to show things to you that you may not even be aware of. Second, thank God for the example of Jesus, who was tempted but never sinned. Third, thank God for always providing a way out of temptation; ask him to show it to you clearly. Close by asking God to help you trust him more, so that when you're tempted, you're able to choose wisely because you trust that God's way is best.

A LITTLE EXTRA

A little accountability goes a long way. Make a list of your top three temptations, and share your list with a trusted friend. Give your friend permission to ask you how you're doing in your areas of temptation. Offer to do the same for your friend.

ONENESS WITH GOD

A LITTLE EXTRA

Spend some time considering the sort of friend you are. Be really honest with yourself (and God). If you want to be really gutsy, ask a friend to give you feedback, telling you what he or she would like you to *continue*, what you should *stop*, and what you should *start*, in order to be a more encouraging friend.

What do you think are the most important qualities of a good friend? Honesty? Loyalty? Humor? Patience? Something else?

Here's some wisdom from Proverbs in response to this question:

There are "friends" who destroy each other,
but a real friend sticks closer than a brother.
Proverbs 18:24

Do you see the answer in there? According to that verse, one of the most important qualities of a good friend is someone who will encourage you and support you. The opposite, as the verse says, is the "friend" who destroys you—which can show up as rumors or lies, competition, discouraging words or names, betrayal, and all sorts of other hurtful tactics.

Which category of "friend" describes the people you spend the most time with? Do they encourage you, or tear you down? Which kind of friend are you?

TALKING WITH GOD

Prayerfully consider your two or three (or more, if you have time) most important friendships. Ask God to help you see clearly if they're constructive or destructive friendships. Thank God for those that are constructive and encouraging, and ask God for courage to do something about those friendships that are destructive and discouraging. Sometimes God can help change these friendships, but sometimes we have to walk away from ones that are leading us in the wrong direction.

"Then, after doing all those things, I will pour out my Spirit upon all people. Your sons and daughters will prophesy. Your old men will dream dreams, and your young men will see visions." Joel 2:28

Today's passage requires going back a few verses to help us better understand its meaning. The "those things" Joel mentions are explained in Joel 2:18-27, and it's all about restoration—God will fix all that is broken.

One of the cool things about Old Testament prophets such as Joel is that their words have "now and not yet" meanings. Put another way, Joel's words meant something real and relevant to his original audience, but his words also have a significant meaning for us today. Joel is describing life after restoration— life as God always intended. Joel describes intimate relationships between God and his people and his people with one another, regardless of age or gender.

TALKING WITH GOD

Pray this prayer today, or one with a similar theme: *God, thank you for your promise of restoration. I trust that when the time is right you will make all things new. Help me live and reveal your kingdom in my daily choices, big and small. I love you; help me learn how to love you more each day.*

VERSE 139:
Joel 2:28

A LITTLE EXTRA

Read Matthew 22:37-38. What connection do you see between Joel's words of promise and Jesus' words of invitation? How does it make you feel to know that Joel's words were written many centuries before Jesus' invitation? More importantly, how will you live into Joel's prophecy, respond to Jesus' invitation, and reveal God's kingdom to those in your life?

GOD HEARS
& RESTORES

A LITTLE EXTRA

Write out the six sentences of the GOSPEL acrostic on a small card. Then work on memorizing each one of them so that you're prepared to share your faith. Once you have them memorized, use the acrostic as a discussion starter with a friend who doesn't know Jesus.

Instead, you must worship Christ as Lord of your life. And if someone asks about your Christian hope, always be ready to explain it. 1 Peter 3:15

What would you say if someone asked you about your relationship with God? Are you prepared to explain it? Can you describe Jesus' gospel message of grace in a clear, concise, compelling way?

There's a simple GOSPEL acrostic from Dare 2 Share Ministries that can help you share your faith. Check it out, memorize it, and then make it your own by adding in your own personal God-stories about your own relationship with Jesus. The acrostic goes like this:

GOD created us to be with him.
OUR sins separate us from God.
SINS cannot be removed by good deeds.
PAYING the price for sin, Jesus died and rose again.
EVERYONE who trusts in him alone has eternal life.
LIFE with Jesus starts now and lasts forever.

The core truths reflected in these six short statements contain the essence of what someone needs to understand in order to make a decision about following Christ. They are not meant to be a "formula" you walk someone through; rather, this is an outline that can help you keep your spiritual conversation with someone on track.

After all, it's tough to clearly explain the message of the gospel to others unless you're prepared to put it into words.

TALKING WITH GOD

Thank God for the gift of salvation available through Jesus. Then spend some time praying about who you should share the gospel with today. Then do it—by phone, online, or face to face!

"If we are thrown into the blazing furnace, the God whom we serve is able to save us. He will rescue us from your power, Your Majesty. But even if he doesn't, we want to make it clear to you, Your Majesty, that we will never serve your gods or worship the gold statue you have set up."
Daniel 3:17-18

It's likely you've heard about Shadrach, Meshach and Abednego. (If not, check out all of Daniel 3.) Rather than a story about punishment and extremely hot temperatures, this story is about radical faith displayed by three dudes who got thrown into a fiery furnace.

After refusing to bow down to the king like everyone else, the three guys were ordered to be thrown into the furnace. Instead of letting the fear of death fill their minds, they continued to pray to God and disobeyed the king. God rewarded their faithfulness and performed an incredible miracle that saved them from the flames. God sent an angel into the furnace to protect them and they came out without a single burn! Isn't it amazing what God can do when we remain faithful to him?

TALKING WITH GOD

Ask God to help you develop the trust, faithfulness, and commitment that Shadrach, Meshach, and Abednego had. We all could take some tips from them and learn how to follow God even when no one else is.

VERSE 141:
Daniel 3:17-18

A LITTLE EXTRA

Think about a time you were afraid that talking about God would get you in trouble. Maybe it was with a teacher at school or a friend who did not have the same beliefs as you. Write out a "what if" story of the best thing that could happen and the worst thing that could happen in that situation. Ask God to help you trust him the next time you face a tough situation.

ONENESS WITH GOD

A LITTLE EXTRA

Spend five minutes looking at yourself in a mirror. Look into your own eyes, instead of looking at your physical characteristics. Allow God's Spirit inside of you to teach you how valuable you are. As you look in the mirror, think about how God created you in his image, and that he loves what he sees. Ask God to help you see yourself the way he does: beautiful and wonderful and amazing.

Then God said, "Let us make human beings in our image, to be like us. They will reign over the fish in the sea, the birds in the sky, the livestock, all the wild animals on the earth, and the small animals that scurry along the ground." So God created human beings in his own image. In the image of God he created them; male and female he created them. Genesis 1:26-27

What do you think it means to be made in God's image? Does it mean we physically look like God? Does it mean we have the same personality characteristics as God? A little of both? Whichever way you understand today's passage, God created you to be his representative in this world. This means two things. First, God must love you dearly if he took the time to make you like him. Second, when you interact with other people, they have a chance to see God in you. You have the opportunity and the calling to be the clearest image of God that you can be.

TALKING WITH GOD

Thank God that you are made in his image, and ask God to help you understand how valuable you are. Ask God to help you represent him well to everyone you meet today.

Mother Teresa is credited with saying this about her work with the poorest of the poor in India: "Each one of them is Jesus in disguise."

When you look around at the people you see each day and when you think about the people who are in great need, do you see Jesus in disguise?

Most of the time we see people for what they can do for us or how they make us feel about ourselves. If we're honest, we'll admit that most of the times we help, it's because it's easy and convenient for us.

"And the King will say, 'I tell you the truth, when you did it to one of the least of these my brothers and sisters, you were doing it to me!'"
Matthew 25:40

Jesus calls us to see people differently. Jesus brings dignity back to people by instructing us to see them as he sees them. When we see people, we need to see their Creator. When we see people in that light and when we decide to serve them, we understand that each act of kindness is greater than just a "simple act"—it's service to our King.

TALK WITH GOD

If you struggle to see Jesus in everyone, spend a moment confessing your sin and asking God to help you see people the way he wants you to see people. Ask Jesus to change your view of those around you who are in need. Pray for an opportunity to serve Jesus by serving people. Ask God to help you trust that his way is best.

ONENESS
WITH GOD

VERSE 143:
Matthew 25:40

A LITTLE EXTRA

Think of at least one way you can serve others in your home, your school, your neighborhood, your team/band/job, or your youth group. Now go try it!

ONENESS
WITH GOD

VERSE 144:
Mark 11:24

A LITTLE EXTRA

Read Mark 11:12-25, and then ask a pastor or leader to meet with you to discuss it. Ask this person what Jesus means in Mark 11:24. Ask them how they've seen God do miracles in their life. Ask them how they've grown in their trust in God. They'll love to share this time with you and help you grow on your faith journey.

"I tell you, you can pray for anything, and if you believe that you've received it, it will be yours."
Mark 11:24

Have you ever thought of God as a genie? Ask him for something, close your eyes really tight, believe, and POOF! There's your fulfilled wish! Isn't that what Jesus says in today's passage?

It might seem that way, but if you read the passage in light of the rest of the chapter—and in light of what else is going on in Jesus' life and ministry—you realize Jesus is talking about something much bigger. Even still, at the heart of Jesus' words is his invitation to trust God. Deeply trust God. Jesus wants us to trust God with everything, even things that seem impossible, believing that he is working everything out in the way that is best for us and for those around us. Do you want that sort of trust today?

TALKING WITH GOD

Pray this prayer today: *Jesus, I trust you, but not completely; help me trust you more. Life is difficult and unfair, and it sometimes feels impossible. Help me trust that you are constantly at work around me to turn every situation into something you know is good. Use my life to reveal your kingdom to the people around me today.*

After this I saw a vast crowd, too great to count, from every nation and tribe and people and language, standing in front of the throne and before the Lamb. They were clothed in white robes and held palm branches in their hands.
Revelation 7:9

Have you ever stared at a piece of art appreciating the beautiful color and admiring the artist's technique, mesmerized by the attention to detail—but then you step back and ask, "But what does it mean?" That's often the reaction people have to John's visions in Revelation upon first read.

But for this particular vision, we find some clarity to its meaning. Hope, unity, and victory in Christ are clearly brushed into this vision. Step closer and discover detail in this vision that directly affects you and the people in your life: Jesus will be shared with every tribe and nation on the earth and in every language. A "vast crowd" of people will believe and will confess that their sins have been washed away by Jesus and will stand in unity before Jesus, clothed in forgiveness and grace praising the Lamb.

Will you be a part of this "vast crowd"? Do you believe God tells the truth? Do you believe that Jesus truly is the only way to life?

TALKING WITH GOD

There are lots of prayers we offer to God, and lots of different ways of offering them to him. But one prayer, one conversation stands out from most: the prayer that adds us to the count of white-robed, palm-branch waivers. See the question in John 3:16.

VERSE 145:
Revelation 7:9

A LITTLE EXTRA

Next time you're part of a large crowd of people, look around you and consider the vast crowd from Revelation 7:9. John's vision may not completely fit in that instance, but it will become a little more real.

SIN &
SEPARATION

VERSE 146:
Judges 2:10-11

A LITTLE EXTRA

Take some time this week to sit down and make a list of the God-moments from your life, including conversations with spiritual mentors, camps, retreats, mission trips—anything that God used to help you trust him more is a God-moment. Find three people this week to share your God-moments with.

After that generation died, another generation grew up who did not acknowledge the Lord or remember the mighty things he had done for Israel. The Israelites did evil in the Lord's sight and served the images of Baal. Judges 2:10-11

When your family gathers at Christmas, do you ever spend some time telling stories of things you did when you were younger? Most of us love to tell stories and remember the good times. Do you ever do that with spiritual things? When was the last time you sat down and told someone what God did or is doing in your life right now?

Do you see what Judges 2 says happened when people forgot the stories of what God had done? If you forget what God has done in your life or why you chose to follow Jesus, you'll likely end up following something else. You can read about people who did just that, time and time again, in the Old Testament.

Your stories of what God has done in your life, and what God is continuing to do, are very important to the spiritual life of those who will come after you. Be a generation that tells the story of God.

TALKING WITH GOD

Consider the ways the culture distracts you from thinking about God. Do you care about movies, music, games, or friendships more than the stories of God's miracles? Ask God for opportunities to share his story with others in your life.

"There is salvation in no one else! God has given no other name under heaven by which we must be saved." Acts 4:12

What a politically incorrect statement! Surely the great Apostle Peter (an apostle is someone who knew Jesus personally) didn't mean what the words in this verse appear to say—that Jesus is the one, true, only way to salvation. How arrogant! How closed-minded! How exclusive and judgmental!

And how inconvenient for us Christians in this day where popular opinion says that every path leads to God.

But there's just no getting away from this sweeping claim of biblical Christianity. *"There is salvation in no one else!"* This simple verse makes it clear that salvation is found only in Jesus.

Actually, it was Jesus himself who first laid out this bold, controversial, unequivocal truth when he said, *"I am the way, the truth, and the life. No one can come to the Father except through me"* (John 14:6).

What does this truth mean for you? It means that it's absolutely essential that you let others know about Jesus and invite them to follow him, because he is *the* way to God. Of course, this shouldn't be done in an obnoxious, overbearing, or holier-than-thou way. No, you love and serve others as you extend Jesus' invitation to trust in him. You live the kingdom of God, and by your words and actions you reveal the kingdom of God to others.

TALKING WITH GOD

Ask God for courage to trust him, to stand on the truth of God's Word, and for boldness to share his message with others. Then find a way to share your faith with someone who needs Jesus.

GOD HEARS & RESTORES

VERSE 147:
Acts 4:12

A LITTLE EXTRA

Entertainer and illusionist Penn Jillette, a staunch atheist, created a video explaining why he respected Christians who wanted to tell others about heaven and hell. Go to YouTube® (make sure it's OK with your parents) and check out the video "Penn Jillette Gets a Gift of a Bible."

ONENESS
WITH GOD

"The Lord doesn't see things the way you see them. People judge by outward appearance, but the Lord looks at the heart." *1 Samuel 16:7*

You rock! Great job taking some time out of your day to take care of your soul. People spend hours each week working on their outward appearance while ignoring the condition of their heart.

Today's verse reminds us that when God sees us, he looks straight into our heart. In other words, God sees the real you—and likes what he sees.

Remembering to take care of your heart is difficult to do in a world that is so focused on your shoes or jeans or phone. Dare to be different. You are worth more than the price tag on your clothes.

TALKING WITH GOD

Ask God to give you the courage to stop judging yourself by your outward appearance. Ask God to help you find your true worth and identity in him. Spend some time confessing any ways you have judged others by their outward appearances. Ask God to help you see people the way he sees them.

A LITTLE EXTRA

Take a risk and simplify. Consider how different life would be if we spent more time caring for our souls (or the souls of others) and less time focusing on our outward appearances. Let today be a day free from makeup, designer clothes, name-brand items, sports team logo, or technology. People will judge you by your outward appearance, so be the right kind of rebel. What matters most is what God sees—and what God sees is your heart. When people ask what's up, tell them that you're taking a break from caring about your outside so you can take care of your inside.

"I am leaving you with a gift—peace of mind and heart. And the peace I give is a gift the world cannot give. So don't be troubled or afraid."
John 14:27

We all love to receive great gifts, don't we? God understands this, and the greatest gifts God gives are the ones that empower us to live and reveal his kingdom.

In today's verse, Jesus was speaking to his disciples near the end of the Last Supper, the meal they shared just hours before his crucifixion. Jesus had just declared that he would send the Holy Spirit to teach them and remind them of what it meant to be a follower of Christ.

Jesus promises to give us peace, and it's the kind of peace our world just doesn't understand. God's peace isn't about the absence of problems; it's about the presence of God's Spirit and strength when you face problems!

TALKING WITH GOD

Ask God for an extra measure of peace today—even if you think it's going to be a problem-free day. God will give you strength if those unexpected challenges arise, and he will fill you with the gift of his peace, which can't be purchased in any store or from any website!

GOD HEARS & RESTORES

VERSE 149:
John 14:27

A LITTLE EXTRA

An olive branch is a traditional symbol of peace. You probably don't have easy access to olive branches, but your family likely has some olives or olive oil somewhere in the kitchen! Eat an olive, dab some bread in olive oil, or use one of those two items to cook a meal. As you consume the olive, its oil, or the finished meal, pray for God's peace to fill you and comfort you and assure you that you're never alone.

GOD HEARS & RESTORES

VERSE 150:
1 John 5:13

A LITTLE EXTRA

Dig out the warranty card or return policy on a recent family purchase. Read it. Yep, really read every word of how the company or store is providing a "just-in-case" option if things don't work out. Notice if there are any exceptions. You can walk with a new confidence today because you know when it's all said and done, you've made the right choice with Christ. He will follow through every time. With no exceptions.

Why do companies offer warranties when you purchase electronics, cars, and even those bizarre products on late-night infomercials? Because the future is uncertain. What if something happens? What if the product doesn't work? What if you change your mind? You might feel better about your purchase if you have options later on.

I have written this to you who believe in the name of the Son of God, so that you may know you have eternal life. 1 John 5:13

Christ will never break down on you. He follows through on everything he says. Period. When you have confessed your sins, have accepted his gift of salvation, and live according to his plan, Christ promises an incredible, eternal life in heaven.

In today's passage, we read that we can *know* we have eternal life—not wonder or hope, but know. There's no question here—no "just-in-case" warranty if things don't work out. Christ is the true answer for everyone. He is the way, the truth, and the life.

TALKING WITH GOD

Do you wonder about your own salvation? Talk to God all about it. Ask him to give you a peace and a confidence about the decision you've made. He's responsible for saving you; you're just responsible for trusting and following him.

And he called his twelve disciples together and began sending them out two by two, giving them authority to cast out evil spirits. Mark 6:7

Have you ever wondered why Jesus chose 12 ordinary men to hang out with and start a movement that would become the church? Why didn't Jesus look for powerful and important people? Why didn't he recruit big-name political or military or religious leaders?

Today's verse comes fairly soon after Jesus invited his disciples to follow him. Jesus divided them up in pairs and said to go—go find someone to help, go look for people who are hurting, broken, and in need of healing. The disciples didn't have years of experience with Jesus' power to give them confidence. They were fresh recruits—yet not long after first calling them to follow him, Jesus sent them out to serve and minister and meet needs. And he sent them out with his authority.

Leading the life Jesus invites us to live can be a lot like this passage. We can spend our time noticing people in need and using the gifts and talents God has given us to serve them. God has given us the privilege of serving and the talents to make a difference. We simply need to go.

TALKING WITH GOD

Ask God to open your eyes to see people in need, and ask God to give you courage to respond in love.

GOD HEARS & RESTORES

VERSE 151:
Mark 6:7

A LITTLE EXTRA

Draw a heart on the palm of your hand. Every time you see it today, remember that God loves you and that he wants you to show his love to others. If you're really brave, invite a friend to take this challenge, too.

VERSE 152:
Psalm 139:13-14

A LITTLE EXTRA

Read Psalm 127:3. Regardless of your birth, your childhood, your parents, or your life now, God sees you as a reward. God created every detail of you and brought you into this life as a gift. Take some time to truly focus on that truth.

When you think about yourself, what things come to mind? Quickly write down the first three words you thought of—and then read today's passage.

You made all the delicate, inner parts of my body and knit me together in my mother's womb. Thank you for making me so wonderfully complex! Your workmanship is marvelous—how well I know it.
Psalm 139:13-14

God created the earth and everything in it. This includes you. When God created you, he knit you together. *Knit* means to form or create. When we set out to form or create something, we think about it first. We decide how it will be and what the end goal is. We spend time thinking of the details of our creation, and then we begin to form it.

This is how God created you. God decided who you were, even before you were born. As you were being formed and created inside your mother's womb, God knew you. He was creating you exactly how he desired.

You are a work of art. You are wonderful, and God knit you together, specially and intentionally. Do you believe that? Look at the words you wrote down. Do they represent God's wonderful work?

TALKING WITH GOD

Ask God to show you his thoughts. Ask God to remove the negative ones to focus on the work he created in you. Ask God to help you live the life he dreamed for you when he was knitting you together.

What is currently stressing you out? What things are taking over your life right now that you feel like you cannot control?

"He must become greater and greater, and I must become less and less." John 3:30

When selfishness and taking care of only ourselves consume us, it usually adds more stress and problems to our lives. While failure in this area can be frustrating to each of us, John the Baptist's words here hint that when Jesus becomes greater and greater in our lives, it is a process. And like any process, it takes time and goes through stages. A good question to ask is whether Jesus is greater in your life today than he was yesterday—and whether you are less.

The more we trust God and allow him into our lives, the more people can see God living in us. To do this, we must surrender daily all the stress and other things that can consume us. It sounds like a big task, but God's Spirit will help us do this as we pray, study, and listen to God.

TALKING WITH GOD

Ask God to teach you to completely open your heart to him so there will be no more room for you. Ask God to cleanse you of all your selfish thoughts and deeds.

CONSEQUENCES & CRYING OUT

VERSE 153:
John 3:30

A LITTLE EXTRA

Make a list of the top three things that are stressing you out right now. Pray over each one and ask God to take control of those areas in your life.

CONSEQUENCES & CRYING OUT

VERSE 154:
John 16:33

A LITTLE EXTRA

Write a thank you note to Jesus. Tell him how much you're grateful for the suffering he endured for you. Put the note in your nightstand drawer or school binder so you can be reminded of Jesus' sacrifice and can make it a habit to frequently thank him for all he has done.

"I have told you all this so that you may have peace in me. Here on earth you will have many trials and sorrows. But take heart, because I have overcome the world." John 16:33

What comes to mind when you think of Jesus talking about overcoming the world? Maybe you picture the empty tomb and the sight of Jesus raised from the dead, walking among the very people that had wanted him dead only a few days earlier. Or perhaps you imagine hearing the accounts of how the curtain in the Temple in Jerusalem was torn in two, symbolizing how we now have direct access to God.

Think of Jesus on the cross fully surrendered to the trials of this world, only to come back to life on the third day. That can immediately help you feel a sense of peace in knowing that Jesus has gone through immeasurably more pain and suffering than you ever will, just so that you can spend eternity with him.

TALKING WITH GOD

The next time you're going through a tough situation and you feel as though you can't recover, remember what Jesus went through. Thank him for all of the trials he endured for us, conquering the sin and sorrows of our world. Allow the peace of God's promises to fill your heart and put your problems in the right perspective.

Let's say you are invited to spend a day volunteering with a local service project. Which of the following would you prefer to do for a day: cleaning bathrooms at gas stations around the city, or painting and repairing a house for an elderly person in your church?

Now imagine you showing up and being asked to do the opposite project of the one you wanted. Then it starts raining. Then your least favorite person shows up to help—and insists on working right alongside you the entire time. And anything else that could go wrong goes wrong.

Yuck.

With that in mind, read today's passage, which offers insight into what our attitude ought to be when we are "doing" anything:

Work willingly at whatever you do, as though you were working for the Lord rather than for people. Remember that the Lord will give you an inheritance as your reward, and that the Master you are serving is Christ. Colossians 3:23-24

Underline the words *whatever* and *for the Lord*. Is this a fair request? Why is it important for Christ-followers to approach everything as if they are working for the Lord?

TALKING WITH GOD

Because sitting is a symbol of rest, today stand as you pray. If you are in your room alone, actually walk as you talk to the Lord. Ask him to show you really what this verse means. Ask God to help you trust him enough to change your attitude when it comes to work—especially work you're not excited to be doing.

ONENESS
WITH GOD

VERSE 155:
Colossians 3:23-24

A LITTLE EXTRA

Tie a piece of string around your thumb. As you go through your day, every time you see the string, let it remind you to do everything as if you're working for the Lord.

VERSE 156:
Mark 14:36

A LITTLE EXTRA

Read the entire account of Jesus and the disciples in Gethsemane in Mark 14:32-42. In verse 38, Jesus said, *"Keep watch and pray, so that you will not give in to temptation."* What temptation are you facing?

How do you pray? Do you go to God with a list of wants and needs and nothing more? Do you keep a list of stresses and concerns to yourself, and only mention that God gets to decide what happens in your life? Does it sometimes feel like you're making your wish after you've blown out the candles on your birthday cake?

"Abba, Father," he cried out, "everything is possible for you. Please take this cup of suffering away from me. Yet I want your will to be done, not mine."
Mark 14:36

Jesus, again, gives us the perfect example of how to pray: He affirms God's greatness. Everything is possible for God. He worked incredible miracles in Bible times, and he's still working miracles today. Jesus then pleads with God to end his suffering. Jesus shows us it's OK to be blunt and honest with God.

In possibly the most important part, Jesus finishes with the main point. Even if God says no to his request, Jesus is OK with it. Jesus trusts God and knows that his will is best. Jesus wants God's will above all else, even his own life.

You can trust God with everything—including your life.

TALKING WITH GOD

Whatever is going on in your life, try praying as Jesus prayed. Focus on how everything is possible with God. Be honest as you share with him a desire you have. You can trust God to make the best decision for your today and your tomorrow. Ask for his will above all else.

Think about some goals that you've set or traits that you want to have. Are they mostly positive or negative?

Many of us try to set good goals to become people with positive traits. We look at ourselves and make judgments about where we are and where we want to be. We strive for good things, and when we see them, we are pleased with ourselves. Does this sound like you? Take a look at today's verse:

Don't be impressed with your own wisdom.
Instead, fear the Lord and turn away from evil.
Proverbs 3:7

In this verse, *fear* doesn't mean to be terrified of God; it means to respect, honor, and admire God. And then we are called to turn away or reject evil.

So instead of focusing on ourselves and how wise we think we are, we can focus on God and how wise we know he is. We can shift our thoughts away from selfish things and instead admire God. And as our thoughts turn from us to God, we will not only turn away from evil, but we will also begin to hate anything that God hates.

TALKING WITH GOD

Many of us spend most of our time being self-focused. Ask God to bring awareness of times that you could be focused on him, instead of yourself. Ask God to help you trust him more and turn to him when you need wisdom.

CONSEQUENCES & CRYING OUT

VERSE 157:
Proverbs 3:7

A LITTLE EXTRA

Read Psalm 66:5. On a sheet of paper, write down five specific things God has done in your life. Think back to these experiences. Remember what happened, where you were, and how you felt. Are you still in awe of God? Remind yourself of the amazing things God has done—and then thank him.

CONSEQUENCES & CRYING OUT

VERSE 158:
Psalm 51:1

A LITTLE EXTRA

Read 2 Samuel 11:1–12:14 to understand the full story of David's sin, including the bad decisions he made and the consequences that came from those choices. Write your own psalm of repentance for a current or past sin you've struggled with.

Have mercy on me, O God, because of your unfailing love. Because of your great compassion, blot out the stain of my sins. Psalm 51:1

Today's verse is part of King David's response after the prophet Nathan confronted him about his sin: committing adultery with Bathsheba and then arranging the death of her husband, Uriah. David was king of Israel at the time, and he could have had Nathan killed for his words. David could have justified his sin and been angry with God. But God used Nathan's words to break David's heart. David repented of his sin and turned back to God. David still faced consequences for his sin, but his relationship with God was restored.

How do you respond when you're confronted with sin? Do you have someone in your life who cares enough about you to speak truth in love into your life? If they do, will you be thankful for them or angry with them? Will you turn to God or toward your sin?

TALKING WITH GOD

If you are struggling with sin today, confess it to God and ask him for help. Ask God to forgive you, and ask him to help you find a true friend who will be a "Nathan" in your life. Ask God to help you receive correction like David did. Commit to never turning your back on God, even in the most difficult seasons of life.

But the Holy Spirit produces this kind of fruit in our lives: love, joy, peace, patience, kindness, goodness, faithfulness, gentleness, and self-control. There is no law against these things!
Galatians 5:22-23

Fruit happens. Trees don't have to gather supplies, follow a recipe, or concentrate on anything to produce fruit. If the environment is right, fruit appears. Fruit is the byproduct and the natural result for a healthy plant. The same is true for us. God's Holy Spirit produces the fruit; we need to focus on creating a healthy environment.

For example: Praying, reading a daily devotion (such as this one), joining a small group, worshipping with other Christ-followers, helping someone in need, sharing your God-story—these are all ways we develop a spiritually healthy environment in which growth can naturally occur. Live a life that allows the characteristics, or "fruit," of the Holy Spirit to fill your life and pour out into the lives of other people.

TALKING WITH GOD

How are you doing on creating a healthy environment for fruit in your life? What changes can you make to do a little better? Ask God to help you develop the discipline to make space for the fruit of God's Spirit to grow in your life.

VERSE 159:
Galatians 5:22-23

A LITTLE EXTRA

Go look at a plant that has fruit on it. (If it's winter, do an online search and find a good picture.) You'll probably notice that fruit-bearing trees are healthy: green leaves, solid branches, and other signs of nutrition and growth. Every time you see a piece of fruit—on a tree, in a grocery store, on the kitchen table, in the cafeteria—remember Paul's words in today's passage. Ask yourself if you see fruit in your life.

CONSEQUENCES & CRYING OUT

A LITTLE EXTRA

Read the accounts of this story in Matthew 19:16-30, Mark 10:17-31, and Luke 18:18-30. What differences and similarities do you notice in the passages? What did God's Holy Spirit reveal to you as you read today? Journal your thoughts or jot them down in the margins.

Looking at the man, Jesus felt genuine love for him. "There is still one thing you haven't done," he told him. "Go and sell all your possessions and give the money to the poor, and you will have treasure in heaven. Then come, follow me." Mark 10:21

Today's passage appears in three Gospels: Matthew, Mark, and Luke. This experience was pretty memorable. Notice that Jesus loved this guy but still told him the truth. And what Jesus told this man was different from what he told others who asked similar questions. And the rest of the passage tells how the man heard Jesus' words and walked away. Jesus did not chase him down or beg him to reconsider; Jesus let him go. Jesus loved the man but let him walk away.

How does that make you feel? If Jesus really loved him, wouldn't he have tried to change his mind? Perhaps Jesus understood that we must be at a place of recognizing our need for Jesus above all else. Since Jesus knows your heart, what might he say you need to give up? Do you trust him to know what's best?

TALKING WITH GOD

Pray this kind of prayer today: *Lord, help me recognize that I need you more than anything else in life. Help me understand that when you ask me tough questions or make tough statements, it's because you love me. Help me not walk away but allow you to love me and lead me. Help me live and reveal your kingdom in my decisions today.*

"Seek the Kingdom of God above all else, and live righteously, and he will give you everything you need." Matthew 6:33

What are you looking for in life? Is it a "toy" such as a car or a cell phone? Is it a relationship: best friend, boyfriend, girlfriend? Is it popularity or influence? Is it musical or athletic accomplishments?

Now consider why you want those things. Is it because you want to do your very best for God? Is it because of a search for identity and purpose and acceptance? Is it somewhere in between? In today's passage, Jesus tells us that what we are truly searching for in life can be found in him. In fact, Jesus tells us that nothing we are truly searching for in life can be found outside of him. If we put our energy into deepening our trust relationship with Jesus, we will have everything we really need in life—perhaps not in the way we originally planned, but in a deeper sense of what's driving us. How hard or easy is it for you to trust Jesus' words in this verse?

TALKING WITH GOD

Pray this kind of prayer: *God, help me recognize that everything I want in life is found in you, and nothing I want in life can be found outside of you. I trust you; help me trust you more today. Use my life to reveal your kingdom to others.*

ONENESS
WITH GOD

VERSE 161:
Matthew 6:33

A LITTLE EXTRA

Ask God to search your heart and help you see the deeper things you desire. It may be helpful to have a spiritual mentor assist you with this. Write today's verse on an adhesive note and put it in a space where you'll see it as a reminder to seek God first and trust him to meet all of your needs.

CONSEQUENCES & CRYING OUT

A LITTLE EXTRA

Find a close friend, and practice insulting one another but responding in a friendly, Christ-like way. This will take some time, but it will prepare you for the real thing.

Think about a recent time someone insulted you or made fun of something you did. How did that make you feel? How did you react? Now think of a time recently that you insulted someone or made fun of someone for something they did. Why did you do that? How did they react? What feelings did you have after you did this?

Don't repay evil for evil. Don't retaliate with insults when people insult you. Instead, pay them back with a blessing. That is what God has called you to do, and he will bless you for it. 1 Peter 3:9

What we're asked to do in today's passage is tough to do, but it's very important that all Christ-followers learn how to react when we feel attacked. Most of us have been taught to stand up for ourselves when someone does something to us or against us. But in this Scripture we are told not to retaliate when someone makes fun of us. We are told that we ought to be kind to them and bless them with our actions, instead of reacting with another insult or finding a way to get revenge. Returning them a blessing is what God is calling us to do, and in the end, God will reward us for doing so.

TALKING WITH GOD

Take a moment and talk to God about a recent time you were insulted. Ask God to help you be a blessing to the person who insulted you.

Yet true godliness with contentment is itself great wealth. After all, we brought nothing with us when we came into the world, and we can't take anything with us when we leave it.
1 Timothy 6:6–7

VERSE 163:
1 Timothy 6:6–7

How can contentment be the same as great wealth?
That seems a bit weird, right?

Think about it, though. If you're never content with what you have, you will always want more, no matter how much you have. The real truth is that wealth means having an abundance of anything. The person who has a wealth of blessing is the one who is content and grateful to God for what he or she has. The world is filled with stories of rich people who are never happy, because they are never content with just having a lot of money or lots of possessions. As a Christ-follower, our greatest treasure lies in Jesus' sacrifice on the cross.

TALKING WITH GOD

Thank God for all you have—and be specific, including family, friends, food, shelter, abilities, and so on. Ask God to help you trust that who he is and what he gives is enough. Ask God to help you find true godliness with contentment.

A LITTLE EXTRA

The next time you are feeling dissatisfied about what you have—or deeply desiring something you don't have—do something to help those who are struggling. Maybe volunteer at a local ministry to the homeless, or serve in a soup kitchen. Visit a website for an organization that helps people in poor nations, and read the stories of the children they are serving. Take note of the great need in the lives of others. Seeing those needs will help you focus less on yourself, and it will grow an attitude of contentment in your heart with what God has given you.

ONENESS

WITH GOD

VERSE 164:
Ephesians 6:10

A LITTLE EXTRA

Read Ephesians 6:10-17. Draw a stick figure, and as you reread about the "armor," draw it on your stick figure. When you're done, thank God that he does such a thorough job preparing and protecting us.

A final word: Be strong in the Lord and in his mighty power. Ephesians 6:10

Make a muscle. You know how. Bend your arm, curl your fist and pump it. What do you think? Look good or is it pretty puny? Stare long and hard at that muscle.

Guess what? No matter how physically strong you are, it will never be enough. Yes, it may give you the ability to tear a phonebook in half with your bare hands, but it probably won't get you through a bad day. We need more than just physical strength to live and declare God's kingdom.

That is why the Apostle Paul gives us this command to be strong in the Lord. This is about the power that comes from God alone. Relying on just our own strength will leave us feeling weak. But God's strength never fails. That is why this is the first verse in a passage that explains our "fight" and how to conquer it. This is a boost, not an end.

Look at your muscle again. Are you strong in his mighty power or your own?

TALKING WITH GOD

Flex a muscle while you pray. It might feel a little weird at first, but it will help you remember the importance of relying on God's strength. Ask God what it means to be strong in him. Ask him to show you his power and how it is greater than your own.

Kids can't wait for Christmas. Adults can't wait until they can retire. Others can't wait for their next paycheck, their loved one to get better, or the latest new gizmo.

What is it for you? The one thing you are waiting for—and you wish it would just happen *right now*?

Habakkuk is such a strange name for a Bible book, it's a wonder you'd find anything valuable in it, right? Not so! Because Hab (surely that's what his friends called him) asks God a question that's common to all of us: Why do you let certain things happen, and when are you going to get around to making things right? Here's God's response to Hab:

"This vision is for a future time. It describes the end, and it will be fulfilled. If it seems slow in coming, wait patiently, for it will surely take place. It will not be delayed." Habakkuk 2:3

God's short answer: Hang in there.

TALKING WITH GOD

Spend a few minutes talking with God about what you're waiting on him to do. It's OK to tell God exactly how you're feeling. When you've shared all your thoughts, reread the verse above, allowing God to speak directly to you through his Word. Then, be still for at least one minute and wait to hear his response to you.

GOD HEARS & RESTORES

A LITTLE EXTRA

It's good to remember that God will work things out in his perfect timing. To help you hang in there, find something you look at every day—maybe the mirror in your room. Take an adhesive note and write a few words that describe what you're waiting for. Underneath those words, write *"Hang in there. — God."* Use as many notes as you need! They'll look great in the shape of a cross.

ONENESS WITH GOD

A LITTLE EXTRA

Each time you see a toddler or young child, ask God to reveal to you something that you have not given up to him—an area where you're still saying "mine."

Don't you realize that your body is the temple of the Holy Spirit, who lives in you and was given to you by God? You do not belong to yourself, for God bought you with a high price. So you must honor God with your body. 1 Corinthians 6:19–20

One of the first words that babies seem to learn is *mine*—a reminder of a pre-existing condition deep within every human being to have possession over things and control them without answering to anybody. When we are kids, it's about a toy; as a person grows up, it's about every area of our lives, including our bodies.

Honoring God with your body means using it to do things that are important to him, not just pursuing the things that are important to you. Sometimes we say with our mouth that we believe in God and he has our allegiance, but we keep areas back from him to ourselves. It's like we've divided our bodies into little compartments. Perhaps we have given him a piece of our mind each day to read Scripture, but we don't think about what clothes God would have us wear. Maybe we give God our bodies on loan as we attend a church service one night a week, but the foods we eat are destroying our health.

Give God every compartment of your body. Hold nothing back. Invite him into every decision you make.

TALKING WITH GOD

Pray that God would open your eyes to see ways that you have been holding on to the ownership of your body. In every way, surrender yourself to God and to his plan.

Don't you realize that all of you together are the temple of God and that the Spirit of God lives in you? God will destroy anyone who destroys this temple. For God's temple is holy, and you are that temple. 1 Corinthians 3:16–17

For generations, God's people encountered his presence in a temple that actually was a tent that was carried around in the desert and was designed by God himself, with many instructions on how every little thing was to be done perfectly—or a high price would be paid. Lots of detail was given to being clean when visiting the place where God dwelled. Later, a temple was built in Jerusalem, and the people continued to follow instructions on how to interact with God.

The idea of God not living in the temple was a crazy new concept to the people who first read this writing in the New Testament. But it also might have been embarrassing. Think of all the things people did that they would never do in the temple around God.

God comes and lives inside of us now. It's so much easier to connect with him, and anyone can do it. Everywhere we go, everything we do, God is with us. We are the place where God lives. How then should we live?

TALKING WITH GOD

Offer this prayer to God, or one with a similar theme: *God, forgive me for not treating my body as a holy place where you live. Help me be aware today that you are a God who lives inside of your people. Thank you for being a God that is always with me.*

VERSE 167:
1 Corinthians 3:16–17

A LITTLE EXTRA

God gave Moses all kinds of instructions for the temple life. Read Exodus 40 to discover some of the things required to enter into God's Old Testament house.

ONENESS WITH GOD

A LITTLE EXTRA

Listen to the song "Every Season" by Nichole Nordeman. Concentrate on the message of the song, and pray through any thought that comes to your mind as you listen.

For everything there is a season, a time for every activity under heaven. Ecclesiastes 3:1

Professional sports have seasons. Television shows have seasons. But have you ever thought about your life passing by in a series of seasons?

What are some things we know about seasons? They are distinctly different from each other. They happen every year. They happen in order. Some are harsh and some are mild. What else can you think of? Make a list.

Things begin anew in spring. Heat and vacation dominate our thoughts of summer. Fall is a time of new school years and changing colors in the leaves. And winter is a time to bundle up, come in from the cold, and hide away from the rain.

Now write down some notable moments in your life: (1) The most difficult thing you are facing right now. (2) Your biggest dream, no matter how crazy other people may think it is. (3) The happiest time in your life. (4) The saddest moment you have ever experienced.

Take each one of these moments and match them to the characteristics of seasons that you wrote down. Can you find any similarities between the two? Are there any consistent patterns or characteristics? If you started to look at the moments in your life as seasons, how would your viewpoint change?

TALKING WITH GOD

Pray that God would give you his perspective on your life. Ask God to help you trust him more as your life moves from season to season.

ONENESS WITH GOD

"My thoughts are nothing like your thoughts," says the Lord. "And my ways are far beyond anything you could imagine." Isaiah 55:8

Has anything in your life not worked out the way you would like? You really wanted to make the sports team, but you didn't. You studied really hard for a test, but you still got a bad grade. It could be something bigger. Maybe you just found out that your family is moving, or your parents are divorcing, or a close friend is really ill.

In these moments, we can blame God that life's not fair or trust that he loves us so much that he wants the best for us. That is why he tells us in Isaiah that he does and sees things differently. God can see our past, present, and future all at the same time. God wants to take everything in our lives and move us toward an amazing plan for our lives—even the bad things that break God's heart. Life isn't fair, but God wants us to know that he is big enough to take care of us, especially when we can't take care of ourselves.

TALKING WITH GOD

Tell God about your hurt and disappointments. Tell him about the things that are overwhelming you. Ask God to help you trust him in the middle of the mess.

VERSE 169:
Isaiah 55:8

A LITTLE EXTRA

Check out claymath.org/millennium/Yang-Mills_Theory and read about the Yang-Mills theory. Once you understand it, figure out how to explain it to your dog. Was that easy or difficult? Now figure out how to get your dog to eat a dog treat. Was that easier? The next time you're stuck with a math or physics or organic chemistry problem, remember today's passage and thank God that his ways are beyond our ways.

GOD HEARS & RESTORES

A LITTLE EXTRA

While you can't "prove" God's existence to anyone, you can be prepared for a reasoned, logical discussion about God. Check out "Does God Exist?" at everystudent.com/features/isthere.html.

Faith is the confidence that what we hope for will actually happen; it gives us assurance about things we cannot see. Hebrews 11:1

What does having faith mean, anyway? Does it mean never having any doubts about your spiritual beliefs or never asking God questions? No, God is relational and is not threatened by our honest search for answers. In fact, King David, whom God described as a "man after my own heart," asked God loads of questions in the psalms he wrote. Questions that often started with "Why O God…?" Questions that we may never know the answers to during this lifetime. Because God is immense and our brains are puny, until we're in heaven there will always be things we just don't get about him.

Faith is trust. Do you trust God? Do you trust that God's way is best? Faith is an unshakeable certainty in a few core truths that the Bible emphasizes over and over. What are they?

1. God. There is one God who is triune in nature— Father, Son, and Holy Spirit.

2. Jesus. Jesus is the Son of God, fully God and fully man, and he came to earth to be the atoning sacrifice for the sins of the world.

3. The Bible. Scripture is the divinely inspired, fully reliable Word of God and is the Christ-follower's guide for living.

4. The Gospel. Jesus died and rose again so we can have eternal life if we put our trust in him alone.

These are the core anchors of our Christian faith that give us assurance and hope.

TALKING WITH GOD

Write a few sentences thanking God for each of these truths that ground your faith.

Don't let evil conquer you, but conquer evil by doing good. Romans 12:21

"They hit me first!" Ever said that? If so, it's probably because you got caught "doing unto others exactly what they did to you." It feels good to pay someone back for something. Or does it? When we repay evil with evil, we allow this cycle to continue, and we become part of the problem.

God knows that we live in a world that is sometimes mean, hurtful, and unfair. But God also knows that the only way to defeat evil is NOT to repay it with evil, but to do the right thing. The next time someone is mean, hurtful, or unfair, choose to conquer evil by doing good. Instead of repaying evil with evil, repay evil with good. You will not regret it.

TALKING WITH GOD

Imagine God is in the room (which he is, but sometimes it helps to picture him actually sitting there with you), and spend some time talking with him about the situations in your life that are hurtful. Maybe it's a relationship, a string of bad decisions, or just the ugliness of the world. God wants you to tell him all the things that hurt you. Once you've shared your heart, ask God to help you respond to each situation the way he wants—not with evil, but by repaying evil with good.

GOD HEARS & RESTORES

VERSE 171:
Romans 12:21

A LITTLE EXTRA

Pick one or two things from your conversation with God, and write them in your journal. Ask God to help you be creative in the ways you can respond to people in each situation. Make a list of the ideas you have, and as you try each one, write out what happens—how people respond—and how the situation changes. Watch what God does when you trust him and his way of living.

IT'S ALL ABOUT TRUST

As you read the Bible, you'll see the word *faith* show up a lot of times. In the Old Testament and in the New Testament, faith seems to be a pretty big deal to God. What is faith? Faith is believing in something so much that you're willing to adjust your life in response to it. In short, faith is trust. Anytime you read the word *faith* in the Bible, you can substitute the word *trust*.

FAITH starts with trusting God to save you from your sin. Some people call this "getting saved," or being "born again," or "giving your life to Christ." We all sin (Romans 3:23), the consequence for our sin is spiritual death (Romans 6:23a), God offers us forgiveness through the sacrifice of Jesus (Romans 6:23b), and we accept God's forgiveness when we invite him into our lives (Romans 10:9-10). *Then Christ will make his home in your hearts as you trust in him. Your roots will grow down into God's love and keep you strong (Ephesians 3:17).* To begin a relationship with God, you have to take a risk to trust him.

TRUST grows over time. Just like in human relationships, trust does not happen overnight. When you trust God with a little, he honors your trust and proves to you that he is trustworthy. As God proves he is trustworthy, you trust him with a little more. As you trust God with a little more, he honors your trust and proves that he is trustworthy. And trust grows. To grow in your trust in God, you have to take a risk to continue to trust him.

If you haven't begun a relationship with God, pray a prayer like this one: *Dear God, I know I'm a sinner and my sin separates me from you. I believe you died for my sins, and I trust that you can and will forgive me. Please come into my life and forgive me of my sin. I trust you today. In Jesus' name, amen.* If you prayed that prayer for the first time, ROCK ON! Go talk to your pastor or another adult you trust.

If you have a relationship with God, ask him to help you trust him more. Take the risk, and watch God do amazing things in your life.

IT'S ALL ABOUT TRUST.

For if we are faithful to the end, trusting God just as firmly as when we first believed, we will share in all that belongs to Christ (Hebrews 3:14).

ONENESS
WITH GOD

A LITTLE EXTRA

Find something that represents God's unending love for you—something that will remind you of God's love on days you don't feel very loveable. Try to pick something that you will see in everyday life, as a repeated reminder that God thinks you're awesome.

And I am convinced that nothing can ever separate us from God's love. Neither death nor life, neither angels nor demons, neither our fears for today nor our worries about tomorrow—not even the powers of hell can separate us from God's love. No power in the sky above or in the earth below—indeed, nothing in all creation will ever be able to separate us from the love of God that is revealed in Christ Jesus our Lord. Romans 8:38-39

Many people consider this passage one of their favorites in all of Scripture. Nothing was left to chance here. Paul didn't just write that nothing can keep us from God's love—he elaborated with a long list of things that won't get in the way: stuff we see every day, stuff we don't see every day, stuff that occupies our thoughts, even the devil himself. Nothing. Nada. Zilch. Zero. A big fat goose egg. Nothing can block God's love. Period.

And God's love is made perfect in his Son, Jesus, who revealed the Father's love when he stood in our place of condemnation, on the cross. If anything were able to separate us from God's love, it would make the sacrifice of Christ worthless.

TALKING WITH GOD

Have you ever just marveled at God's love for you? Have you ever asked God why he loves you so much? Have you ever thanked God for his amazing, unchanging love for you? Spend some time doing that today. And then listen—God might just sing you a love song.

Then the angel showed me a river with the water of life, clear as crystal, flowing from the throne of God and of the Lamb. It flowed down the center of the main street. On each side of the river grew a tree of life, bearing twelve crops of fruit, with a fresh crop each month. The leaves were used for medicine to heal the nations. Revelation 22:1-2

GOD HEARS & RESTORES

VERSE 173:
Revelation 22:1-2

For the most part, the people who wrote the Bible were more concerned with writing passages that would help people get to heaven than they were about writing passages that described heaven. So when the writer of Revelation takes a moment to actually tell us what heaven will be like, it's like getting a sneak peak at an upcoming movie. We don't get a ton of information, but we get enough to make us want to know more.

The amazing part of today's passage is the promise that we will no longer be broken. Water, the symbol of eternal life, will satisfy our spiritual thirst once and for all. We will be able to eat freely from the tree of life. The leaves from the tree will be used as a medicine to heal all of our relationships. All things will be restored and made new.

A LITTLE EXTRA

The next time you drink filtered or bottled water, think about the pure, crystal-clear water that God promises in heaven—and take a moment to thank God for that promise!

TALKING TO GOD

Pray this kind of prayer: *God, I look forward to the day when I no longer thirst for the things of this world. I'm so worn out from the struggle. Thank you for giving us a life eternal with you. Thank you that this life isn't all there is. I'm homesick for you, God. I love you.*

VERSE 174:
Mark 4:31-32

A LITTLE EXTRA

You might be one person in a large school or a large city, but there's no reason you can't have a huge impact. Think about a way you could spark something for God in your school or in your community. Could it be a Bible study at lunch or a prayer meeting before school? Or maybe you're supposed to run for a class office, so you can affect change throughout the entire school? Or perhaps God has a calling for you that will impact your whole city!

Think about the last time you were sick. Really, really, puking sick. Now consider that whatever bacteria or virus knocked you out for days was something you can't even see without a microscope. Size doesn't matter. Small things can affect us in huge ways.

"It is like a mustard seed planted in the ground. It is the smallest of all seeds, but it becomes the largest of all garden plants; it grows long branches, and birds can make nests in its shade." Mark 4:31-32

The "it" that Jesus is talking about here is God's kingdom. So how is it that God's kingdom starts small? Well, it doesn't get much smaller than a baby born in a small town. Or a small group of ordinary guys following a rabbi from town to town. And of course, that small "mustard seed" turned out to be the biggest thing ever—the fulcrum upon which the entire universe rests.

Don't assume that because something (or someone) is small, it (or that person) can't have a huge impact.

TALKING WITH GOD

God uses mustard seeds every day. Ask him to bless your mustard-seed efforts as you seek his will.

O Lord, you alone are my hope. I've trusted you, O Lord, from childhood. Psalm 71:5

Read the verse aloud.

Read the passage aloud again. What word stands out to you?

Read the verse a third time. Let God show you which phrase is most important for you today.

There are times when a message from Scripture is fairly obvious and similar for most everyone. There are other times, like this, where God speaks something different to each person. And it takes practice to hear him speak. It can be a feeling deep in your spirit. Or you could hear the same point in your quiet time, from friends, and at church all in the same week. It can be a sudden recollection as you're walking down the street. Be open to God speaking into your life.

What is God telling you today? Is God allowing you to recall a time he was trustworthy in your past? Is God calling you to put your hope in him—specific to something going on in your life?

TALKING WITH GOD

Just God. Just you. It's OK to sit in silence and wait. Tell him what's on your mind, what you're excited about, and what stresses you. Wait and listen to what he has to say. He has a word for you today.

GOD HEARS & RESTORES

VERSE 175:
Psalm 71:5

A LITTLE EXTRA

If possible, set aside an extended quiet time, or retreat, today. It can be a drive away from the city or just a half-hour in your favorite reading chair. Remove as many distractions as possible (turn off your phone, TV, music). Sit. Listen. If God seems extra silent, grab your Bible and read through some of the psalms. Enjoy your time with God, just like you do with a good friend.

VERSE 176:
Mark 14:9

A LITTLE EXTRA

Read 2 Corinthians 8:19. Spend some time praying about a way you can make an offering or give a gift to someone, in honor of Jesus. Think about how Jesus gave so much lavishly to us. Ask God to allow you to have a glimpse into the woman in Bethany, who poured the perfume on Jesus.

Think of something that you really cherish—a gift or a possession that holds a special place in your heart, or something you saved up your money for months to buy. Think about why this item means so much to you.

In today's verse, we read about a woman who came to Jesus with a jar of expensive perfume. She broke the jar and poured the perfume on Jesus' head. In these times, this perfume was said to be worth more than a year's wages!

"I tell you the truth, wherever the Good News is preached throughout the world, this woman's deed will be remembered and discussed." Mark 14:9

People ridiculed this woman, but Jesus was honored by her lavish gift to him, knowing that she had given everything she had. This woman poured out everything she had and honored Jesus with it. Jesus, too, has given everything to us—including his life. He chose to die for our sins, so that we could live lives of freedom. He poured out his love when he died on the cross and continues to do so as we walk in relationship with him every day.

TALKING WITH GOD

We sometimes take advantage of the things we have. We forget that God is the giver of all good things. Ask God to reveal the things that you are holding on to too tightly. Ask God to reveal ways you can honor him with your possessions, remembering that Jesus gave everything for us.

Therefore, since we are surrounded by such a huge crowd of witnesses to the life of faith, let us strip off every weight that slows us down, especially the sin that so easily trips us up. And let us run with endurance the race God has set before us. We do this by keeping our eyes on Jesus, the champion who initiates and perfects our faith. Because of the joy awaiting him, he endured the cross, disregarding its shame. Now he is seated in the place of honor beside God's throne. Hebrews 12:1–2

GOD HEARS & RESTORES

Imagine competing in the marathon at the Olympics and arriving in the stadium to the deafening applause of the crowd. Can you feel the rise in confidence and strength as they cheer you on?

This amphitheater or stadium-type setting is what the writer of Hebrews is painting as he describes the "cloud of witnesses" that have gone before us—generations of people who have loved God and followed Christ. We can gain confidence because there are many who have gone before us and faced great challenges yet finished well.

TALKING WITH GOD

Take time to pray through this passage. Write down some of the weight and sin that slows you down in your faith—and then give those things to God today. Ask God to give you strength and endurance for your "race." Ask God to give you focus to keep your eyes fixed on Jesus this week.

A LITTLE EXTRA

With your parents' permission, search online for videos showing champions winning an Olympic race. Focus on people in the crowd and how they cheer on the athlete. Then read back through the passage and imagine being cheered on by a huge crowd of witnesses.

GOD HEARS & RESTORES

A LITTLE EXTRA

Look around your school, neighborhood, or community and notice any groups of people that are often overlooked. How can you show love to them? Talk to your parents and friends and church leaders about reaching out to them. When you serve the overlooked, you are living and revealing God's kingdom.

"He ensures that orphans and widows receive justice. He shows love to the foreigners living among you and gives them food and clothing."
Deuteronomy 10:18

When you think of the word *orphan*, what comes to mind? We often think of children living in poverty on the other side of the world—and yes, that is one example. But an orphan is simply someone without parents. A widow is someone whose husband has died.

Many people in our society seem to not belong. They are "foreigners," even if they were born and raised in this culture. Verse 17 of this passage tells us that God is in charge and that he loves us all equally. Anyone who is in need, who is desperate, who doesn't seem to belong—God will take care of them, and he often uses us to do it!

God wants us to remember the orphans, widows, and foreigners. If this is you, know that the Lord loves you in a way that undoes all of those things that seem unfair. If this is not you, look around and find the unnoticed people in your life.

TALKING WITH GOD

Ask God to show his justice to those that are poor or feel like their world is falling apart. Ask him to take care of them in a very real way. If this describes your life, ask God to come in and show you what this means in a personal way.

You're running late. You grab what you need and rush out the door. As you start the car, you realize you have just 10 minutes to make the 15-minute trip. Traffic's not too bad, and your adrenaline is pumping. You can make it; you're pretty close. Then your heart stops cold: You see the police officer on the side of the road running radar. Ugh, how could you have missed it? You keep glancing in the rear-view mirror praying the officer doesn't pull out. Whew—you're safe.

Don't be misled—you cannot mock the justice of God. You will always harvest what you plant. Those who live only to satisfy their own sinful nature will harvest decay and death from that sinful nature. But those who live to please the Spirit will harvest everlasting life from the Spirit.
Galatians 6:7-8

God isn't waiting to zap you when you do wrong. It's not like that at all. God wants what's best for you and has a plan for you. If you stray from that plan, you will endure consequences. But there's good news! You can always make it right with God and get right back in line with his plan.

TALHING WITH GOD

Confess to God anything you're trying to get away with. Honestly take a look at how those decisions have caused consequences and worse things to happen in your life. Even if no one else knows or sees what's happening, you and God both know. Take the time to make it right with God.

CONSEQUENCES
& CRYING OUT

VERSE 179:
Galatians 6:7-8

A LITTLE EXTRA

Talk with a trusted Christian friend or mentor about an area where you've made poor choices, and ask for accountability in making right choices. You could even give him or her a list of questions to ask you each week. And be sure to celebrate as God helps you make better choices.

ONENESS
WITH GOD

A LITTLE EXTRA

If you're not already in the habit of memorizing Scripture, commit to memorizing one verse each week. Start with today's verse and see what happens.

Have you ever tried walking or running in the forest at night? Maybe you have been to a youth group or a camp that plays night games such as Capture the Flag in the woods. If you have done any of these (or if you can imagine doing them), you know it's not easy to run or walk at night without tripping, falling, or running into stuff.

In a similar way, life is full of obstacles, snares, and hazards that can cause us to fall. Whether it's poor decisions in our relationships, or some kind of failure, there are many things that cause us to stumble. King David, who wrote much of the book of Psalms, knew this all too well. He was a man who tripped and was ensnared by sin and mistakes. He learned fully that God's Word and truth were his only light in a dark and deceptive world.

Your word is a lamp to guide my feet and a light for my path. Psalm 119:105

Are you able to see where God is leading you, or are your decisions causing you pain as you fall? Are you seeking God's light and path in the midst of the darkness? Specifically, how is God's Word leading you? How are you reading, learning, and applying the truths of God's Word in your life?

TALKING WITH GOD

Ask God to lead you in your daily decisions, as well as your future plans. If there's a specific decision you need to make, ask God to help you make the right decision. Spend time being still and allowing God to speak to your heart.

Get wisdom; develop good judgment. Don't forget my words or turn away from them. Proverbs 4:5

Did you catch that? Most of us are not born with deep wisdom or good judgment. Those are skills that are acquired over time by people who are intentional about seeking them out. *Get* wisdom; *develop* good judgment. That's great—but how?

According to this verse, it happens when we hang on to the words of the Father, which we find in the Bible. Wisdom and good judgment don't just develop automatically as we grow older; they come from trusting God more as we study, memorize, and obey the words from the Father found in the Bible. It isn't just about acquiring more knowledge to fill our brains. It's about taking the truths of Scripture and letting them sink deep within us. It's about leading lives that are built on what God values most.

So great job! By reading today, you've spent some time investing in acquiring true wisdom and good judgment. It's a valuable habit to maintain for the rest of your life!

TALKING WITH GOD

Pray that as you read the Bible, God would plant the words of Scripture deep in your heart and begin producing solid wisdom and good judgment in you. The books of Psalms and Proverbs are good places to start!

ONENESS WITH GOD

A LITTLE EXTRA

Look through Psalms and Proverbs. Write some verses about wisdom and judgment on index cards and hang them in your locker or bathroom, or set them as reminders on certain dates in your phone or calendar. When they pop up or come to mind, spend some time meditating on the good judgment and wisdom God is nurturing in you.

ONENESS
WITH GOD

A LITTLE EXTRA

Read what James says about the strength of a real person, in James 4:13-16.

We now have this light shining in our hearts, but we ourselves are like fragile clay jars containing this great treasure. This makes it clear that our great power is from God, not from ourselves.
2 Corinthians 4:7

Describing our lives like clay jars makes perfect sense because like clay jars, we can chip or break. Clay jars would be used to hold simple things but would never be used as a weapon or to hammer with. Clay shatters when it gets hit. It is vulnerable.

None of us has superpowers. In fact, the strongest man on earth, when compared to the power of God, would seem as brittle as a clay jar. The good news, however, is that even though we are fragile containers, we get to hold the power of God. That is great news. Because of this great privilege, we need to be on guard against pride.

When God's power is at work in us, he wants to get the glory. Pride tells us to take the credit for anything that this power of God is accomplishing through us. Pride is the oldest of all sins. Pride may disguise itself as something else, but at the root, pride is seeking to destroy people. We are not the power! We are only holding it. When we take any credit for what God is doing, we are destroying the oneness that God wants with us.

TALKING WITH GOD

Offer this prayer or a similarly themed one today: *Thank you, God, for putting your Holy Spirit inside of me. I want to give you all the credit for the light that shines inside me. Help me be OK with my weaknesses, knowing that as I trust you, you show your power through my life.*

"Your name will no longer be Jacob," the man told him. "From now on you will be called Israel, because you have fought with God and with men and have won." Genesis 32:28

On several occasions in the Bible, God gave people new names when they had a life-changing experience with him. For instance, Abram (which means "high or exalted father") became Abraham ("father of many nations") when God promised he would have many descendants. The name Jacob means "deceiver," and that is exactly who Jacob was. He lied and cheated his way through life.

However, God saw more than that in Jacob, and after their wrestling match here in Genesis 32, God renamed him Israel, which means "power with God." You see, God renames us based on how he sees us, not how we see ourselves. We may think we are weak, ugly, dumb, weird, or inadequate. Perhaps we've even had people in our lives who've used those kinds of words to describe and identify us. But not God—he sees you as he created you to be: strong, faithful, compassionate, intelligent, someone who can change the world. God has a name for you that defines who you will become.

TALKING WITH GOD

Thank God that he sees you as you were created to be. Ask God to help you see yourself as he sees you. And ask God to give you an opportunity to help people see themselves as he sees them.

ONENESS
WITH GOD

VERSE 183:
Genesis 32:28

A LITTLE EXTRA

With parental permission, watch youtube.com/ watch?v=7-xavMhcZK8. Also check out yoursecretname.com/ test to see how the name you've been "given" by this world might be different from the name God has given you.

GOD HEARS & RESTORES

A LITTLE EXTRA

Draw a stop sign somewhere you'll see it regularly. When you see it, stop and pray, asking God to help trust him more and do the right thing. And every time you see a stop sign around town, let it remind you that God is always at work around you, inviting you to trust him more.

"You have made me look like a fool!" Balaam shouted. "If I had a sword with me, I would kill you!" "But I am the same donkey you have ridden all your life," the donkey answered. "Have I ever done anything like this before?" "No," Balaam admitted. Then the Lord opened Balaam's eyes, and he saw the angel of the Lord standing in the roadway with a drawn sword in his hand. Balaam bowed his head and fell face down on the ground before him. Numbers 22:29-31

In this story, Balaam was stubbornly going somewhere that God did not want him to go. As a result, God sent an angel in his path to kill him. Had it not been for the warning from an unlikely source—his donkey—Balaam would have been killed.

Sometimes, when we are being disobedient to God, we don't listen to the warnings that tell us we're headed for trouble. In those times, God lovingly puts friends and family in our way to turn us around. Are there people in your life today who are trying to tell you something for your own good? Maybe it's time to listen to their advice.

TALKING WITH GOD

Pray that God would help trust him and his plan for your life. Ask for God's help in hearing the warnings of your family, friends, and church, so you can be the person he wants you to be.

Then they began to argue among themselves about who would be the greatest among them. Luke 22:24

Have you ever had a conversation with a friend, sharing your heart with them, only to find them not really focusing on what you're saying? Or you're telling them about a tough time you're having, and they're not really getting the point?

In today's passage, Jesus is having that experience with his closest friends. Jesus had just told the disciples that one of them would betray him and that this betrayal would cost Jesus his life. Instead of digging into what Jesus had just revealed, the disciples began fighting over who was the best. Jesus takes the opportunity to talk about what makes someone great in God's kingdom.

Two observations: First, we should pay attention to someone when they are sharing things that are important. Second, in God's kingdom, being great means something radically different from what our culture teaches. Jesus invites us into a deeper trusting relationship with him. Are you ready to serve?

TALKING WITH GOD

Pray this kind of prayer: *Lord, sometimes I miss the point. I want to be close to you, to trust you, to obey you, but sometimes I don't get it. Please help me be more connected to you, so that when you speak, I recognize and understand your voice. And help me reject the culture's definition of great and embrace your definition. Help me trust you more as I live and reveal God's kingdom.*

SIN & SEPARATION

VERSE 185:
Luke 22:24

A LITTLE EXTRA

With parental permission, borrow a washcloth from your bathroom and carry it around with you today as a reminder to be a servant to others. Every time you see the little towel, let it be a reminder that followers of Jesus are to lead lives of sacrifice and service.

ONENESS WITH GOD

A LITTLE EXTRA

Proverbs 27:17 says this: *As iron sharpens iron, so a friend sharpens a friend.* Think about some ways friends can sharpen each other. How can the sharpening make relationships harmonious? Have you ever told your friends how they sharpen you? Write them a note or post a thought via social media telling them how their relationship has been a blessing to you.

How wonderful and pleasant it is when brothers live together in harmony! Psalm 133:1

Lots of beautiful music includes harmony—distinctly different notes coming together to complement one another and produce a wonderful and pleasant sound.

Think about your relationships with other Christ-followers. Would you consider your interactions with them the creation of pleasant music, or are they more like the sound of a hundred preschoolers singing the most annoying song ever? (Yes, we realize many songs are candidates for that title!)

How can you develop friendships that go deeper than the surface and reveal true relationship? Sometimes we think if others would change, relationships would be easier. What would it take for you to make changes so your relationships with others would be more harmonious?

Why do you think it's important for Christ-followers to live together in harmony? What are some of the consequences of disharmony among those who follow Jesus? What part can you and your friends play in creating the kind of harmony Scripture discusses and God desires?

TALKING WITH GOD

If you have strong Christian friendships, thank God for each of your friends by name and pray for them today. If you don't have deep Christian friendships, pray that God will give you friends who share your faith that you can walk with in harmony.

God saved you by his grace when you believed. And you can't take credit for this; it is a gift from God. Salvation is not a reward for the good things we have done, so none of us can boast about it. For we are God's masterpiece. He has created us anew in Christ Jesus, so we can do the good things he planned for us long ago. Ephesians 2:8–10

Can being good earn you a place in heaven? Reread those verses to find the answer to this common question. (Really, read the passage again.)

Contrary to popular opinion, the Bible makes it clear that sins cannot be forgiven by doing good deeds. No amount of "trying" to be good on our part can get us there.

But Jesus saved the day—literally. He did the work for us and presented salvation to us as a free gift!

And once you've accepted this free gift, something amazing happens. In the original language of the Bible, the word *masterpiece* is *poeima*, which is where we get our word *poem.* So when this verse says that *"we are God's masterpiece,"* it's saying that we are God's poetry. You are a living work of art that God is "writing" as you live out the *"good things he planned for you long ago."* Are you letting God write his poetry into your life as you show people around you how much God loves them?

A LITTLE EXTRA

Write a short poem to God expressing your appreciation for the free gift of salvation he's given you through Jesus. If you're really brave, post your poem publicly via social media.

TALKING WITH GOD

Pray for and then talk to one of your non-Christian friends about this free gift of salvation that Jesus offers all who trust in him.

VERSE 188:
Deuteronomy 10:19

A LITTLE EXTRA

Read the entire section of Deuteronomy 10:12-22. (It's only 11 verses!) After reading it, see if there are any other people that come to mind, or actions of love that God is calling you to in your life.

"So you, too, must show love to foreigners, for you yourselves were once foreigners in the land of Egypt." Deuteronomy 10:19

Well, today's devotion is easy. Show love. Done. Stop! We can't move forward before we go back. Look back at the verse, and you'll see a tiny word that should flag you down any time you see it in the Bible: "too." In this case, when you see "too," think "who?"—and look back to the verse or two before. It will help you get the big picture. If you add Deuteronomy 10:18 to today's verse, you get this: *"He [God] ensures that orphans and widows receive justice. He shows love to the foreigners living among you and gives them food and clothing. So you, too, must show love to foreigners, for you yourselves were once foreigners in the land of Egypt."* This passage is really about responding to people the same way God responds to us. God is always fair, kind, just, and loving. Simply put, God treats people right—especially those who need the most help. We can remind ourselves to show love (treat people right) when we remember that we, too, need someone to treat us right—and God does. Every time.

TALKING WITH GOD

Ask God to bring to your mind at least two people who need to be shown love. Write their names down. Then spend one minute praying for each person, plus one minute quietly listening for God to tell you how you can show that person his love. Write down anything God puts on your heart so you can remember—and do it.

Have you ever gotten a prize or reward for doing a good deed or helping someone in need? Do you like getting something for your accomplishments? Is it wrong to be rewarded for doing something well—or for doing the right thing?

"Watch out! Don't do your good deeds publicly, to be admired by others, for you will lose the reward from your Father in heaven." Matthew 6:1

Jesus challenges us to do great things, but he wants us to stay centered in him. Jesus does not want us boasting about ourselves when we do things for the kingdom of God. Everything we do ought to be rooted in our love for God. Sometimes we try to impress others by boasting about the things we have accomplished in life or the kind, honorable, generous things we have done. But we must remember that we cannot serve both God and the world. When do the right thing, we need to do it for the right reason—not for attention or notoriety or other people's praise.

TALKING WITH GOD

Ask God to help you from today forward to find ways to serve others without boasting about yourself. Ask God to keep you humble in all that you do in life and to help you do the right thing for the right reason.

ONENESS
WITH GOD

VERSE 189:
Matthew 6:1

A LITTLE EXTRA

Be honest and take a look at yourself and see how you look for praise in the things you do. Do you always look for praise and rewards from people around you? Read Matthew 6:19-21 and ponder Jesus' teachings in those verses.

GOD HEARS & RESTORES

A LITTLE EXTRA

Learn more about how to live out THE Cause at your school at dare2share.org/thecause.

"Therefore, go and make disciples of all the nations, baptizing them in the name of the Father and the Son and the Holy Spirit. Teach these new disciples to obey all the commands I have given you. And be sure of this: I am with you always, even to the end of the age." Matthew 28:19-20

Jesus calls *all* of us to share his message and make disciples! This is not just the job of your youth leader or your pastor—it is at the very center of *your* job description for life, too. This great cause that Jesus presents in these verses truly is THE Cause.

Why does Jesus give us this command? Because the eternal destiny of every soul hangs in the balance. Consider Jesus' words in John 3:16: *"For God loved the world so much that he gave his one and only Son, so that everyone who believes in him will not perish but have eternal life."*

In Romans 10:14, Paul tells us: *But how can they call on him to save them unless they believe in him? And how can they believe in him if they have never heard about him? And how can they hear about him unless someone tells them?* That's where you come in. Sharing your faith is the entry point for making disciples. And you can take courage from Jesus' promise: *"I am with you always."*

TALKING WITH GOD

Have a conversation with God about your willingness to share his message with others and make disciples. If you're reluctant, ask for a heart that feels compassion for people who don't know Jesus. If you're scared, ask for boldness. If you're clueless, ask for wisdom.

You are the God of great wonders! You demonstrate your awesome power among the nations.
Psalm 77:14

GOD HEARS & RESTORES

Praise God, from whom all blessings flow! God is still performing miracles today. God gives a second burst of energy for a late-night study session. God allows your family's food budget to stretch just a bit further this week. God provides a job—just in time. God causes people to meet at the most unexpected time to begin a great friendship. God allows a verse of Scripture to jump off the page and relate to what you're going through.

Do you see the common thread here? God. God's plan. God's power. How has God demonstrated his power to others? How has God shown his great wonders to only you?

God is all-powerful but also incredibly personal. God cares about what matters most to you. Something God does might seem insignificant to someone else, but it makes a huge difference in your life. Watch for the little and big ways God is at work—specifically for you.

Be thankful and hold your head high today. The God of great wonders is at work for you!

TALKING WITH GOD

Praise God for his incredible works. List the ways God has demonstrated his power to you. Keep going, and list some more. You can't run out. God is just that good—all the time! In the midst of living in a fallen and broken world, thank God for his goodness to you and to all who turn to him.

VERSE 191:
Psalm 77:14

A LITTLE EXTRA

Grab some adhesive notes. On each note, write something God has done to demonstrate his awesome power. These can be big things to everyone, or just big things to you. Place these notes around your home and car to remind you of his awesomeness.

VERSE 192:
John 4:13-14

A LITTLE EXTRA

Choose a day, and for that whole day drink only water. (Check with your parents first, though.) And whenever you're tempted to drink something else, think about Jesus and how he's promised to be the only thing we'll ever need. For more info, do some research on the topic of fasting. Talk to your parents and consider fasting from something for a season. It doesn't have to be food!

Jesus replied, "Anyone who drinks this water will soon become thirsty again. But those who drink the water I give will never be thirsty again. It becomes a fresh, bubbling spring within them, giving them eternal life." John 4:13-14

You've probably been told to drink more water. You're supposed to drink eight glasses per day, experts say, but that's hard to do. Plus, we often take water for granted. You just walk to the faucet, and bam! Water! But in Jesus' time, it was more difficult to obtain good, drinkable water. You had to travel—maybe a long distance—to get it.

From a spiritual perspective, if you drink of the "water" Jesus is offering, you'll have a "spring of water" inside. Think about someone you've met who seemed different—a person whose faith and spirit seemed so strong, who seemed to have this water that Jesus talks about. What might it take for you to become this type of person to someone else?

TALKING WITH GOD

Thank God for the living water he provides. Just as Jesus shared with the thirsty woman, ask God to bring to mind people in your life who are thirsty for something real, and pray for courage to share about the water with them.

ONENESS WITH GOD

"But the time is coming—indeed it's here now—when true worshipers will worship the Father in spirit and in truth. The Father is looking for those who will worship him that way. For God is Spirit, so those who worship him must worship in spirit and in truth." John 4:23-24

What do you think of when you hear the word *worship*? Is it music, singing, praise songs, and worship leaders? When it comes to worship, God is not just looking for people to sing about him or even to him. Worship encompasses so much more—it's about how we live our lives. We can worship God when we're driving to school, practicing with the team, having dinner with our family, or even reading a book.

We can worship God every moment of every day. In today's passage, Jesus tells us that God wants us to worship in spirit and in truth. Sure, this applies to how we sing to God during a church service, but it also applies to how we talk to friends online or what we do during the weekend. We are called to live as though the Spirit of God is inside of us (which he is), and we ought to do everything in truth. That's what true worship looks like.

TALKING WITH GOD

Ask God to teach you new ways to worship him; he wants you to worship him no matter what you're doing. Ask God to show you new times to worship him; Sunday morning and Wednesday night aren't the only times to worship. Ask God to teach you what it means to worship in spirit and in truth.

VERSE 193:
John 4:23-24

A LITTLE EXTRA

Write out your daily schedule, and break it down by the hour. Write down something you can do in each hour to worship God.

ONENESS WITH GOD

A LITTLE EXTRA

Keep a pen and a notepad with you today. When God gives you an opportunity to help someone, do it, and write it down. At the end of the day, thank God for the opportunities you had to live and reveal his kingdom.

"Give, and you will receive. Your gift will return to you in full—pressed down, shaken together to make room for more, running over, and poured into your lap. The amount you give will determine the amount you get back." Luke 6:38

"Get rich quick." "If it sounds too good to be true, then it probably is." Have you ever heard either of those phrases? Rarely do get-rich-quick schemes work, so is this what Jesus is talking about in today's verse?

No way. Jesus says nothing about getting rich or being quick. In fact, he doesn't put any detail or timeframe on how or when your gift will be returned to you. And unlike those sayings about getting rich overnight, everything Jesus says comes true. And for what it's worth, following Jesus isn't a risky investment or a foolish scheme; it's the best decision we can make.

Jesus asks us to lead our lives with an attitude of giving. We have the privilege of giving our time, our talents, and our treasures. And we can give without limitations, motivated purely by our gratitude for God's love for us. Jesus asks us to do this to live and reveal the kingdom of God, but today's passage includes an added bonus: We will be rewarded when the time is right.

TALKING WITH GOD

Ask God to help you live life as a giving person. Ask God to show you opportunities to give to others.

Jesus called out to them, "Come, follow me, and I will show you how to fish for people!" Mark 1:17

Jesus said the words in today's passage to a group of men who were fishermen. It's likely that their fathers fished. And their grandfathers fished. It was the family occupation. They lived near the water. They probably knew 100 ways to cook a fish. They must have always smelled like fish. Fish, fish, fish.

Maybe they took some tests when they were younger to see if they were priest material. But they must not have done well, because they were fishing.

Why was Jesus' invitation so compelling that these men were willing to give up everything?

For starters, he was Jesus—fully God and fully human. And it's very likely that he was really charismatic. People recognized that he was different from the other religious leaders they'd encountered.

What would it take for you to give up the life you're used to and pursue Jesus fully? He wants you to fish for people, too.

TALKING WITH GOD

Maybe God has called you to something, and you're hesitating. Maybe you're not exactly listening—afraid of what God might say to you or where he might call you. Be open to what God is saying to you, and trust that where he calls you is right where you should be.

VERSE 195:
Mark 1:17

A LITTLE EXTRA

Talk with your parents about having fish for dinner one night this week. While you're eating, think about those fishermen from long ago, and talk with your parents about why they made the decision to follow Jesus. Talk about your own journey of following Jesus.

ONENESS WITH GOD

VERSE 196:
Genesis 1:1

A LITTLE EXTRA

Tonight, find some alone time in a location with no interruptions. Focus on an object if you're in a room or gaze into space if you're outside. Contemplate how that object or space is ordered. God pays attention to every detail from the smallest quark to the supernova billions of miles away. God is interested in the details that form you: your joys, sorrows, doubts—all of it. Just start sharing it with him. Lay it down before God, and then spend a minute in quiet. Just listen.

In the beginning God created the heavens and the earth. *Genesis 1:1*

Creatio ex nihilo is a Latin phrase meaning "out of nothing." From nothing to something is a mind-bending thought, yet we experience the process in small ways all the time.

An empty page before becoming a great story and a blank canvas before becoming a masterpiece are examples of a creation process that all started in Genesis. In fact, the very idea of creating was created "in the beginning."

God created all the pieces and the parts for a life-giving relationship with Jesus. God created everything that gives us purpose and meaning. But the ordering of it all only comes through our relationship with Jesus and how we live it all out. All the "stuff" for finding our purpose and living out the gifts God created in us only takes form with our decision to follow Jesus and become more like him.

TALKING WITH GOD
Creation began with the visual and spoken word—art before science. Try a prayer time that's a little different. As you spend time with God, doodle—just grab what's available and draw with it. Makes some marks on an adhesive note, pour some salt on the table and move it around with your fingers, or do something else artistic.

Then he said to the crowd, "If any of you wants to be my follower, you must turn from your selfish ways, take up your cross daily, and follow me."
Luke 9:23

Following Jesus is all about knowing him and making him known. Becoming a serious Christ-follower is not an easy road. It takes surrender, sacrifice, and, well, spunk. You have to be willing to go against the crowd—all while trying to reach out to the crowd with his message of grace.

How is this even possible? It may sound trite, but it's possible because of love. Yes, love is the answer. God's love for you and your love for God will transform you into a dedicated follower, no matter the cost. And God's love lived out in you will motivate you to reach out to others and rescue them from a life apart from God.

Love and a moment-by-moment dependence on the power of the Holy Spirit will carry you through. It's the Spirit living in you and through you that enables you to love and live for Jesus.

Knowing him and making him known. That's what it's all about.

TALKING WITH GOD

Is following Jesus the most important thing in your life? Is he your heart's most passionate desire? You can handle any "cross" that comes your way if your love for God drives everything you do and you stay plugged into his Holy Spirit through prayer, worship, and time in Scripture. Talk to God about your love for and commitment to him. Tell God the things you're willing to surrender and sacrifice for the greater cause of knowing him and making him known.

GOD HEARS & RESTORES

VERSE 197:
Luke 9:23

A LITTLE EXTRA

Read Philippians 3:7-14 and pray it back to God. Draw a doodle of what the passage says to you.

ONENESS
WITH GOD

Even so, dear brothers and sisters, we urge you to love them even more. Make it your goal to live a quiet life, minding your own business and working with your hands, just as we instructed you before. Then people who are not Christians will respect the way you live, and you will not need to depend on others. 1 Thessalonians 4:10-12

In today's passage, Paul challenges and invites us to live in a way that causes people to respect God and our trust in Christ. When people respect us, we have more opportunities to tell them what it means to follow Jesus, and our actions are consistent with what we say we believe.

One way to earn people's respect is to avoid gossiping and talking poorly about others—in other words, mind your own business. Another way is to work hard at whatever you do.

Are you being mean to people or talking about them behind their backs? Are you being lazy in your schoolwork, practice, or chores? If so, choose today to stop doing that and to begin focusing on being a better example of Jesus.

TALKING WITH GOD

Ask God to help you lead a life that will point other people toward him. Ask God for ideas and direction on how you could begin doing that today. Ask God to help you trust that his way is best.

A LITTLE EXTRA

Find an hour today when you can take a temporary vow of silence. (Bedtime doesn't count!) Choose a time when you would normally be talking with people, and instead, be silent. You may want to write out some note cards that explain what you're doing. Then watch how people respond to your time of silence, and see if your example helps your friends, too.

Think about the biggest temptation you've ever faced. Maybe it was a desire to get revenge on someone who wronged you. Maybe it was going too far with your girlfriend or boyfriend. Maybe it was spending money on something you shouldn't have purchased. Maybe it was spreading a juicy piece of gossip to everyone who'd listen. When we're tempted, no matter what it is, we need to remember that we're not alone.

The Spirit then compelled Jesus to go into the wilderness, where he was tempted by Satan for forty days. He was out among the wild animals, and angels took care of him. Mark 1:12-13

Even Jesus was tempted. That's right: Jesus was God in the flesh, but he still had to choose to overcome sinful desires. Hebrews 4:15 tells us that Jesus was tempted in every way, but he didn't sin. Because of that we can confidently bring our struggles to him. He knows what it's like to face sin. And the good news is, he knows the secret to resisting it. No, we won't be able to lead a sinless life like Jesus did, but we can become more resistant to temptation and more reliant on God's power working in our lives.

TALKING WITH GOD

Be honest with God about the things that tempt you. Ask God to help you avoid those situations, and ask God to give you the strength to do the right thing, even when it's really difficult.

CONSEQUENCES
& CRYING OUT

VERSE 199:
Mark 1:12-13

A LITTLE EXTRA

Take out a piece of paper and write down your biggest temptations. Be honest about your struggles. Want to make it more personal? Share your list with someone else and ask that person to hold you accountable.

209

ONENESS WITH GOD

VERSE 200:
Matthew 11:11

A LITTLE EXTRA

Draw or print the
Superman shield,
and put it somewhere
you'll see it regularly.
Every time you see it,
remember that God is
inviting you to be super
as you live and reveal
his kingdom.

"I tell you the truth, of all who have ever lived, none is greater that John the Baptist. Yet even the least person in the Kingdom of Heaven is greater than he is!" Matthew 11:11

John the Baptist was the greatest ever? Who would have thought? The Bible describes him as a wild man who lived in the wilderness and ate bugs and honey. (Can you imagine that on the menu at your favorite restaurant?) But he lived a highly disciplined life, and he was always telling others about Jesus. Truly, his life was devoted to pointing people toward Jesus.

Now go back and read that verse again. Check out what Jesus says about us. We have the chance to be greater than John the Baptist! We don't have to dress like him or eat like him (that's great news!)—we simply have to learn to live with the Spirit of God in our lives and to actively pursue God's kingdom. Do you believe God can help you to live and reveal his kingdom? Walk out the door today in confidence, knowing that God has created you to live an amazing story that points people back to Jesus.

TALKING WITH GOD

Thank God for his Spirit. Ask him to lead you and guide you as you live and reveal the kingdom of God with the people in your life. And maybe even offer thanks to God that you don't have to wear camel's hair and eat locusts!

ONENESS
WITH GOD

"In the same way, let your good deeds shine out for all to see, so that everyone will praise your heavenly Father." Matthew 5:16

Unlike other religions, Christianity is not based on our "good deeds." Regardless of whether or not we help the old lady across the street or share our lunch with the lonely kid at school, if we have a personal relationship with Christ and commit to following his path, we can go to heaven!

But what good is our faith if we don't help other people decide to follow Christ, too? If you are walking around cursing all the time or treating your parents badly, what will people think of you? Even though our eternity in heaven isn't based on what good deeds we do, it is important to lead our lives in a way that can bring other people to Christ so that they may see the light of him in everything that we say and do.

TALKING WITH GOD

Ask God to show someone his love through your actions today. Pray something like this: *Lord, allow my actions to be evidence of my faith in you. I pray that everyone I encounter throughout my day will see my love for you in everything that I do. Please give me an opportunity to show my trust in you today.*

A LITTLE EXTRA

Commit to do something today that will give others a glimpse of the kindness in your heart that God has given you. Maybe write an encouraging note to a teacher at school, or offer to roll your neighbor's trashcans out to the curb. One of these small and simple "good deeds" could be a conversation starter that gives you an opportunity to share God's love with that person!

SIN & SEPARATION

VERSE 202:
Romans 13:1

A LITTLE EXTRA

Turn on the news channel for a few minutes. Perhaps a presidential speech or a high-speed police chase will be aired. "Governing authorities," such as our president or other members of government, along with police officers, are another example of people we must obey because of their position of authority. Take a moment and pray for these people. No matter how mad they make you or what decisions they make, pray that they find wisdom and use their authority to benefit those around them.

In today's passage, Paul gives us some instructions that can be very difficult to follow. Before you read it, you need to understand two phrases. To "submit" to someone means a lot of things, but essentially it means to obey them. "Governing authorities" means any person or group who is in charge of a part of your life.

Everyone must submit to governing authorities. For all authority comes from God, and those in positions of authority have been placed there by God. Romans 13:1

The list of governing authorities in your life could include your parents, teachers, coaches, police officers, pastors, and babysitters. But sometimes those people are wrong—surely Paul doesn't mean submitting to people who are wrong, or people who aren't Christ-followers, or people who are mean to you. But he does.

In Paul's time, the government was actively persecuting Christ-followers, but he still wrote this passage. It doesn't mean disobeying God in order to submit to others, but recognize that all authority comes from God. We can learn something from every leader God has placed in our lives—even the ones we don't like.

TALKING WITH GOD

To whom in your life do you find it difficult to submit? Ask God to soften your heart toward them and allow you to submit fully to their authority in your life.

So he got up from the table, took off his robe, wrapped a towel around his waist, and poured water into a basin. Then he began to wash the disciples' feet, drying them with the towel he had around him. John 13:4-5

Imagine what was going through the minds of Jesus' disciples. They'd seen Jesus heal people, drive out demons, and raise people from the dead. They still didn't seem to quite understand him, but they knew he was different and amazing and *surely* sent from God.

And suddenly he starts to wash their feet.

Consider for a moment just how dirty and messy their feet would have been. They didn't have socks or athletic shoes—they wore sandals, which were basically leather straps holding something on the bottom of their feet. Roads weren't paved. And there are animals everywhere, doing the, well, things that animals do. Right there in the street. And it gets on your feet.

It wasn't enough for the Son of God to come and become human; now he's stooping even lower and doing something only servants would do. Why? As an example.

Whose feet could you wash this week? Who would be amazed to see you "stooping" to help them? If Jesus— the Savior of the universe—can wash the feet of those he loves, maybe you can, too.

TALKING WITH GOD

Thank God for the people he's placed in your life who have, in some way, washed your feet.

A LITTLE EXTRA

Wash your parents' feet this week. OK, you don't have to actually wash their feet (though that would be super cool), but think of something you can do that would blow them away. Don't draw attention to it. Just quietly and humbly help them, and see how they react.

213

GOD HEARS & RESTORES

A LITTLE EXTRA

Memorize this passage. Start by reading the whole thing out loud. Then read one sentence at a time. Keep at it until you've got it down. Now, when something discouraging happens, quote this passage to yourself to remind you of who God is and how he loves you.

It's OK to cry out to God. He wants you to talk to him whether you're having the best day or the worst day. On the worst days, hold tight to promises like this:

He sang: "The Lord is my rock, my fortress, and my savior; my God is my rock, in whom I find protection. He is my shield, the power that saves me, and my place of safety. He is my refuge, my savior, the one who saves me from violence."
2 Samuel 22:2-3

Read through the passage again, but slow things down. Read just the first sentence. How has God proved himself as a rock (a stable foundation), a fortress (a protective structure), or a savior (a rescuer)?

Read the second sentence. Can you picture God as a shield? a saving power? a safe place? Reflect on a time when he protected you and kept you safe.

Now read the last sentence. How has God provided a safe escape in a time of physical, verbal, or emotional violence?

Slowing down and asking yourself questions is a practice that allows you to make better sense of Scripture and grasp what God is saying to you.

TALKING WITH GOD

Do you need God's work and protection in a situation right now? Talk with him about it. Tell him how you feel and how you're afraid. Ask him to protect you and rescue you. He's promised to do just that.

For a child is born to us, a son is given to us. The government will rest on his shoulders. And he will be called: Wonderful Counselor, Mighty God, Everlasting Father, Prince of Peace. His government and its peace will never end. He will rule with fairness and justice from the throne of his ancestor David for all eternity. The passionate commitment of the Lord of Heaven's Armies will make this happen! Isaiah 9:6-7

VERSE 205:
Isaiah 9:6-7

Isaiah is a huge book in the Bible—and much of it is devoted to foretelling the coming of Jesus hundreds of years before it actually happened. Whole books have been written just about Isaiah and its importance. The people of Israel were looking for some specific traits in the Messiah—someone to rule and reign and deliver them. This passage speaks volumes about who Jesus is: He's a counselor, he's mighty, he's our daddy, he's everlasting, he's peaceful, he's passionate—Jesus really is all in all. And he knows exactly who you need him to be each moment of your life.

TALKING WITH GOD

Tell God some of his attributes that have been most important to you. That list might include Rescuer, Healer, or Provider. What is that list for you? Thank God for who he has been in your life—and who he will continue to be in the days to come.

A LITTLE EXTRA

Check out wordle.net. Begin entering the words that describe God in your life—everything you can think of. Generate a word cloud that reminds you who God is in your life. Print it and hang it where you spend most of your private time with him—a reminder of all the attributes God brings to your relationship with him.

GOD HEARS & RESTORES

A LITTLE EXTRA

Watch *Soul Surfer*, or do an online search for "Bethany Hamilton." What can you learn from her life?

For I can do everything through Christ, who gives me strength. *Philippians 4:13*

What are some of the greatest challenges you have faced? What are some of the greatest challenges ahead of you?

The movie *Soul Surfer* tells the true story of teenage surfing sensation Bethany Hamilton. She lost her arm in a shark attack, and her dream of being able to surf again seemed all but lost. The movie includes a powerful scene where she asks her dad when she will be able to surf again. He tells her soon, but she doesn't see how she could possibly be ready. Her dad begins by saying, "you can do all things..."—and Bethany completes the verse saying, "through him who gives me strength."

The rest of the movie shows how Bethany defies the odds by getting back into competitive surfing and bringing incredible glory to God. Bethany knew that her own strength was not enough, but God provided for her in her weakness.

Paul wrote these words to the Philippians while in prison and facing death, so these are not just shallow words aimed to create hype. Paul had discovered firsthand what it meant to completely depend on God.

Even though you feel weak and unable to tackle certain challenges in life, how can your dependence on God's strength help you?

TALKING WITH GOD

Tell God about the challenges you are facing and any fear surrounding the challenges ahead. God already knows, but he wants a relationship with you where you can share anything with him. Ask God to fill you with his strength to help you through this week's challenges.

"God blesses those whose hearts are pure, for they will see God." Matthew 5:8

After reading that verse, you might be asking, "What does it mean to have a pure heart? What does it mean to see God?"

There are times and areas in our lives when we put up boundaries and rules to guard against sin. If you have a girlfriend or boyfriend you might have talked about which lines you won't cross physically. You might have told yourself what type of music you won't listen to, or which TV shows you won't watch.

Having a pure heart isn't only about boundaries you won't cross, music you won't listen to, or TV shows you won't watch. It's about your trust in God. Do you trust that God's way is best? Will you trust him enough to live the way he wants you to live?

God wants your heart to be pure in all things, and he wants you to see him. When your heart is pure and you're running after God, you'll see him show up more and more in your life.

TALKING WITH GOD

Ask God to give you eyes to see him today. God is present and active in your life—but are you looking for him? Ask him to open your eyes and reveal himself to you.

VERSE 207:
Matthew 5:8

A LITTLE EXTRA

If you really want to be challenged with seeing God, ask him to challenge you in a way today that you have never been challenged before. Ask him to make it a big challenge. Then as you're in that challenge, rely on him and look to him. If you say this prayer with sincerity and a pure heart, God promises that he will show up. It won't be easy, but you'll be running hard after him.

GOD HEARS
& RESTORES

A LITTLE EXTRA

Read John 10:10 to understand the kind of life you get with Jesus. Does this description of life match up with what you are experiencing now as you follow Jesus? What changes do you need to make to allow God to show you real life?

Do you love math? Addition is pretty simple. A + B = C, right? That's the beauty of addition—it's straightforward.

John gives us an easy equation to understand.

Whoever has the Son has life; whoever does not have God's Son does not have life. 1 John 5:12

Jesus + you = life. Pretty simple.

And you (or anyone else) without Jesus equals no life. Simple math. Not only is it a simple equation, it is a simple reality.

To make it reality, we simply need to accept that Jesus is God's Son and that he came to give us life through his death and resurrection. We believe and we accept and we receive life. A full life in the here-and-now—and eternal life with Jesus.

The amazing part of this equation is that our part is so minimal and God's part is essentially everything. Not only is it a simple equation, it is a miraculous equation!

Are you experiencing the life that Jesus offers— eternal life in heaven, and abundant life here on Earth? Are you missing out on this glorious math equation?

TALK WITH GOD

There are two options for this moment. First, if you have experienced this glorious equation in your life, then thank Jesus again for life and commit to living and revealing his kingdom. If you haven't experienced the glorious equation, consider taking a moment now to confess your belief in Jesus as God's Son and start living the life. If you need some help with this decision see pp. 180-181.

You say, "I am allowed to do anything"—but not everything is good for you. You say, "I am allowed to do anything"—but not everything is beneficial. Don't be concerned for your own good but for the good of others. 1 Corinthians 10:23-24

Have you ever said, "But this is my right" or demanded your freedom of expression? We are quick to stand up for the things we are allowed to do. Sometimes we call these things gray areas in Scripture. For instance, there isn't anything in the whole Bible about playing video games too much, right? Are these areas really gray, or are we throwing a fit about what our rights are supposed to be?

We no longer live under the Old Testament law, and there are freedoms in Christ. The big caution we see in this passage comes at the end. It's not about us; it's about other people. If we do something that is allowed, but it hurts someone else, then that hurts God. If we knowingly do that thing anyway, it becomes an act of selfishness, which is sin.

Don't build a case as to why you are allowed to do something. Instead, ask if it is going to hurt another person that God loves.

A LITTLE EXTRA

Read what the brother of Jesus said in James 4:17 about not doing the good things we know we ought to do.

TALKING WITH GOD

Consider praying a prayer like this: *Jesus, thank you for your example in thinking of me first. You could have stayed in heaven and avoided the cross. Instead, you put me first and made a way for me to be free. So give me the wisdom to make decisions that help others around me, regardless of what my freedoms are.*

GOD HEARS
& RESTORES

A LITTLE EXTRA

Find 10 medium rubber bands. As you get ready in the morning, put all 10 rubber bands on your left wrist. Spend the day being mindful of what you say. Is it positive? Is it abusive? Is it good? Each time you catch yourself using negative or abusive language, move one rubber band to your right wrist. How long did it take you to go through all 10 rubber bands? Did you make it all day, or did you go through all 10 before breakfast? By the way, it's OK to share what you're doing when someone asks about the rubber bands. Share your story.

Don't use foul or abusive language. Let everything you say be good and helpful, so that your words will be an encouragement to those who hear them.
Ephesians 4:29

You might be thinking today's devotion will be just about curse words. It's much bigger than just that.

Words are powerful. *All* words are powerful. In 2012, Matthias Mehl, a researcher at the University of Arizona, reported that men and women speak around 17,000 words a day, give or take a few hundred.

Of those 17,000 words each day, you can encourage someone with a kind word, offend others with a curse word, embarrass a friend with an insult, or alienate others with an unspoken word. What we say matters.

You've been torn apart by unkind words, and you've been encouraged by good and helpful words. What impact do you have on your friends with the words you are using?

TALKING WITH GOD

Thank God for the power of words. Thank him for those who have spoken encouragement into your life. In the same way, pray for those who have said unkind things to you. Pray that God helps you be more aware of what you say.

I pray that God, the source of hope, will fill you completely with joy and peace because you trust in him. Then you will overflow with confident hope through the power of the Holy Spirit.
Romans 15:13

Hope comes from God. Real hope, anyway. You may be able to find hope if everything in life is going right. Or you may feel hopeful if all the people in your life are being nice. But if you find hope in circumstances, what happens when things in life aren't going right? What happens when people in your life treat you badly? True hope comes from God, who will always work things out for the good of those who love him, because God is always good. We can experience hope because we trust God. As we grow in our trust in God, our hope grows with it. So grow your hope!

TALKING WITH GOD

Hope isn't something we bake in the oven or build in the workshop. Hope comes because we trust God. The more we trust, the more hope we have. Ask God to help you trust him more today, so you can live a life of hope. Also ask God to give you opportunities to share the reason for the hope that you have with your family and friends.

VERSE 211:
Romans 15:13

A LITTLE EXTRA

With parental permission, watch the video "With a Piece of Chalk" at youtube.com/watch?v=mBZAFJ-Q6Mw. As you watch the video, write down all of the things that steal the boy's joy, hope, and peace. What are the things that steal your hope? Ask God to help you trust him more and continue to grow in your trust, so nothing can steal your hope.

A LITTLE EXTRA

Take a walk around your block. As you walk along this path, consider the rewards of following God's path for your life. During your walk, ask God to help you trust him more.

Trust in the Lord with all your heart; do not depend on your own understanding. Seek his will in all you do, and he will show you which path to take. Proverbs 3:5-6

What kind of career do you want when you're older? What kinds of dreams about the future fill your mind? Take a second and draw a little picture of it in the margins here.

Have you ever considered what God wants you to be when you grow up? What will you do if your plan for your life is different from God's plan for your life? Do you trust that God wants what's best for you and knows what's best for you?

In today's passage, we are told to trust God even if we don't understand everything. And if we pursue God, he will keep us going in the right direction. Take another look at the picture you drew in the margin. Now draw a question mark underneath. Do you trust God enough to follow his plan even if you don't fully understand it?

TALKING WITH GOD

Today as you pray, lift your hands over your head as a sign of trust—just like a little kid might raise her arms as she asks to get picked up. Ask God to reveal more of his plan for your life. If you struggle trusting God, ask him to help you trust him more. God loves you, wants what's best for you, and is trustworthy. It may take time, but it's always worth it.

Everyone enjoys compliments. OK, you might get embarrassed if it's said in public or in front of lots of people. But it makes you happy to know someone likes you, appreciates you, and notices you. How much better is it when people appreciate you for who you are, not just for what you've done?

Everywhere—from east to west—praise the name of the Lord. Psalm 113:3

Praising God is different from thanking God. You praise God for who he is; you thank God for what he does. Read the statements below, and consider specific examples of how you have experienced God's greatness:

- God is the creator.
- God is fair and just.
- God is open and communicates with us.
- God is mighty in power.
- God is caring.
- God is the one and only God.
- God is love.
- God is protective.

What's missing? Is there another way in your life God has revealed his power and greatness? God is perfect and just what you need—every day.

TALKING WITH GOD

Praise God for who he is. Be specific. Who is God to you? While you're doing this, ask God to help you get a sense of his awesomeness. Seriously consider who he is, and enjoy talking to the Creator of the universe, who loves and cares about you.

GOD HEARS & RESTORES

A LITTLE EXTRA

Get a map or a globe, or look at a map online. Choose a continent or country that means something to you (past vacation, interesting culture, or your home). Do some research on that area and see how God is present. This can be done online—through the news, mission agencies, or blogs. Reflect on how your God—the mighty and only God—is present from the east to the west.

ONENESS
WITH GOD

A LITTLE EXTRA

Get parental permission, and fast for one meal. Instead of eating, spend the time inviting God to show himself to you. Do something you like: take a walk, play guitar, ride your bike, shoot hoops. It doesn't matter; the important thing is to invite God to be with you.

The Lord passed in front of Moses, calling out, "Yahweh! The Lord! The God of compassion and mercy! I am slow to anger and filled with unfailing love and faithfulness." Exodus 34:6

Moses is a rock star in the Bible. No person had as many experiences in the presence of God as Moses until Jesus himself walked on the planet. This verse occurs as Moses was spending 40 days with God high on a mountain getting instructions on how to lead the people of Israel. God decided to give Moses a glimpse of who he was.

This was still at the beginning of the nation of Israel's history. Throughout the history of God's people the same thing happens again and again. The people forget about the goodness of God and turn away. God then punishes the people until they repent and turn back to him.

God knew that there would be no way for him to be in relationship with these people who would continue to forget him and wander away. Of all the things God could have said as he passed by Moses on the mountain, he chose to tell Moses about his compassion and mercy. Throughout Israel's history, God would remind his people that he is indeed slow to anger and filled with unfailing love and faithfulness.

TALKING WITH GOD

Thank God for being slow to anger. Thank him for how his compassion and mercy have made the way, through Jesus Christ, for us to be in relationship with God.

Love never gives up, never loses faith, is always hopeful, and endures through every circumstance.
1 Corinthians 13:7

People sometimes throw around the phrase, "I love you," yet they may not realize how powerful those words are. Love is not a feeling; it's a choice. Feelings come and they go, but choices become a lifestyle. When love is built on a temporary, emotional feeling, it changes with circumstances. When love is built on a choice, it is faithful to do the right thing.

True love is sacrificial. True love cares about the other person's well-being. True love is humble and thoughtful and lasting. True love can be identified through actions and faithfulness and generosity and kindness.

Our culture bombards us with unhealthy images of "falling" in and out of love. But culture has no comment on the kind of love we discover in the Bible. The kind of love we read about in today's verse can only be understood if you've received this kind of love from Jesus.

TALKING WITH GOD

If you've never put your trust in Jesus, open your heart and ask God to fill you with his love today. If you know Jesus' love personally, ask God to help you show it better as you live and reveal his kingdom. Pray for opportunities to display God's true love to the world around you.

ONENESS
WITH GOD

VERSE 215:
1 Corinthians 13:7

A LITTLE EXTRA

Pay attention to the messages you hear about love in music and on TV and in movies. Compare it to the Bible's message about love in the whole chapter of 1 Corinthians 13. What are the differences between our culture's description of love and God's description of love? What kind of love do you want in your life?

Should I start reading the Bible from the beginning?

Because the Bible is not just one book, but a collection of books, we suggest being intentional in the way you begin reading. Any order is a good order if you're reading the Bible, but instead of starting in Genesis, we recommend following this order:

- Gospel of John
- Proverbs
- James
- Genesis
- Romans
- Psalms

Once you've read these books, talk to your pastor or a trusted friend and get their input on where to go from there. And be encouraged—you've begun a lifelong journey of deepening your trust in God, and you'll never regret it!

 What's the difference between reading the Bible and studying the Bible?

Reading the Bible is faster, similar to reading a book. It's sort of like when you swap stories with a close friend; you're not memorizing names or dates or places, but you're reading to get a sense of God's love for all people. Studying the Bible is slower and more thoughtful. You're still not memorizing names or dates or places, but you're really focusing on words or phrases that seem to jump out at you (that's the Holy Spirit highlighting God's truth). It's not a requirement, but a good study Bible can be really helpful as you study God's Word.

3. **Which Bible translation is best?**

Every Bible translation has strengths and weaknesses, and we find great value in reading a variety of Bible translations. Generally, we suggest using the Bible translation recommended by your pastor and church.

4. **How do I find passages that talk about specific situations?**

When you find a verse that deals with something specific, write it down in your journal, highlight it in your Bible, or use some other method to keep track of themes or helpful wisdom. Lots of Bibles have topical indexes (sometimes called concordances), which list verses that talk about specific things. The Internet can be an amazing resource, of course. With your parents' permission, check out biblegateway.com or blueletterbible. org. You also can buy an "exhaustive concordance," which lists every word in the Bible and every verse that uses that word.

5. **Why do we have an Old Testament and a New Testament?**

The Bible is the story of God's relationship with his people. The 39 books of the Old Testament (OT) tell the story of God's relationship with his people before Jesus Christ. The 27 books of the New Testament (NT) tell the story of God's relationship with his people during Jesus' time on earth as well as after Jesus' death and resurrection.

GOD HEARS & RESTORES

Technology seems to change every couple of months, professional sports teams battle for the top spot every week, and the local radio stations update their top lists almost daily. It's hard keeping up with an ever-changing world, and sometimes we just want some consistency. Today's verse reminds us that God is the same yesterday, today, and forever.

VERSE 216:
Daniel 6:26

A LITTLE EXTRA

Find an old globe (or an old map online) and look at the countries in Eastern Europe and the northwest side of Asia. Compare it to a modern map, and notice how countries' names and borders have changed. This is how our world is—but God never changes. Imagine living in a time when everything you knew was changing. In the midst of this, God wouldn't change. No matter what happens in your life, big or small, God is there for you and with you, and his love never fails.

"I decree that everyone throughout my kingdom should tremble with fear before the God of Daniel. For he is the living God, and he will endure forever. His kingdom will never be destroyed, and his rule will never end." Daniel 6:26

The good news, in the craziness of life, is that God is eternal. God never changes and never ceases to exist. God was there before the earth was created and will be there when the new earth descends from heaven. You can always count on him, and his words are true.

TALKING WITH GOD

Begin by thanking God for always being there for you. Even during your most difficult times, God is never far away from you. He is the living God who ready to draw near to you.

Then he looked at those around him and said, "Look, these are my mother and brothers. Anyone who does God's will is my brother and sister and mother." Mark 3:34-35

Once again, Jesus was shocking the crowd, making a scene, and upsetting the rules. In Bible times, family was one of the most important things. Children didn't move away and go to college to start their lives, only returning on holidays. Instead, adult children stayed with the family—often in the same house. Your family was your identity as well as your livelihood. If your dad was a carpenter, you would grow up and be a carpenter to help with the family business. You were born into a family, and you were loyal to that family forever. Jesus here declares there's a loyalty in life greater than the loyalty of a family. This was incredibly shocking to the culture.

To what are you loyal? How do you show your loyalty, your devotion, your faithfulness? Is it weird to think you're called to be more loyal to Christ than to your own friends? How about than your own family?

TALKING WITH GOD

How do you choose between one good opportunity and another good opportunity? How can you plan ahead to intentionally show loyalty but also make unexpected decisions to show loyalty? Thank God for the opportunities in your life. Identify what good things in life are competing for your top priority and greatest loyalty, and ask God for wisdom as you make daily decisions.

GOD HEARS & RESTORES

A LITTLE EXTRA

Take out a sheet of paper or turn to a new sheet in your journal. List the top three things that take your time (other than sleeping). Also list the top three things on which you spend money. Think about how these lists reflect what's most important to you.

VERSE 218:
Ephesians 4:11–12

A LITTLE EXTRA

Go online and take a spiritual gifts test—or see if your youth pastor has one that you can take. Once you see what your spiritual gift(s) might be, talk with one friend and one adult about what you're learning about yourself and how you can begin developing your gift(s) as you serve in a ministry.

Now these are the gifts Christ gave to the church: the apostles, the prophets, the evangelists, and the pastors and teachers. Their responsibility is to equip God's people to do his work and build up the church, the body of Christ. Ephesians 4:11–12

One of the cool things about being a child of God is that you get to be part of his huge family that extends into eternity. Yet while you're part of this amazing family, God created you to be an individual. God wants you in his family, but he also has a plan for you that's unique and specific.

God doesn't look at people and declare, "All of you will become pastors who wear ugly suits and sing songs only in the key of G!" No, God looks at each one of us and gives us special gifts to be used as a blessing to other Christ-followers and to the world.

You are part of the family of God. You are a special and unique individual. You are the only you the world will ever see. You have a gift that only you can live out.

TALKING WITH GOD

Pray this kind of prayer: *God, help me know you more so I can know myself. Help me discover my gifts as an individual in your family, and help me not compare myself to others. And then, when you've made your plan clear to me, Lord, help me use my gift to be a blessing.*

Jesus turned to Peter and said, "Get away from me, Satan! You are a dangerous trap to me. You are seeing things merely from a human point of view, not from God's." Matthew 16:23

Perspective matters. How you see the world matters. Because God invites us to live and reveal his kingdom, he wants us to have his perspective on the world. Ever wonder why John 3:16 is perhaps the best-known Bible verse? What does it say? Take a moment to look it up, or say it out loud if you already have it memorized.

So what was Jesus really saying in today's verse? Jesus was telling Peter that following him was not just about walking along, straggling behind. Following Jesus is about learning to look at the world from *his* perspective—to see people, situations, hardships, and blessings as God sees them. God's perspective is big, amazing, and often stretches us to work hard to find it. But it is good. In it you can find forgiveness for the worst of sinners, joy in suffering, and salvation in the midst of a crucifixion.

TALKING WITH GOD

Ask God to give you eyes to see his perspective. Think about situations that challenge you—interactions with friends, confrontations with parents, disappointments while playing sports—and ask God to help you understand how he views those situations and how he wants you to act and react.

SIN & SEPARATION

A LITTLE EXTRA

Think of a decision that you're struggling to make. What if you did exactly what *you* wanted? What's the best that could happen— and worst that could happen? What if you did exactly what *God* wanted? What are the best and worst that could happen? How does playing the "what if" game help your perspective?

ONENESS WITH GOD

A LITTLE EXTRA

Wear your favorite thing today and use it as a reminder to dress yourself in the things of God. Or wear that ugly or unwanted item to remind you of the spiritual clothes worth avoiding!

Since God chose you to be the holy people he loves, you must clothe yourselves with tenderhearted mercy, kindness, humility, gentleness, and patience.
Colossians 3:12

Do you have a favorite hoodie, T-shirt, or pair of jeans? You know what we're talking about: that one go-to item you wear that fits and feels and looks just right.

We spend a lot of time thinking about the physical clothes we wear, but God wants us to pay attention to our spiritual "clothing," too. God wants us to wear tenderhearted mercy, kindness, humility, gentleness, and patience with the same ease as wearing our favorite T-shirt. God wants to fill our wardrobe with heart-changing characteristics designed for a perfect fit.

Now think about what you hate to wear—that piece of clothing that's too small, too itchy, or too ugly. You never wear it. You keep trying to get rid of it. You don't want people to associate you with it. Just as God has certain spiritual clothes he wants us to wear, he also wants us to avoid other kinds of clothes—selfishness, meanness, greed, pride, and impatience that can be as ill-fitting as that shirt, dress, or pair of shoes that never seem to fit right.

TALKING WITH GOD

Pray this prayer today, or one with a similar theme: *God, cover me with so much tenderhearted mercy, kindness, humility, gentleness, and patience that wearing these things becomes as comfortable to me as my favorite pair of jeans. And God, strip away the things that don't fit right. Throw it all in the trash.*

People can be brutal with their words. You're too tall or too short, too skinny or overweight, you wear nerdy clothes or you're too trendy. Or maybe you've been ridiculed or rejected because of your skin color, or your ethnicity, or your family's history, or where you live in town. Hurtful comments can cause people to believe that they are not as good as others. And if you hear enough of those comments, you may begin to believe that God doesn't like you either. But this belief isn't true, and it doesn't have to be your story.

Then Peter replied, "I see very clearly that God shows no favoritism. In every nation he accepts those who fear him and do what is right."
Acts 10:34–35

Peter spoke the words in today's passage to Cornelius. He was Roman, while Peter was Jewish—two very different groups of people. But God loved Peter, God loved Cornelius, and God loves you.

You are a wonderful creation in God's eyes. No matter what life throws at you, find strength in God. No matter what others may say about you, remember that God loves and accepts you.

TALKING WITH GOD

Pray that you can trust God more today than you did yesterday. Pray that you will begin to believe that you are accepted no matter what your situation may be. Allow God to be who he promises to be in your life.

GOD HEARS & RESTORES

VERSE 221:
Acts 10:34–35

A LITTLE EXTRA

Find a way to support the underdog today. If you're in school, sit with someone who seems to be alone. If you're at work, talk to someone who is struggling. If you're just living life, tell someone that God loves him or her. Let God's love for you overflow into the lives of others as you live and reveal God's kingdom.

SIN &
SEPARATION

A LITTLE EXTRA

The next time you're in a conversation with a friend, try to keep the conversation going by using as few words as possible. See if you can get your friend to do most of the talking while you do most of the listening.

"If only you could be silent! That's the wisest thing you could do." Job 13:5

Job was having the worst day ever. He had lost his all of his children, his possessions, and his health—all in one day. Things could not get any worse.

When Job's friends heard the news, they went to his house as soon as they could, to support him. They were great friends to Job until they made one tragic mistake: They started talking. Their hearts were in the right place, but the more they spoke, the more they hurt Job. The three friends kept saying all the wrong things. Job compared them to being doctors who did not know what they were doing. They were like foot doctors trying to do heart surgery. Epic fail.

Sometimes the best thing you can do to support a friend is to simply be there and say nothing. When people talk about friends who helped them through a tough time, they typically say things such as, "He was there for me when I needed a friend" or "She spent time with me and gave me lots of hugs." Never underestimate the power of being present with a friend.

TALKING WITH GOD

Pray this kind of prayer: *God, help me know when to talk and when to keep silent when I'm with a friend. I only want to use words that help, heal, and encourage. I trust you to help me be a good friend.*

"No one can serve two masters. For you will hate one and love the other; you will be devoted to one and despise the other. You cannot serve both God and money." Luke 16:13

The older you get, the more you'll discover the truth of this statement: Money wisdom is one of the most important lessons you can learn. It'll pay off—literally!

Today's verse implies that money has the ability to master you. Jesus didn't say, "It'll be really tough to serve God and money." He said you *cannot* do both.

What if instead of letting money master you, you mastered money? What if you graduated from college with no debt? What if you *never* got a credit card? What if you paid cash—that you actually saved up and had in-hand—to pay for things? And most importantly, what if you tithed and gave offerings that honored God?

You'd be different. You'd be weird. You'd be the "strange" one of your friends who isn't worried about his finances all of the time. You'd be the "weirdo" who isn't up her neck in debt because she bought things she "needed" with money she didn't have.

You won't be devoted to money—leaving you to be devoted to God. And if you're wise with your money and devoted to God, he will bless you.

TALKING WITH GOD

Thank God for all he has given you. Everything you have and everything you ever will have comes from him. Ask God to help you have a heart of thankfulness, and to always give back to him as he's commanded.

GOD HEARS & RESTORES

VERSE 223:
Luke 16:13

A LITTLE EXTRA

Have a frank and open discussion with your parents about finances. Ask them about mistakes they've made, wise decisions they've made, and advice they have for you. *And then listen to them!*

ONENESS
WITH GOD

VERSE 224:
Isaiah 26:3

A LITTLE EXTRA

Every person will go through hard things at some point. Read Psalm 112:7. On a piece of paper, draw two columns. In one column, write your "bad news." In the second column, write some words with similar meanings to *steadfast* and *confident*. Spend a minute noticing the difference between the two columns. Add "God" to the top of the second column. Tear off your "bad news" and throw it in the trash. As you do this, pray that God would give you peace as you trust in him above your circumstances.

You will keep in perfect peace all who trust in you, all whose thoughts are fixed on you! Isaiah 26:3

When you walk through difficult circumstances or unexpected challenges, God is there right next to you, and he knows exactly what you are dealing with and facing. God knows every thought that comes into your mind. And God will walk with you every step of the way. He will never leave you. When you don't feel like you can continue, you can focus on God's strength, voice, and guidance.

When you do that, God will give you peace. It's peace that you might not understand. But because he loves you unconditionally, you can rest in the fact that he has your best in mind. When you trust God with your thoughts, your life, and your tough circumstances, you will have a peace that can only come from him.

TALKING WITH GOD

Spend a minute quieting any thoughts of fear, exhaustion, or sorrow. Then ask God to reveal himself in your circumstances. Ask God for a "perfect peace" despite the emotions you are feeling. Lay your hardship at his feet and let go of it. Trust God to bear your burden.

"At last!" the man exclaimed. "This one is bone from my bone and flesh from my flesh! She will be called 'woman,' because she was taken from 'man.'" This explains why a man leaves his father and mother and is joined to his wife, and the two are united into one. Genesis 2:23-24

Some people believe that if you cross your fingers behind your back when you make a promise, you can break the promise and not have to worry about the consequences—a "free pass" to tell a lie or not keep your word if it isn't what you want.

Our culture believes this when it comes to relationships. We make promises that last as long as it's good for us, but once things get tough, we break them off—and then come the consequences.

In this passage of Genesis, we see that God's design is for husbands and wives to make promises that last forever. God wants promises that connect two people together so tightly that they begin to look and act like one person. God doesn't want us to experience the pain of broken promises—or to cause pain for others.

TALKING WITH GOD

As you spend time with God, take a moment to pray for each one of your relationships, including your parents, siblings, and friends. And pray for your future spouse.

VERSE 225:
Genesis 2:23-24

A LITTLE EXTRA

Research the various ways in which God makes promises to us. You can find God's promises throughout the Bible, but a simple online search (with your parents' permission) could also help you find some of God's promises. Now think about your relationships and how you can be more intentional about keeping your promises this week. The more you practice keeping your promises today, the more you'll be set up to win in the future.

SIN &
SEPARATION

VERSE 226:
Romans 1:21

A LITTLE EXTRA

Spend some time today worshipping God the right way, rather than the way the Israelites chose to worship a false god. Listen to worship music, spend time in prayer, or worship God by using some of your musical or artistic talents—anything to show God that you are choosing to worship him the way he deserves.

Yes, they knew God, but they wouldn't worship him as God or even give him thanks. And they began to think up foolish ideas of what God was like. As a result, their minds became dark and confused.
Romans 1:21

Are you familiar with that story in the book of Exodus about the Israelites worshipping the golden calf? (Check out Exodus 32 if you don't know the details or just need a refresher.) The men and women of Israel began to doubt God, and, instead of trusting Moses, they decided to create a false idol to worship.

Here in Romans 1:21, the Apostle Paul talks about people who ignore the reality of God. Sometimes we become so doubtful of God that we refuse to believe he even exists anymore. We let our fears conquer our trust in God. Numerous times throughout the Bible, doubt leads people to do some crazy things. When things get too difficult, we have a tendency to abandon God and do things on their own, which always leads to a road of sin and confusion.

TALKING WITH GOD

Dedicate your entire day to God—the good and the bad. Pray for help in trusting that God will hold you through every situation and will never abandon you. Even though it sometimes feels that way, pray for assurance that God will never leave your side.

Each time he said, "My grace is all you need. My power works best in weakness." So now I am glad to boast about my weaknesses, so that the power of Christ can work through me. That's why I take pleasure in my weaknesses, and in the insults, hardships, persecutions, and troubles that I suffer for Christ. For when I am weak, then I am strong.
2 Corinthians 12:9-10

This may seem like a backward idea at first glance. Who brags about being weak? "Hey everybody, I am the smallest and weakest, so please insult me!" Nobody says that! Do we naturally take pleasure in hardships? No way. If we ever heard someone talking like this, we would suspect they were up to something.

In today's passage, the Apostle Paul is trying to bring something to light: When we don't rely on our own strength, we leave room for Christ to be strong in our weakness. Oneness with God grows when we make the story about him and not us. This idea may seem backward but it is a secret to tapping into a strength that will never let us down.

TALKING WITH GOD

Offer a prayer like this: *God, I want to stop trying to be strong on my own. Help me leave room for you to be my strength. When troubles, persecution, hardships, and insults come my way, help me trust you, knowing I can take pleasure in being weak while you are strong.*

ONENESS
WITH GOD

A LITTLE EXTRA

Make a list of your strengths. Write a small prayer surrendering those to God for his glory. Now write a list of things that you see as weaknesses. Remember that these weaknesses can be a hardship, trouble, or any situation where you feel powerless. Write a prayer asking that God would be glorified through your weaknesses.

ONENESS
WITH GOD

A LITTLE EXTRA

Try to visit a park or ball field to observe parents who are watching their children play sports. You'll see some very animated and very excited parents. This is the way God looks at you and cheers for you. When you're faced with a difficult situation today, think about God sitting in the stands cheering you on and encouraging you to do great things for his kingdom.

"For you are a holy people, who belong to the Lord your God. Of all the people on earth, the Lord your God has chosen you to be his own special treasure."
Deuteronomy 7:6

Think about a time when you were picked first for the dodgeball team, or when someone chose you to help with an important project. Think about how you felt in that moment. You probably felt like you were the best at something, and someone wanted you to be there.

God has done more than select you to be first on his dodgeball team; he's chosen you to be his own special treasure, his prized possession. It's an amazing feeling when someone loves you, cares for you, and is proud of you no matter what you've done. If you go to any middle or high school sports game, you'll see players' parents in the stands. And no one is cheering harder than they are. It doesn't matter if the player is a starter or barely in the game, those parents will cheer louder than anyone else. That's how God looks at you.

TALKING WITH GOD

Write out a prayer of thanks to God. Thank him for being there for you when you mess up and when you do well. God's already proud of you, but tell him that you want to continue to live for him. Thank him for being your biggest fan.

Wherever the message of Jesus spreads rapidly, it threatens those in power. This was true in the book of Acts, and many Christ-followers lost their lives because of it. But this is also true today. Right now, around the world, Christ-followers are persecuted because of their faith. From the Middle East to South America, some government leaders want to kill the church and silence anyone who declares their trust in Jesus. Why? Well, the issue is complicated, but it can always be traced back to one fact: The gospel of Jesus undermines their power.

In the face of extreme physical and social pressure, these persecuted Christ-followers respond today much like the apostles did thousands of years ago.

But Peter and the apostles replied, "We must obey God rather than any human authority." Acts 5:29

You might never have to make a similar stance. Perhaps you'll face some ridicule or rejection, but you'll probably never be persecuted. But you will have to decide to whom you pledge your allegiance. People demand your loyalty every day. These people may not be evil, but that's not the point. The bottom line is: Who will you obey above all else? God wants to be in first place and at the center of your life.

TALKING WITH GOD

Pray for Christ-followers who are currently being persecuted around the world. Ask God to give them strength to endure. Also pray that God will give you boldness to follow him in all situations.

CONSEQUENCES

& CRYING OUT

VERSE 229:
Acts 5:29

A LITTLE EXTRA

With your parents' permission, check out lovecostseverything. com for a peek at what modern-day persecution looks like. You can also read the story of the three Hebrew slaves in Daniel 3 to find encouragement in the account of people willing to die for their faith.

ONENESS WITH GOD

A LITTLE EXTRA

Pick one thing you're good at, and find a way to use it to show love to someone this week. Maybe use your art skills to create a homemade card and tell someone that you were thinking about them. Or go to a local playground and play games with kids. Or wash your parents' car just because you love them.

"Your love for one another will prove to the world that you are my disciples." John 13:35

Ever had to prove yourself to someone? Maybe you did one of your chores around the house without being asked and had to convince your parents that you really did it. Maybe it was during practice for band, or in one of the sports you play, or in class to one of your teachers. How did it feel when you were finally proved right?

As Christ-followers, it is an honor to be considered a disciple of Jesus. But how do other people know that we're disciples of Christ? Jesus makes it clear in this verse: our love for one another.

You might think that people would see you as a disciple of Jesus because of how much time you spend reading the Bible, how much Christian music you listen to, how many Scripture verses you can recite, or how many Jesus T-shirts you wear. But Jesus says the way to prove you are his follower is to love one another.

TALKING WITH GOD

Think of one adult and one teenager in your life that you see a lot, but you're not sure if they are Christ-followers. Think of at least one thing you can do the next time you see them that will let them know you care about them. Ask God to give you the courage to act when that opportunity arises.

The Lord helps the fallen and lifts those bent beneath their loads. Psalm 145:14

What's weighing you down today? Do you believe you can trust God with those concerns?

In most religions, people view their god(s) as distant or even angry. They believe that the world was created because of war, and that human history is just a story about people trying to please god(s) out of fear.

But our relationship with God is not like that. We serve a God who created the world out of love. Perhaps you know the Bible's description of the Garden of Eden in the book of Genesis. It was a place God created so he could be near his people. It was a place of conversation and fellowship. God is not angry with you; he desires to be near to those who are hurting.

Throughout his life, Jesus constantly encouraged people who were hurting to come to him and give him their burdens. The same can be said today. No matter what you're facing and no matter how overwhelming your feelings are, God wants you to bring those concerns to him. In fact, you can do it right now.

TALKING WITH GOD

Talk to God about your concerns. What's worrying you? What's stressing you out? What's making you afraid? Tell God, and be honest. God wants to help you.

VERSE 231:
Psalm 145:14

A LITTLE EXTRA

Take out a journal or a piece of paper, and write about the hardest day of your life. Did you feel God's presence that day? Why or why not? Think about ways that you can take a step back from those situations and find a quiet place to seek the peace of God.

ONENESS WITH GOD

VERSE 232:
Acts 2:42-47

A LITTLE EXTRA

Type the word *church* into an online search engine (with your parents' permission, of course). What words come to mind when you look at the pictures? How do those words match up with the words in Acts 2? Journal your thoughts.

All the believers devoted themselves to the apostles' teaching, and to fellowship, and to sharing in meals (including the Lord's Supper), and to prayer. A deep sense of awe came over them all, and the apostles performed many miraculous signs and wonders. And all the believers met together in one place and shared everything they had. They sold their property and possessions and shared the money with those in need. They worshiped together at the Temple each day, met in homes for the Lord's Supper, and shared their meals with great joy and generosity—all the while praising God and enjoying the goodwill of all the people. And each day the Lord added to their fellowship those who were being saved. Acts 2:42-47

Want proof that Jesus really did die and rise again? Look no further than the early church. No other phenomenon explains how a group of people could come together like the first Christ-followers did. No other organization on the planet has a more diverse following than the church of Jesus. Young and old. Rich and poor. All races, all ethnicities. All of these groups find love and support in churches around the world. That common bond, which far outweighs all differences, cannot be explained without something supernatural.

When the church acts like those early Christ-followers did, needs are met and lives are changed. Notice the last sentence of the Scripture above: *the Lord added.* Why does that matter? It shows that community is the best evangelism. When your church takes care of people like the church in Acts did, people will show up!

TALKING WITH GOD

Ask God to help you love the church and find ways to serve. If you aren't currently connected to the church, ask God to help you find a church home. If you are connected to the church, make sure you're building relationships with people outside of the youth group, too.

He escorts me to the banquet hall; it's obvious how much he loves me. Song of Songs 2:4

What if your friends held a surprise party for you this afternoon? No reason—they just think you are awesome. Your best friend keeps you busy until it's time. The doors of a huge ballroom open, and there is a table filled with your favorite foods. Your friends tell you it's all for you! How would you feel? You might feel happy, excited, wowed, but most of all you would feel adored.

Today's verse comes from Song of Songs (also known as Song of Solomon), a book in the Bible that describes the love between a husband and wife. And as great as that love is, it still falls short of the amazing love God has for us! God wants it to be obvious how much he loves us. Imagine that the one who threw the party for you was God. That is what it is like when we will go to be with him forever.

TALKING WITH GOD

Is it obvious that God loves you? God wants you to know the incredible depth of his love for you. As you talk with God today, tell him 10 ways you know he loves you. If you are struggling to identify that long of a list, ask him to specifically and undeniably show you today one way that he loves you.

VERSE 233:
Song of Songs 2:4

A LITTLE EXTRA

Find something that reminds you of your last birthday party—a photo, a card, a specific gift you received, or anything else that's connected to that event. As you look at this object, think of reasons to celebrate God's love. What does it feel like to know that God loves you so deeply?

VERSE 234:
2 Corinthians 4:8-9

A LITTLE EXTRA

Sometime this week, make cookies (even the break-and-bake kind). Watch them in the oven as the heat affects them. Then read today's passage. How does the heat of our lives affect how others see Christ in us? What do those cookies tell us about the way God is with us even when stuff seems to go wrong?

We are pressed on every side by troubles, but we are not crushed. We are perplexed, but not driven to despair. We are hunted down, but never abandoned by God. We get knocked down, but we are not destroyed. 2 Corinthians 4:8-9

Have you ever watched cookies bake? The heat presses in and causes what seems to be destruction. The dough bubbles up and expands, getting flat and brown. The flames seem to be harming that awesome, gooey dough. But when you pull the cookies out of the oven, they have been transformed into something wonderful.

When bad things happen in life, it can feel like we are in an oven. The rising temperatures try to crush us and pull us apart. Trouble, confusion, and enemies knock us around. We have moments where everything seems to be pulling, prodding, and stretching. Yet we can choose to remember that even in the oven, God is protecting us. In the midst of the heat, God is right there with us.

TALKING WITH GOD

What things in your life seem to be pressing in on you these days? Do you have some friend or family drama? Do you have problems of some other kind? Make a list of those problems on the bottom of this page or in a notebook. Then go through each one and ask God to help you trust him to take care of things.

God replied to Moses, "I Am Who I Am. Say this to the people of Israel: I Am has sent me to you."
Exodus 3:14

God told Moses to call him "I AM."

I AM? Doesn't that seem weird? Of all the names God could choose, he chose I AM? What does that even mean?

God uses the name "I AM" because the name describes who he is in our everyday lives. Our world is full of empty promises; God's answer promises that he will never leave us or forsake us. Our world is full of broken hearts; God's answer pledges that he will always be true to who he is—a good, loving, faithful God. Our world is full of lots of different religions with lots of different gods; God's answer declares, "I AM the one true God." Our world is full of changes and uncertainty; God answers by promising, "I AM unchanging. I AM the same today, yesterday, and tomorrow."

I AM. That's the kind of name that instills hope and confidence.

TALKING WITH GOD

Pray this kind of prayer: *Thank you for being my eternal, all-powerful God. Everything in my life seems to be changing all at once. I can hardly keep up. Thank you for remaining the same today, yesterday, and tomorrow. You are the only unchanging thing in my life right now. I love you, I AM.*

ONENESS
WITH GOD

VERSE 235:
Exodus 3:14

A LITTLE EXTRA

Keep something in your life unchanged for 40 days. It could be your profile picture, a ring tone, a nail polish color, or something like that. (Please don't wear the same socks or go 40 days without showering. Sometimes change is a good thing!) Every time you see the unchanged item, let it remind you that God is I AM.

ONENESS WITH GOD

Take delight in the Lord, and he will give you your heart's desires. Psalm 37:4

What does it mean to *take delight in the Lord*? What words come to mind? How would people act if they were "taking delight" in each other?

Some people think this verse means that God will give you anything you want—whatever your heart desires. But that idea is rooted in a misunderstanding of what our desires will be if we're truly delighting ourselves in God. The truth of it is this: When we take delight in someone, the things we want begin to fade into the background. What we start to desire is whatever *they* desire. Think about a couple hopelessly in love. They delight in one another, and what makes them happiest is serving each other. That's the main theme in this verse: When we delight in the Lord, we become so focused on the Lord that our desires become aligned with what he desires. We change, and our heart reflects God's heart more and more.

TALKING WITH GOD

Have you ever asked God what his desires are for you? Ask him now. Seriously, stop reading and do it! As you begin to understand God's dreams and plans for your life, some of the things you have taken delight in will start to seem less important to you.

VERSE 236:
Psalm 37:4

A LITTLE EXTRA

Taking delight in someone requires an investment of time. How much time are you investing in your relationship with God? Grab your MP3 player or your phone, and enjoy some personal worship time today. Turn off your computer or television and just spend some time praying. Meditate on something God has shown you in the Bible this week.

But you, O Lord, are a shield around me; you are my glory, the one who holds my head high.
Psalm 3:3

The word *shield* in this verse isn't just a plate of metal held on your arm to block the enemy's arrows. No, this shield is protecting the entire body from the top, below, left, and right. Completely protected. God is your shield protecting you from Satan's arrows. It's almost like an umbrella, but covering your whole body. The choice is yours if you want to stand under the umbrella protected. Once you stand outside the umbrella, outside of God's plan for your life, you're exposed. Satan can then get a clean shot into you and your life with his lies.

If you find yourself out from under God's umbrella, it's OK. God has made a way for you. Ask God for forgiveness and step right back into his plan for your life. God wants to protect you and provide for you.

While you live under God's umbrella, you have that full-body protection without fear. You can do anything through Christ, who gives you strength. You can hold your head high with God-given confidence.

TALKING WITH GOD

Take a look at what's going on in your life—both the good and the bad. Ask God to forgive you for stepping outside his will, and ask God to help you remain under his umbrella and in his plan.

GOD HEARS & RESTORES

A LITTLE EXTRA

Grab an umbrella and go outside. (Of course, this *really* works if it's raining.) Once outside, open the umbrella and stand underneath. What do you notice? Are you protected from the rain (or the warm sunshine, or the strong wind)? Now, set the umbrella aside. Staying outside, think of ways you'd escape the rain (or sun or wind)—without an umbrella. Consider how this relates to God's plan for your life.

ONENESS
WITH GOD

VERSE 238:
1 Peter 2:11

A LITTLE EXTRA

A key to avoiding sticky situations is to have a friend hold you accountable. Find a Christ-following friend, share with them the areas you think are your weakest, and invite them to help you make good decisions, especially when things get tough. Make sure you offer to help your friend, too.

Dear friends, I warn you as "temporary residents and foreigners" to keep away from worldly desires that wage war against your very souls. 1 Peter 2:11

Have you ever traveled to a place where you didn't speak the local language? It can be a beautiful experience, especially if you worship or pray with other Christ-followers in their language. But there are some scary parts, too: looking for a restroom, reading highway signs, and trying to figure out why everyone is laughing at something you just said but have no idea what it means! You can quickly feel like you don't belong.

Peter is telling Christ-followers the same thing in today's verse: We live in a world where we don't belong. Part of trusting Jesus means that his priorities become our priorities, and what's important to Jesus is radically different from what's important to our culture. Peter warns us to avoid unwise decisions that produce sticky situations, which can tempt us to do bad things. Doing bad things hurts us, and when we're hurting, we forget about living and revealing the kingdom of God.

TALKING WITH GOD

Ask God to help you remember who you are: a follower of Christ, a child of the king, and a citizen of the kingdom of God. Commit to making good decisions that keep you out of tempting situations. And when things get really tough, remember that this world is not your home, and part of your life mission is to help as many people as you can change their citizenship, too.

He looked around at them angrily and was deeply saddened by their hard hearts. Then he said to the man, "Hold out your hand." So the man held out his hand, and it was restored! Mark 3:5

In today's verse, Jesus confronts two types of brokenness. The Pharisees and other religious leaders used the Old Testament law to separate the "good" people from the "bad" people; they were broken. The man in this passage had a deformed hand that may or may not have been caused by his sin, but the religious leaders assumed it was; the man was broken. In one brief act, Jesus addressed both types of brokenness and gave everyone a glimpse of the kingdom of God.

We're all broken. Most people have something about themselves that they want to change. Some may be physical, some emotional, or some spiritual. God loves us enough to help us face our struggles, no matter what they are. Whatever your struggle is today, hold it out to God and invite him to bring healing.

TALKING WITH GOD

Hold out your hands to God as you pray: *God, thank you for loving me, even when my brokenness is ugly. I confess that sometimes I don't know how to be unbroken; I'm glad that you know what to do and that you're willing to do it. Help me trust you enough today to hold all of my brokenness out to you and give you space to fix it. Use my life to reveal your kingdom to someone else who's broken.*

GOD HEARS & RESTORES

A LITTLE EXTRA

Carry a broken toy with you today as a reminder to offer your brokenness to God. Ask God to give you his eyes, so you can see your own brokenness as he sees it, and to see others' brokenness as an opportunity to reveal God's kingdom to them.

ONENESS
WITH GOD

A LITTLE EXTRA

With parental permission, go online to research the qualities of God. You could start online at theopedia. com/List_of_God's_ known_attributes. Choose several of these attributes and spend time celebrating God for each one. Another idea: The Greek letter for God is a theta, ⊖. Draw a small theta on your hand or school binder as a reminder that God is worthy.

"You are worthy, O Lord our God, to receive glory and honor and power. For you created all things, and they exist because you created what you pleased." Revelation 4:11

If your family is like most families, when a special guest is coming to visit, you frantically scramble to clean the house. You might dress up, use special dishes, or put music on in the background. Why don't we do stuff like this every day? Because special guests are worthy of special treatment.

What is God worthy of? God is worthy of our trust, because he's proven himself trustworthy over and over again. God is worthy of our best, because he gave us his best through Jesus. God is worthy of glory (undivided attention and celebration), honor (respect), and power (ability to do what he wants) because he is the creator of all things. God is worthy of special treatment every day, because he is an honored guest in our hearts. God created us and loves us, and he wants a deep relationship with us.

TALKING WITH GOD

Pray this kind of prayer: *Thank you, God, for creating me to be in relationship with you. I don't deserve it, but your love is always there. Help me trust you enough to give you everything I am and everything I have, because you are worthy of it all. Help me live and reveal your kingdom today as an act of worship. Give me opportunities to worship and serve you.*

When he came to the village of Nazareth, his boyhood home, he went as usual to the synagogue on the Sabbath and stood up to read the Scriptures. The scroll of Isaiah the prophet was handed to him. He unrolled the scroll and found the place where this was written: "The Spirit of the Lord is upon me, for he has anointed me to bring Good News to the poor. He has sent me to proclaim that captives will be released, that the blind will see, that the oppressed will be set free, and that the time of the Lord's favor has come." Luke 4:16-19

VERSE 241:
Luke 4:16-19

Don't you love it when the teacher asks a question, and you know the answer? Beautiful!

Just by knowing Christ, you have good news to share. You know the answer. You know how captives will be released, the blind will see, and the oppressed will be set free. How cool is that?

The key is to share the good news of Christ's salvation with others. You don't have to know everything about the Bible or be able to talk like the leaders at your church. God just needs you to be you and to share what Christ has done in your life.

A LITTLE EXTRA

Grab your journal or some paper that you can keep handy. Make a list of people in your life who need to hear the good news. Even if you're intimidated, commit to praying for them and for chances to talk. God will give you opportunities to share!

TALKING WITH GOD

Thank God for this good news. Reflect how your relationship with Christ has changed your life. Think about times you shared this good news with others—and times when you kept it to yourself. Commit to sharing more.

GOD HEARS & RESTORES

VERSE 242:
2 Corinthians 9:8

A LITTLE EXTRA

Paul had some words to say about living in need. Check it out in Philippians 4:11-13.

And God will generously provide all you need. Then you will always have everything you need and plenty left over to share with others.
2 Corinthians 9:8

This teaching section on giving came from Paul because the church in Jerusalem needed some help from other Christ-followers, and many people in Corinth were excited to give. Paul thanked them for their willingness and then gave some guidance on how we should give.

First, we serve a giving God who calls us to give. We are urged to decide in our own hearts what we want to give and then give that amount happily. We can happily give lots of money and receive a huge blessing back— sometimes money, sometimes other blessings—because we were able to a part of helping in some way.

It's not necessarily bad to give little. If a little is all that you have and you give that amount, that is equal to a person who has lots and gives lots.

The ideas of giving and giving glory to Christ are bound together in this passage as one thing that cannot be taken apart. When we give in a way that costs us something, God knows, and he receives glory. We are also promised in this verse that if we give, we will have all we need and will be able to help others.

TALKING WITH GOD

Pray this prayer or one similar to it: *God, you know the decisions in my heart. I want to give in such a way that you receive glory. I trust you to hear and know the needs that I do have. I believe that you will meet all my needs and give me extra to share with others in your name.*

"Bring all the tithes into the storehouse so there will be enough food in my Temple. If you do," says the Lord of Heaven's Armies, *"I will open the windows of heaven for you. I will pour out a blessing so great you won't have enough room to take it in! Try it! Put me to the test!"* Malachi 3:10

Let's say you have a friend who owes you money. You bring it to their attention, and they play dumb about owing you. It's unlikely you'd say this: "Listen, just pay me what you owe me and I will totally make it worth your while: I'll give you even more. In fact, I'll blow your mind with just how generous I'll be to you. All you have to do is give me one little portion of what I've already given you." Most of us would write them off as a friend—or take by force what was owed us.

God wanted to bless Israel, even though the Israelites were withholding God's offering and using it for themselves. God invited them to put his promise to the test.

Even if you don't have much, everything you have ultimately comes from God. Giving is not just an act of obedience; it's a chance for God to reveal something about himself.

TALKING WITH GOD

Commit your money and possessions to God. Offer a prayer of thanks, and ask for God's help in trusting him more and becoming an even more generous person.

VERSE 243:
Malachi 3:10

A LITTLE EXTRA

The "tithe" as mentioned in this passage is 10 percent. You might not be confident giving 10 percent to God, but start somewhere. Try to find a piggy bank, and put it in your room as a way to remind you to always be ready to give to God.

GOD HEARS & RESTORES

A LITTLE EXTRA

Make a list of people who need to know that God loves them just as they are. Ask God to give you opportunities this week to make them feel honored or special—to treat them as Christ would treat them.

"He lifts the poor from the dust and the needy from the garbage dump. He sets them among princes, placing them in seats of honor. For all the earth is the Lord's, and he has set the world in order."
1 Samuel 2:8

Have you ever stood in line at the grocery store and looked at the magazine covers? If so, you know which movie stars are dating, what food certain musicians eat, and how much weight the hottest reality TV star has lost. We live in a culture obsessed with celebrities. We can't get enough news about them. For some reason we are impressed by the rich and famous.

Not God. He doesn't care more about someone because of how much money they make or how many fans they have. God cares about all people equally. God has compassion on the poor and the needy; he sees them as royalty, placing them at the seat of honor.

Have you ever given someone special treatment because she was popular? Have you ever wished you were like someone else because he had lots of friends, money, or fame? Just remember, these things don't matter to God. He loves you just as he created you, and he wants you to see others the same way.

TALKING WITH GOD

As you spend time with God today, ask him to help you see others as he sees them. Ask God to give you a heart to care about people that everyone else seems to overlook.

On the third day after Jesus' death, Mary Magdalene and the other Mary (probably the mother of James) went to his tomb. An angel greeted them.

Then the angel spoke to the women. "Don't be afraid!" he said. "I know you are looking for Jesus, who was crucified. He isn't here! He is risen from the dead, just as he said would happen. Come, see where his body was lying. And now, go quickly and tell his disciples that he has risen from the dead, and he is going ahead of you to Galilee. You will see him there. Remember what I have told you."
Matthew 28:5-7

Jesus predicted his death and resurrection to his disciples and friends. They believed what he taught. They supported him as he ministered. They followed him as he traveled from town to town.

When Mary Magdalene and the other Mary heard the angel's news, they were overjoyed for two reasons:

- Jesus is, in fact, *alive*. They didn't need to mourn his death any longer.
- They could trust Jesus to do what he said he would do. He predicted his death and resurrection—and that's just what happened.

TALKING WITH GOD

Thank God that Jesus is alive. It's incredibly powerful to embrace the fact that Jesus died for your sins, and he lives today. But don't stop there. Thank God that he can be trusted—with everything. He always does what he promises. Period. Give him the areas of your life where you need to trust him more.

GOD HEARS & RESTORES

VERSE 245:
Matthew 28:5-7

A LITTLE EXTRA

Grab your journal or a clean piece of paper. Make a list of areas in your life where you need to trust Jesus and trust what he has said. Then take time in prayer to give those things to Jesus. He can—and will—handle them.

GOD HEARS & RESTORES

VERSE 246:
James 1:22

A LITTLE EXTRA

During the next sermon you hear, write down one way you can translate what you're hearing into action. If the message is a "fill-in-the-blank" sermon, don't be content with that. Figure out a way to make a tangible action from the words in those blanks. If you're really brave, email your youth leader and ask him or her to hold you accountable to follow through. True faith comes from doing, not just hearing.

But don't just listen to God's word. You must do what it says. Otherwise, you are only fooling yourselves. James 1:22

How does your relationship with Christ look when you aren't with your church or sitting in a Bible study? That's really the question in this verse. God's influence in our lives—through church, friends, the Bible, and the Holy Spirit—ought to be something that shows in how we act in everyday life. How do we treat people? Where do we invest our time and money? Do the stories we tell during the week match the songs we're singing on Sundays?

If we're living inconsistently, we're fooling ourselves. But fooling ourselves about what? A little later in this chapter, in verse 26, James says we're fooling ourselves if we aren't practicing all that we're listening to—and our religion is worthless. We're fooling ourselves into thinking that our relationship with God is real and life-changing, if our actions don't match our words.

TALKING WITH GOD

Ask God to show you if your life doesn't match your words. It's probably going to sting a little bit. But it's worth it. As you read through this book, make it part of your quiet time routine to ask how you can put each day's truths into practice in your life.

Think of the person who knows you best—that person who most intimately knows your hopes and fears and dreams and secrets. Maybe that person is one of your parents? Or maybe a really close friend?

Here's a really interesting Bible verse about how well God knew an Old Testament prophet named Jeremiah—and how well God knows you:

"I knew you before I formed you in your mother's womb. Before you were born I set you apart and appointed you as my prophet to the nations."
Jeremiah 1:5

While the verse is specifically about God knowing Jeremiah, they're words to us also, words to you about how well God knows you.

God knows you so well that he has *always* known you. That's pretty wild, huh? Think of friends who've known you for years. Think of all the people who've known you since the day you were born. Well, God knew you before anyone of them even knew you, and God knows you better than anyone else knows you! In fact, God knows you better than you know yourself.

TALKING WITH GOD

God knows you *that* well—and loves you. Thank God for that. Acknowledge that there's nothing you can hide from God. Ask God to help you trust him enough to bare your soul to him, telling him everything you think and feel and dream.

ONENESS
WITH GOD

VERSE 247:
Jeremiah 1:5

A LITTLE EXTRA

Spend some time thinking and praying about this: Is there anything you've been trying to hide from God, anything you wish God *didn't* know about you? If you can think of anything, turn that over to God, and express that you won't try to keep secrets from him (since you can't anyway!).

GOD HEARS & RESTORES

VERSE 248:
Luke 17:6

A LITTLE EXTRA

You could translate Jesus' words in this verse as, "If you trust me just a tiny bit, I will do amazing things in your life and through your life!" In what areas of life do you struggle to trust Jesus? Every decision you make comes down to your trust—or lack of trust—in Jesus. As you make decisions throughout your day, ask yourself if your choices reflect your trust in Jesus.

If you could have any superpower, what would it be? Would you fly, be invisible, walk through walls? Sure, this would be impossible in real life, but play along. How would you use your superpower?

Jesus gave his disciples a sort of superpower—the power to heal. A father brought his son to the disciples for healing, but they couldn't heal the boy. So the family went to Jesus for healing. Later the disciples asked Jesus about faith.

The Lord answered, "If you had faith even as small as a mustard seed, you could say to this mulberry tree, 'May you be uprooted and thrown into the sea,' and it would obey you!" Luke 17:6

God gives his followers the power to walk through each day with confidence and peace as he's in control.

Are you using this power? Do you have enough trust in God to walk in confidence? This means joyfully going through each day, not obsessing over past decisions and not worrying about what the future holds. You can do this; God has already given you this gift!

TALKING WITH GOD

Thank God for his incredible power—and that he doesn't keep all the power to himself. Thank God for the times today he will help you walk in confidence.

ONENESS
WITH GOD

"You must be holy because I, the Lord, am holy. I have set you apart from all other people to be my very own." Leviticus 20:26

Holy (adjective): exalted or worthy of complete devotion as one perfect in goodness and righteousness; set apart for God's purposes.

When we think of being "set apart" from everyone else, a negative image might come to our minds: a girl wearing different clothes and being ridiculed, or a guy sitting all alone at lunch. However, when God decided to "set us apart" from the rest of the world, he had the most beautiful image in his mind! God wanted us to be completely devoted to him and to live a life of holiness rather than a life of sin.

Most of the world chooses to do what they want and ignore what God wants, but God chose us to be his very own followers who are set apart from everyone else! God handpicked YOU to be holy as he is holy and to do all that you can to live your life according to his Word.

TALKING WITH GOD

When you chose to follow Jesus and trust him with your salvation, God called you to live a holy life and stand out from the rest of the world. What are you doing to be "set apart"? Pray that God will allow others to see you differently and notice how you live rather than how most people around you live.

VERSE 249:
Leviticus 20:26

A LITTLE EXTRA

Wear a new bracelet, style your hair differently, or even wear a crazy-colored shirt to school one day! Someone probably will ask you about it, and you can use that opportunity to explain that you are choosing to be different. It may end up being a great conversation that will let you share Christ!

SIN &
SEPARATION

A LITTLE EXTRA

Go to a gym or a gymnastics facility, put some cushions under a balance beam, and try to walk across it. First try to do it while looking around at anything but the beam. Pick yourself up, and then try to cross while concentrating on the beam and nothing else. Think about how your experience at the gym relates to following God on that narrow path.

"You can enter God's Kingdom only through the narrow gate. The highway to hell is broad, and its gate is wide for the many who choose that way. But the gateway to life is very narrow and the road is difficult, and only a few ever find it."
Matthew 7:13–14

It's interesting that in today's passage, Jesus doesn't say, "If you don't tell my message to as many people as we can, it's possible some of them might not make it to heaven." He just flat-out tells us that only a few will find that road.

Becoming like Christ is hard. When you're walking on a narrow path, you have to keep your eyes straight ahead. If you get distracted, you'll probably fall. And the enemy throws all kinds of distractions at us. But as followers of Christ, we have to keep our eyes on Jesus and on the narrow path.

Jesus knew that a lot of people would opt for the wide path that allows leeway and distraction and the opportunity to look at everything *but* him. You have a choice. Choose the narrow way.

TALKING WITH GOD

God wants you to be on that narrow path to him. So talk to him about it. Ask God to help you focus on him. Ask God to give you strength to withstand the temptations and distractions Satan will throw down in your way.

I don't mean to say that I have already achieved these things or that I have already reached perfection. But I press on to possess that perfection for which Christ Jesus first possessed me. No, dear brothers and sisters, I have not achieved it, but I focus on this one thing: Forgetting the past and looking forward to what lies ahead, I press on to reach the end of the race and receive the heavenly prize for which God, through Christ Jesus, is calling us. Philippians 3:12-14

GOD HEARS & RESTORES

A LITTLE EXTRA

Read Matthew 25:14-28 and make a list of ways you can live your life for God.

Have you ever watched an Olympic athlete compete? Even the most uncoordinated klutz can appreciate their training, focus, discipline, passion, and determination. They give it their all to win the prize.

In these verses, the Apostle Paul tells us the same should be true for us as we run the race of life God has set out before us. We're not just on some casual, random stroll through the park; Jesus has a plan and purpose for our lives. It's all about knowing him, trusting him, loving him, and sharing him with others.

Running our race to win means learning to live for him, in the power of God's Spirit, every minute of every day.

Just like an Olympic athlete, our race also requires passion, focus, and endurance. But Paul makes it clear here that it doesn't require perfection. Part of running well is showing a gritty determination to keep our eye on the prize and continually lean on God as he helps us get back up after each stumble or fall.

TALKING WITH GOD

What's the biggest challenge you face as you seek to run your race well? Talk to God about this thing that makes you stumble or fall.

GOD HEARS & RESTORES

A LITTLE EXTRA

Make a list of five things that you know Jesus has forgiven you for. Breathe prayers of thanks for God's forgiveness throughout your day today. Ask God to help you forgive others in the same way he's forgiven you.

"I tell you, her sins—and they are many—have been forgiven, so she has shown me much love. But a person who is forgiven little shows only little love." Luke 7:47

Think for a moment about something bad that you've done. Maybe it was an accidental spill on the carpet, or maybe you intentionally hurt a friend through gossip. You knew the moment you did it that you were wrong, and you had an ache in the pit of your stomach that wanted everything to be all right. What do you feel when the person forgives you?

We are more likely to understand our own imperfections when we know what brokenness feels like. That is the source of this verse. This particular woman had lived so sinfully that she thought there was no way out. When Jesus forgave her, her response was to fall on her face before him, crying for joy and kissing his feet.

Every act of God's grace deserves a response. When we understand the significance of our sin—what it cost Jesus—we are overwhelmed with gratitude.

TALKING WITH GOD

Pray this kind of prayer today: *God, thank you for the unbelievable gift of forgiveness. I don't deserve it, but I'm thankful for it. Help me always be aware of my sinfulness and your grace. I trust you, but help me trust you more. Use my life to reveal your kingdom.*

Always be full of joy in the Lord. I say it again—
rejoice! Philippians 4:4

Always be full of joy in the Lord? Always? Really? Is
Paul delusional? How can we rejoice when bad things
are happening all around us? Divorce. Hunger. Abuse.
Cancer. Death. Betrayal. Are we supposed to be happy
about these things?

Paul was in prison when he wrote this passage, and
he wasn't super stoked about being behind bars.
Paul wasn't saying that Christ-followers ought to be
fake, but he was encouraging us to not let our outer
circumstance influence our inner attitude.

Yes, heart-breaking tragedy is part of being alive, but
we can rejoice in knowing that with Jesus we never
walk alone. We can find joy in understanding that while
this world is full of heartache, there will come a day in
heaven when there will be no more weeping, hurt, pain,
suffering, sickness, or death.

Our past, present, and future relationship with Jesus is
the only thing that makes rejoicing possible.

TALKING WITH GOD

Talk with God about the things in this world that bring
you down. Take your time. Tell him everything. Once
you have given him all of your burdens, pray this kind
of prayer: *God, fill me with your brand of joy. Not a*
happiness that is dependent on my circumstance, but a
kind of joy that trusts in you and dreams of a better day.
I want to rejoice in you always. Teach me how. I trust
you, Lord.

ONENESS
WITH GOD

VERSE 253:
Philippians 4:4

A LITTLE EXTRA

With your parents'
permission, download
the song "You Hold Me
Now," sung by Hillsong
United. As you listen to
the lyrics—especially
the chorus—ask God to
transform your broken
heart into a rejoicing
heart.

VERSE 254:
Luke 12:21

A LITTLE EXTRA

Write down five expensive things that you own or want to own. These could include a car, your phone, your baseball card collection, a fancy piece of jewelry, and so on. If it's something you own, talk with your parents, and pray about trading it in for something less expensive and using the money to make a difference for God's kingdom. If it's something you want to own, ask God to help you keep your focus on him and not be distracted by a bunch of stuff. Possessions fade, but a rich friendship with God lasts forever.

"Yes, a person is a fool to store up earthly wealth but not have a rich relationship with God."
Luke 12:21

Think of someone who has a lot of stuff. It could be someone you know personally, someone you've heard about, or even a celebrity. They probably have all the new gadgets, phones, cars, and other possessions. And every year, there's something that is newer, bigger, and better, which means they have to continue to upgrade.

In today's verse, Jesus is telling us that it's far more important to have a deep relationship with God than to have a bunch of stuff on earth. Our culture says our worth is based, in part, on how much stuff we have. But God has a different standard. Instead of spending so much time thinking about all the stuff you want, spend your time investing in your relationship with God.

TALKING WITH GOD

Ask God to look into your life and see if anything you're focusing on is distracting you from him. Ask God to help you turn your attention away from those things and spend your time building your relationship with him.

And he said to her, "Daughter, your faith has made you well. Go in peace. Your suffering is over."
Mark 5:34

What is the worst sickness you have ever had? Maybe it lasted a day, a week, or even longer. It was one of those times you thought you would never get past. Or perhaps you are in the middle of one of those times now. All you want is to be well. Maybe you thought (or do think) there is no way you could ever be better.

That is what happened to the woman in today's verse, who had been to doctors but only got worse. She knew that if she could even get near Jesus and touch his clothes she would well. But a magic formula or a special garment isn't what healed her. It was Jesus.

Are you in a time where you need to reach out for him? God will meet our suffering. Sometimes it happens on this side of heaven, and sometimes it happens on the other side. Sometimes he makes us well physically, and sometimes he gives hope. Either way, God is the one that heals us as we trust in him.

TALKING WITH GOD

Does something in your life need to be made well? If not in your life, what about in the life of a friend or loved one? Talk to God today about it. Ask him to help you or the person who needs help. Allow God's presence to cover the suffering.

GOD HEARS & RESTORES

VERSE 255:
Mark 5:34

A LITTLE EXTRA

Find a small twig outside, and break it. Carry it in your pocket today as a reminder of your brokenness—or the pain of someone else in your life. Every time you see it, let the broken twig remind you that God is the one who heals and restores.

GOD HEARS
& RESTORES

A LITTLE EXTRA

Do something generous for someone who doesn't know Jesus. Then talk to that person about Jesus' generosity to us. Do an online search for "random acts of kindness" for some creative ideas.

"For God loved the world so much that he gave his one and only Son, so that everyone who believes in him will not perish but have eternal life. God sent his Son into the world not to judge the world, but to save the world through him." John 3:16–17

It blows your mind, actually, when you try to really grasp what Jesus did for us on the cross.

These verses capture the audaciousness (look up the word if you don't know its meaning) of the gospel: God's lavish love, Jesus' atoning death, and the eternal life available to everyone who trusts in him alone.

Jesus' work on the cross can change us forever. And this message is news too good to keep to yourself.

So look for opportunities today to talk about him. Try taking an "Ask, Admire, Admit" approach during a conversation. Start by **asking** something like, "From what I can tell, I think you may look at things from a different viewpoint than I do, so I was wondering what you thought about _____ (a specific topic)?" Keep asking questions to get the dialogue going. Listen carefully to the person's response and find something to **admire** in what they believe—and compliment them on it. Then when the time is right, interject a simple "Can I tell you what I believe?" This is your chance to **admit** that you need a Savior and to explain Jesus' free gift of salvation that's available to those who trust in him.

Remember that you can never argue someone into faith. Just try to paint a picture of what a trusting relationship with Jesus is like.

TALKING WITH GOD

Thank God for his immense love, and pray for an opportunity to tell someone about Jesus today.

"I am the good shepherd; I know my own sheep, and they know me, just as my Father knows me and I know the Father. So I sacrifice my life for the sheep." John 10:14-15

GOD HEARS & RESTORES

Imagine being a kid in a crowded mall and getting separated from your parents. It is very noisy, with people having numerous conversations all around you. Everything is just a jumble of sounds. Then you hear it. Somewhere off to the left is the sound of your mom calling your name. Her voice is completely distinctive from the other voices around you. She is frantically trying to find you. You cry out and move in her direction. After a few steps you see her, pushing her way toward you. You are found. Though it seemed like a few hours, it was only a few seconds, and your mother was searching for you the whole time.

Jesus reminds us that we are his sheep. He knows everything about us. If we listen, his voice is clear and distinguishable from all others. Best of all, he is the shepherd who would do anything to come to your rescue—even die on a cross.

TALKING WITH GOD

God knows our needs and wants to care for us. Spend time thanking him for being such a loving father. Sit in silence for two minutes and listen carefully for God's voice or leading. It takes practice to learn to hear him, but he will speak to you. What is God telling you today?

VERSE 257:
John 10:14-15

A LITTLE EXTRA

Research the duties of a shepherd at historicjesus.com/character/shepherd.html. Think about the work it took to watch a flock of sheep. Each day was long, hard, and even dangerous. Why do you think Jesus wants us to think of him as our shepherd? Write some thoughts in the margins of this page.

Studying the Bible can be intimidating. Asking the right questions can help. As you continue to grow in your trust in God, you will begin wanting to read more of the Bible. When you do, ask yourself these six questions to help you get the most out of your time:

1. **What do I learn about God?** Do I see God's love, compassion, justice, anger, or some other character quality? How do I know God more after reading this passage?

2. **What do I learn about myself from this verse/passage?** Do I see my successes, my brokenness, my stubbornness, my potential, or something else? How do I know myself more after reading this passage?

3. **What do I learn about God's love for humanity?** Do I see forgiveness, protection, consequences for sin, restoration?

4. **How do I become more like Jesus?** What example does he set by what he does (or doesn't do) or says (or doesn't say)? How will I live differently after reading this passage?

5. **How do I become a stronger part of the church?** How did God shape me to serve others? What is my role in the body of Christ?

6. **How do I become a stronger example in the world?** What is my role in helping others begin to trust Jesus?

The Bible is one of the main ways we get to know God and understand what it means to live and reveal God's kingdom. These questions can help you think more deeply about the Bible, and your trust in God can grow. Where do you want to go today?

THE KINGDOM OF GOD is a big deal. It represents God's plan for his creation—living life the way God dreamed for us, filled with wonder, purpose, passion, joy, and God! We first see what God's kingdom is like in Genesis 1–2. Adam and Eve lived in perfect relationship with God, perfect relationship with one another, and perfect relationship with the rest of creation.

Then sin entered the picture, and everything changed. All relationships were messed up. God's plan for creation was hijacked. And everyone was left trying to figure things out in a broken world.

Then Jesus entered the picture, and everything changed again. Jesus lived exactly the way God wanted—in perfect relationship with God, other people, and the rest of creation. And now as Jesus' followers, we are invited to trust Jesus enough to live the way he lived—the way of God's kingdom.

We are to do the right thing, because we trust that it's the best way to live. We are to treat people the way Jesus did, because we trust that it's the best way to love. We love, we serve, we give, we forgive, we laugh, we grieve, we live well. It's really difficult, but it's worth it. Because as we live the kingdom of God, others will see it, and maybe they will want in on it, too.

Everything we do as followers of Jesus ought to be about living and revealing God's kingdom. Everything. We. Do. And the best news of all: Jesus has given you everything you need to do it (2 Peter 1:3).

LARK—Live And Reveal the Kingdom!

CONSEQUENCES & CRYING OUT

VERSE 258:
Acts 18:9

A LITTLE EXTRA

Do you know someone who doesn't know Jesus? Try fasting from food for 24 hours and praying for them every time you feel hungry. Ask your parents or youth leader for more information.

Have you ever been frustrated? Have you ever thought that despite your efforts, God was not coming through for you? If so, you're not alone. The Apostle Paul had a lot of successes during his ministry. He saw a lot of people come to trust in Jesus, and he lived an adventurous life. But that doesn't mean his travels were without frustration.

In fact, there was one city he almost gave up on. When he arrived in the Greek city of Corinth, the people rejected his message. They refused to listen to him preach, and this made Paul extremely angry. But before he could catch a ride out of town, God stepped in.

One night the Lord spoke to Paul in a vision and told him, "Don't be afraid! Speak out! Don't be silent!" Acts 18:9

Just like Paul, we sometimes need to be reminded that even when things appear difficult, God wants us to keep at it. Maybe you've been trying to tell a friend or parent about Jesus for months or years. Maybe you think they'll never get it. If so, don't be discouraged. Remember that you have to keep speaking out!

TALKING WITH GOD

Tell God about the times you've been frustrated recently. Don't be afraid to express how you truly felt. Ask him for the strength to press on through those frustrations. Also, don't be afraid to ask him to remind you of some successes. God loves to encourage us when we're working to live and reveal his kingdom.

For we are not fighting against flesh-and-blood enemies, but against evil rulers and authorities of the unseen world, against mighty powers in this dark world, and against evil spirits in the heavenly places. Ephesians 6:12

SIN & SEPARATION

Even though you may not hear it talked about every week during church services, there's a spiritual realm out there that is part of your everyday life. And the evil forces of this spiritual realm hate you, God, and anything associated with God.

VERSE 259:
Ephesians 6:12

It's interesting that in today's verse, Paul says we aren't fighting against flesh-and-blood enemies—but then he uses the metaphor of armor to describe what we need to combat these forces. His analogies help us understand the physical parallels to the spiritual battle. We need truth, righteousness, and peace. We need faith. And finally, we need God's Word.

A LITTLE EXTRA

Paul was very specific with the words he used here. Read through the entire passage, Ephesians 6:10-17, and go through each piece of the armor of God. Think about how truth is a belt. And how righteousness is a protective covering for your heart. And how Scripture is a sword. And so forth through the whole armor. This can help solidify the importance of these pieces of our faith.

Sometimes it can be hard to believe in this "unseen world," but it is real, and those in it would love nothing more than for you to think they don't exist.

TALKING WITH GOD

Talk to God about the piece (or pieces) of the armor you feel you're most lacking. Just as with physical battles, the enemy will look for a weakness and exploit it. Ask God to help you strengthen each piece of his armor in your life.

ONENESS WITH GOD

A LITTLE EXTRA

Post this message on social media: "I am not the person I used to be. Ask me why." Be ready to tell the story of how your old self has been crucified with Christ. And the next time a friend jokes about zombies or talks about a zombie movie, talk about the spiritual transformation that has happened in your life because of Jesus.

My old self has been crucified with Christ. It is no longer I who live, but Christ lives in me. So I live in this earthly body by trusting in the Son of God, who loved me and gave himself for me.
Galatians 2:20

Have you ever seen a zombie movie? Even if you haven't, you probably know that zombies are gross, creepy creatures who walk around half-dead with slimy things hanging from their pores. Not a pretty sight at all!

Do you ever wonder if that's how we looked spiritually before choosing to follow Jesus? Before Christ, we limped around half-dead with sin oozing all over us. Now that we trust Jesus, our old, sinful, zombie-like life is dead. We no longer carry the shame of our sin because it has been crucified with Christ. We no longer walk around half-dead because in Christ we are made fully alive. Because Jesus loved us enough to pay the price for our sins by dying on the cross, we are not the people we used to be.

TALKING WITH GOD

Pray this kind of prayer: *Jesus, thank you for dying on the cross to save me from my sins. Thank you for destroying my old self so I can live freely with you. Because of you, I will never be the same. I love you.*

God is our refuge and strength, always ready to help in times of trouble. Psalm 46:1

Life isn't easy.

We get tired. We lose focus and energy. We encounter unexpected challenges. We feel like we're under attack spiritually, emotionally, or relationally.

Fortunately, as Christ-followers we are never alone. God is with us. And today's verse reveals so much about God's character and God's relationship with us, his people.

Sometimes we just need a place to withdraw. During those times, God is our refuge, our shelter, our tower, our fortress, our place of protection.

Sometimes we just need a source of strength. During those times, God is our encourager, our supporter, our comforter, our provider, the one who renews and revives and restores us.

Here's another important truth tucked into this powerful verse: God isn't occasionally ready to help us; he is *always* ready. When you need God's help, call out to him. When you need his refuge or strength, pray for it. God won't let you face life's challenges alone.

TALKING WITH GOD

Turn today's verse into a prayer of declaration—that God is *your* refuge and *your* strength, that God is always ready to help *you* during troubled times. Talk with God about the places or the moments or the settings where you need an extra measure of strength, or an extra shield of protection, or an extra time of calm and shelter.

GOD HEARS
& RESTORES

VERSE 261:
Psalm 46:1

A LITTLE EXTRA

Spend time in a place of protection: under a covered patio, behind a tall fence, beside a large rock, or anything else that offers some kind of shelter. Even if today is a beautifully sunny day, consider how God protects and provides for you during life's biggest storms and toughest challenges.

ONENESS WITH GOD

VERSE 262:
Matthew 19:26

A LITTLE EXTRA

Go outside and find a cool-looking rock that's small enough to fit in your pocket, but big enough that you'll notice it while you're carrying it around. Carry it in your pocket on days when life seems too difficult, as a reminder that with a little trust in Jesus, you can move a mountain.

Have you ever attempted something that you really wanted to accomplish, but you failed because it was just too hard or demanding? Or maybe you've encountered a situation that you couldn't handle, and it seemed like things couldn't change. Think of a time when you have felt like that and you didn't know what to do. Now think of that situation with God in the mix. How would God's involvement in this situation change the outcome for you? After reading this passage you might just find your answer.

Jesus looked at them intently and said, "Humanly speaking, it is impossible. But with God everything is possible." Matthew 19:26

The words that Jesus spoke were short and simple. If we, as humans, are doing things in life that we can't complete on our own, we can always count on God to provide guidance to us. All we have to do is open up our hearts and ask him to.

TALKING WITH GOD

Talk to God about how you're feeling right now. It's OK to express any anger or frustration or confusion that you might be experiencing in your life—especially when those feelings come from an impossible situation you're facing. Ask God to help you with the decisions and situations in your life that seem impossible on your own.

There is no longer Jew or Gentile, slave or free, male or female. For you are all one in Christ Jesus.
Galatians 3:28

Throughout history, many wars were started because one group of people didn't like another group of people. In today's verse, Paul says that we are all children of God, and we are all one in Jesus. No matter if you're from Mississippi or Mongolia, Jesus loves you, and we should be united in Christ.

You might be thinking, "This is a great verse for Bible times, but it doesn't apply today. It talks about slaves, and there's no slavery anymore in our country—and this verse only applies to way back then." But if you think about our culture today, you see how some people are treated differently because of race, religion, handicap, or even the groups or organizations in which they participate. We ought to look at everyone as a child of God.

Why would Paul write these words? Because anytime we believe we're better than someone else, it makes it impossible for us to love our neighbors as we love ourselves. Examine your heart. Is there someone you believe doesn't deserve your attention? Perhaps God wants to change your heart today.

TALKING WITH GOD

Pray today that God would allow you to look at everyone as his children. We are all one in him. Ask God to forgive you for being judgmental and to remove the obstacle of pride, which can hinder you from seeing all people as his children.

SIN & SEPARATION

A LITTLE EXTRA

Try to say something kind to every person you speak with today. Can you make it all day? If you mess up, ask God to forgive you, and start over tomorrow.

VERSE 264:
Titus 2:11

A LITTLE EXTRA

With parental permission, watch this video by The Skit Guys for a picture of grace: youtube.com/watch?v=EhoFEuw2GPA. Christ's sacrifice on the cross took what was unforgivable and made it forgivable. If you have any sins that need forgiveness, today is the day to trust Jesus to forgive them and leave them behind.

For the grace of God has been revealed, bringing salvation to all people. Titus 2:11

There are many definitions for grace. Grace can be considered an undeserved gift. Some people say it's **G**od's **R**iches **A**t **C**hrist's **E**xpense. Dictionary.com says grace is a pardon or issuing of mercy. Whatever definition you prefer, one truth remains the same: God's grace offers salvation to all. No one can do enough good acts to earn the favor that God offers. It is only through his generosity—through Jesus' death on the cross and his resurrection—that our relationship with God is restored. God offers grace, and we need to respond with trust and invite Jesus to be our Savior. What amazing grace!

TALKING WITH GOD

If you have never made the decision to follow Jesus and receive his gift of forgiveness, you can do it today. Tell God you are sorry for your sins and you need the gift of forgiveness that he offers. Commit to follow him for the rest of your life. Thank him for saving you. If you have already made this decision, thank God for the gift of salvation that he has given you. Ask for his daily help to be a follower of Jesus. Ask God to help your trust in him grow every day as you live and reveal his kingdom.

"But be sure to fear the Lord and faithfully serve him. Think of all the wonderful things he has done for you." 1 Samuel 12:24

It may seem a little weird to talk about fearing God and realizing he is wonderful at the same time. Which is it? Are we supposed to be afraid of him, or are we supposed to be listing the wonderful things he has done? The answer is YES! Fearing God and remembering the wonderful things he has done can actually happen at the same time!

Sometimes fear can also mean awe. In today's verse, God didn't want people to be cowering in their homes afraid of him. Quite the opposite: God wanted the people to be constantly mindful of the times he had been faithful in the past.

Consider the pattern of God's people in the Old Testament: God would do wonderful things. They would forget and experience consequences. Then the people would remember God and turn to him again. This would repeat for generations. The prophet Samuel was giving a warning to the people, who wanted a king so they could be like other nations. God gave them the king they asked for but cautioned them to not forget that he alone was the one who had provided for them.

TALKING WITH GOD

Spend some time thanking God for the wonderful things he has done for you. Start with things he's done today, then things he did yesterday, then this week, then this month, and so on. Get into the habit of thinking about God's faithfulness, and your trust in him will grow.

VERSE 265:
1 Samuel 12:24

A LITTLE EXTRA

Read the story in Acts 4 about two men captured for preaching about God. When the men were questioned, they had a great answer about fearing God vs. fearing people.

GOD HEARS
& RESTORES

A LITTLE EXTRA

For more help
sharing your faith,
go to facebook.com/
dare2share and click on
Soul Fuel.

But they couldn't reach him because of the crowd. So they went up to the roof and took off some tiles. Then they lowered the sick man on his mat down into the crowd, right in front of Jesus. Seeing their faith, Jesus said to the man, "Young man, your sins are forgiven." Luke 5:19-20

Do you know the whole story? This group of guys desperately wanted to bring their disabled friend to Jesus for healing. But the place was packed out. They couldn't even get in the door. So they got creative. They went up on the roof, ripped a hole in it, and lowered their friend's stretcher down right in front of Jesus. And it worked! Jesus saw their faith and healed their friend, both physically and spiritually.

Do you have friends who are in desperate need of physical, emotional, relational, or spiritual healing? Friends you need to get to Jesus? Are you being creative about finding a way for them to meet up with him?

Try one of these ideas or come up with one of your own:

- Invite them to youth group
- Watch a movie together that will open the door to a serious spiritual conversation
- Buy them a ticket to join you at a Christian concert
- Take them for a latte and talk candidly about Jesus

Get serious about helping your friends meet Jesus. Make a plan. Don't just leave it to random chance—because their very lives depend on it.

TALKING WITH GOD

Talk to God about how you could creatively introduce your friends to Jesus. Then step out and do it.

"The eyes of the Lord search the whole earth in order to strengthen those whose hearts are fully committed to him. What a fool you have been! From now on you will be at war." 2 Chronicles 16:9

When you look close at the sin committed against God in the Bible you will see that people in our world today struggle with the exact same kinds of sins and temptations and pitfalls.

This verse about having a heart fully committed to God comes from a sin that many kings made, starting with the very first king of Israel, Saul. The sin that caused Asa to be called a fool was the sin of not relying on God. Asa instead chose to rely on other things that he could control. God wants us to rely on him. Not relying on him is sin.

Does this specific sin sound familiar to you? Have you been guilty of relying on other things instead of being fully committed to God? God wants us to trust in him to be our provider.

However, there is really good news in this verse! God is searching the earth and wants to strengthen those whose hearts are fully committed to him.

VERSE 267:
2 Chronicles 16:9

A LITTLE EXTRA

Read 1 Samuel 15 and see the mistake that the first king of Israel made by not relying on God.

TALKING WITH GOD

Pray this kind of prayer today: *God, I want to have a heart that is fully committed to you. Open my eyes to ways I need to rely on you and not on things that I think I can control. I do not want to repeat the sins of others that led to separation from you.*

SIN &
SEPARATION

VERSE 268:
Isaiah 65:1

A LITTLE EXTRA

Some of the most famous and poetic descriptions of Jesus were written by Isaiah hundreds of years before the birth of Christ. Read Isaiah's description of Jesus in Isaiah 52:13–53:12.

The Lord says, "I was ready to respond, but no one asked for help. I was ready to be found, but no one was looking for me. I said, 'Here I am, here I am!' to a nation that did not call on my name."
Isaiah 65:1

It's easy to criticize the people of Israel because of their inconsistent relationship with God. The reality, however, is that we often act just like them. When another country invaded Israel, they would run back to the Lord and repent. Similarly, when we have what we think we need, we wander from God and almost forget that he exists—but then return when we face problems.

During the time of today's verse, the people were sinning more and more. God used his prophet Isaiah to warn the people. The consequence for turning from God would be very difficult for Israel: They would be conquered, and many would die. The young men would be carried off to other countries.

God didn't want this to happen. In fact we see God almost pleading in this verse for someone to look to him for help. He was there waiting and ready to deliver them. But no one asked. In time, though, they would cry out to him for deliverance, but only after many years and difficult consequences.

TALKING WITH GOD

Pray this kind of prayer today: *God, open my eyes to see you calling out to me every day. Forgive me for not hearing you. Forgive me for not calling on your name in every situation. I want to be someone who is constantly looking for you.*

> *"Then if my people who are called by my name will humble themselves and pray and seek my face and turn from their wicked ways, I will hear from heaven and forgive their sins and restore their land."* 2 Chronicles 7:14

What's the last movie you saw where the main character realized they were wrong and asked for forgiveness? You probably can think of a few. How about songs that are all about being sorry for a wrong that has been done? You may be able to think of a few of these, too.

Now try and think about a song or movie where a main character gets revenge for something that's been done against them. This is a common storyline, isn't it? We are used to seeing stories or hearing songs where people take control of a situation or get their sweet revenge.

Now try and remember a movie where the main character gets on their knees and repents to God for sin and asks God to intervene or to restore their situation. Yeah, that one doesn't happen very often, does it? God's instructions usually go against what we normally see around us in our culture. Anyone can read them but few people do. God's instructions bring life and healing.

TALKING WITH GOD

Pray this prayer, or one with a similar theme: *God, I realized that healing in my life only comes from humbling myself, turning away from wickedness, and turning to you. You are a God who hears his children from heaven and restores all things.*

GOD HEARS & RESTORES

VERSE 269:
2 Chronicles 7:14

A LITTLE EXTRA

Think you're too young to make a difference? Read about an 8-year-old king who led his entire nation back to God, in 2 Chronicles 34.

GOD HEARS & RESTORES

A LITTLE EXTRA

Check out the website everystudent.com. You'll be better prepared for your follow-up conversations with your friends.

"In the same way, there is joy in the presence of God's angels when even one sinner repents."
Luke 15:10

Just imagine it! There's a party in heaven whenever someone puts their trust in Christ! Pretty incredible, isn't it? And God has made it clear that you have a part to play in helping the angels party on—you get to invite everyone in your life to come meet the Jesus you know and love.

So here's a simple way to do just that. Try sending the following message to your friends who don't know him. You can do this via social media, email, or a handwritten personal note:

There's something very important that I want to tell you about. Yeah, you might think this is kind of a weird thing for me to do, but I believe this is the most important truth in the world…and because you mean a lot to me, I want to be sure you know about it.

Please go to gospeljourney.com and watch the video there called Life in 6 Words: The GOSPEL. *Please just check it out. It will mean a lot to me if you're willing to do this.*

I'm not saying you'll necessarily agree with this video, but I feel like it's something you should at least think about. I'd like to talk to you in the next day or two about what you think of it. So expect a call from me and we'll talk about it then.

Like I said, you mean a lot to me. That's why I want to share this with you.

TALKING WITH GOD

Pray for your friends who will be receiving this note.

All Scripture is inspired by God and is useful to teach us what is true and to make us realize what is wrong in our lives. It corrects us when we are wrong and teaches us to do what is right. God uses it to prepare and equip his people to do every good work. 2 Timothy 3:16–17

VERSE 271:
2 Timothy 3:16–17

Have you ever had a really big decision to make but you didn't know if it was right or wrong? Which way should you go, or what should you do? Did you ask other people to help you make the decision? Did you weigh the good and bad with a chart outlining the pros and cons? Did you pray? Did you search your Bible for an answer?

Look at the first words of this passage. Scripture is a written word inspired by God. It's the primary way he communicates with you. God's words can help you when you have big decisions to make. And those words can teach you how to live.

The more you know the Bible, the more you can discover God's wisdom. God is ready to help you lead a wise, Jesus-centered life.

TALKING WITH GOD

Pray that God would begin to use Scripture in your life the way today's passage describes. Pray that your first step in making decisions would be to seek God through his Word. Pray that God would prepare you and equip you to do good works as you live and reveal the kingdom of God.

A LITTLE EXTRA

Read today's passage, and make a list of the things that Scripture can do in our lives. Beneath each word, write a specific instance where God has used the Bible in that way in your life.

VERSE 272:
Judges 7:7-8

A LITTLE EXTRA

Read 1 Samuel 17 for another story of God doing something surprising and risky. What needs to happen for you to be ready to trust God enough to take a risk and live and reveal his kingdom?

The Lord told Gideon, "With these 300 men I will rescue you and give you victory over the Midianites. Send all the others home." So Gideon collected the provisions and rams' horns of the other warriors and sent them home. But he kept the 300 men with him. Judges 7:7-8

God likes to surprise us. He likes doing things that make people look and say, "What just happened?!?" God likes getting involved in a situation where everyone thinks they know what will happen next—and then doing something completely unexpected.

In today's passage, God redefines the concept of a battle plan. Military leaders would argue that in most situations, you want to have the larger number of troops. In Gideon's situation, God disagrees. Why? Two possible reasons: First, instead of the people looking to their own strength when the situation got sticky, God wanted them to look to him. Second, God wanted everyone who saw the battle to know that Gideon's army didn't defeat the Midianites because of their own manpower or tactical advantage; Gideon's soldiers won the battle because they trusted God, and God fought for them.

And God wants the same for you. It's risky to follow God, but it's worth it.

TALKING WITH GOD

Pray this kind of prayer: *God, help me look to you in all situations. Please forgive me for trying to solve problems on my own without first talking with you. Help me trust you more, and help me make decisions that cause people to recognize your strength in my life and not my own.*

For the more we suffer for Christ, the more God will shower us with his comfort through Christ.
2 Corinthians 1:5

It's crazy how life can be so wonderful yet painful at the same time. All people suffer in some way because difficult things happen in life. There is no escaping it. People don't go looking for opportunities to suffer. That's because suffering is painful. We are not guaranteed that there will be no suffering when we follow Christ; in fact, Jesus said that if he suffered we would also suffer.

Jesus was the promised Messiah, but his message and ministry didn't line up with what many people expected. The people anticipated a king who would deliver them from the countries that ruled over them. But Jesus provided a different kind of deliverance. When he came he talked with power. He said things that no person who ever walked on the face of the earth had said. He had real powers to heal. He was legit!

But Jesus had a different way to take over the world that didn't involve weapons and armies and battles. He would use suffering.

The suffering of Jesus would provide a way for God's kingdom to be built—a kingdom that would never fall. That kingdom continues to grow, and people have shared in Christ's suffering. Every time a person has suffered for Jesus he has been there and comforted them.

TALKING WITH GOD

Pray that when you experience times of suffering, God would help you suffer with honor for his glory. Thank God for the promise that he is with you to comfort you every time you suffer.

VERSE 273:
2 Corinthians 1:5

A LITTLE EXTRA

Read what James says about trials and suffering in James 1:2-4.

287

GOD HEARS & RESTORES

A LITTLE EXTRA

Take a piece of toilet paper. Write on it the sin that you want to stop dragging around behind you. Now flush it down the toilet as a symbol of God's faithfulness to forgive you.

If we claim we have no sin, we are only fooling ourselves and not living in the truth. But if we confess our sins to him, he is faithful and just to forgive us our sins and to cleanse us from all wickedness. 1 John 1:8-9

Trying to hide sin from God is like having toilet paper stuck to your shoe. You might ignore it, but everyone around you can see the evidence. It's obvious that you are not completely clean. Confessing your sins means admitting your struggles to God (which he already knows anyway), and asking for his forgiveness and his help.

Are there sins in your life that you are pretending don't exist? Are there sins you realize you are committing but need to stop? Is there anything in your life that you know you should be doing but you are avoiding instead? Do you have unresolved issues in any of your relationships? Is there any unforgiveness in your life? Share them with God now.

We can confess our sin to God every day. One by one. There is no shame in admitting to God that we need his forgiveness.

TALKING WITH GOD

If there is anything you were too ashamed to admit to God earlier, now is the time to confess. You are only fooling yourself if you think that you can hide anything from God. God knows the truth and wants you to live in the truth as well. Make a commitment to confess your sin every day, one by one.

Before reading this passage today, think about your friendships. Write down the names of your two or three closest friends. What makes these friendships so special? What qualities of your friends do you value the most? Take a few moments to really think about these friendships, and then read the following verse:

A friend is always loyal, and a brother is born to help in time of need. Proverbs 17:17

In this passage, the word *brother* is used as a synonym for a true friend. In other words, the mark of a true friend is someone who acts like a true blood relative and is deeply concerned about you. This person is loyal to you and committed to you like a brother or sister when things are tough or aren't going well for you. It's easy for a friend to spend time with you when it's all the fun and games, but what about during tough days?

As you think about your friendships, here are two things to consider:

1. What kinds of friends surround you? Are they the kinds of friends who are loyal, committed, and will stick with you like a brother or sister?

2. What kind of friend are you? Are you the most loyal and committed friend you can be?

TALKING WITH GOD

As you talk with God today, ask him to show you who your true friends are. Ask God to teach you how to be a good friend and to help you trust that his way of friendship is best—for you and for your friends.

ONENESS
WITH GOD

VERSE 275:
Proverbs 17:17

A LITTLE EXTRA

Read Proverbs 17:17 with the friends you listed at the start of today's reading, and ask them how you can be a better friend. As a group, commit to becoming the kinds of friends described in this passage.

VERSE 276:
John 4:34

A LITTLE EXTRA

Jesus was teaching the disciples to focus on living and revealing God's kingdom and to avoid distractions. What things are distracting you right now? Write them down and ask God to remove them from your life.

Jews and Samaritans did not like each other—in fact, it isn't an exaggeration to say that they often hated each other. So when Jesus and his disciples traveled through Samaria, it sparked a surprising encounter and unusual conversation.

Everyone was hungry, so the disciples headed off to go find food, while Jesus stayed behind at a well. He began a conversation with a woman who ended up coming to faith in Jesus, and she experienced forgiveness for her sins. She ran off to tell people in her town.

Meanwhile the disciples returned and offered Jesus the food they obtained. But Jesus made a statement that must have left his disciples feeling really frustrated:

Then Jesus explained: "My nourishment comes from doing the will of God, who sent me, and from finishing his work." John 4:34

They went all the way to get food and someone already fed Jesus? What was Jesus talking about here?

Jesus was teaching the disciples what it looks like to be urgent about living and revealing God's kingdom. Jesus cared more about the mission than food. Yes, we need physical food to keep our bodies nourished, but we cannot live a life that reveals God's kingdom if we aren't being fed spiritually, too.

TALKING WITH GOD

Focus your prayer on the kingdom of God. Ask God to fill your heart and mind with very specific ways that he wants you to live and reveal his kingdom today. Write down whatever thoughts come to your heart and mind.

And so he did only a few miracles there because of their unbelief. Matthew 13:58

Did Jesus need people to believe in him in order to do miracles? No. Jesus' ability to perform miracles was based solely on his power as the Son of God, not on people's ability to believe in him. So what happened in today's verse? The people didn't want to believe. They would've rejected anything Jesus did in their midst because of their unbelief. They would have explained it away or just refused to believe their eyes. They were not ready to receive what he had for them.

How can you make yourself ready to receive what Jesus has for you? How can you make yourself more open to the unexpected things God wants to do in your life? Do you struggle to believe he can do anything with a specific area of your life?

TALKING WITH GOD

Ask God to show you if you have an attitude of unbelief that is keeping you from experiencing all that he has for you. Open your heart to receive the miracles God has for you by believing that he can do all things.

A LITTLE EXTRA

Think about one area of your life where you need a miracle, but you struggle to believe it could happen. Create a calendar event one week away, and name the event "miracle." Spend this week praying that God would grow your trust in him to believe he can do a miracle in the area you need. When the calendar event arrives, if your trust in God has grown in this area, mark it as completed. If you're still struggling with unbelief, postpone the event for another week. Keep postponing the event until your trust in God has grown and you're waiting for the miracle God might want to do.

GOD HEARS & RESTORES

VERSE 278:
Isaiah 40:31

A LITTLE EXTRA

The next time you see a bird soaring high in the sky, stop and watch. If the bird is *truly* soaring, you won't see much flapping of wings, because unseen currents of air keep the bird in the air. Let that sight remind you that when you learn to *truly* trust God, he will provide strength—maybe even unseen strength—for you to live and reveal his kingdom.

But those who trust in the Lord will find new strength. They will soar high on wings like eagles. They will run and not grow weary. They will walk and not faint. Isaiah 40:31

There you are, lined up with the rest of your classmates. Someone had the great idea that all students should run a mile in gym class. So here you stand, preparing to test yourself against the clock and your peers to see if you have what it takes. The coach yells, "Start" and off you go.

After a few hundred feet you marvel at how easy it is. You're not even breaking a sweat. After another minute or so, it happens. All of the energy drains from your body. Your muscles turn to rubber. You wonder if you can even finish the race.

We have those moments in our walk with Jesus, too, when we are tired and feel like we can't go on. The good news is that if you trust in the Lord, he will give you new strength. God may not give you what you expect, but he will give you exactly what you need.

TALKING WITH GOD

If you are tired today because of difficult situations, don't ask God to remove the problems; ask him to help you to trust him more. As you trust him more, you will find new strength to live and reveal God's kingdom.

Prayer can be one of the most rewarding and stressful things we do as Christ-followers. Have you ever been afraid to pray? Have there been times when the sin in your life made you ashamed and embarrassed to talk to God? Or maybe you struggle with feeling God doesn't know who you are and that you're wasting his time?

This High Priest of ours understands our weaknesses, for he faced all of the same testings we do, yet he did not sin. So let us come boldly to the throne of our gracious God. There we will receive his mercy, and we will find grace to help us when we need it most. Hebrews 4:15–16

In today's passage, we're reminded that even when we are afraid to come to God because of our sin, we'll find grace and mercy. Grace is an undeserved favor that we can never earn, no matter how good of a person we are. Mercy means not receiving the eternal punishment for our sin that we have earned. We can come boldly because God knows who we are and what we've done but loves us anyway.

TALKING WITH GOD

When you talk with God today, resist the temptation to introduce yourself. Simply speak from your heart and share your excitement, concerns, and fears with God as you would a trusted friend.

SIN &
SEPARATION

VERSE 279:
Hebrews 4:15–16

A LITTLE EXTRA

Make a list of all the temptations you face. Once you've got a thorough list, spend some time thinking about today's passage— and remember that Jesus was tempted by the same things. Jesus, God's Son, was tempted, just like you. Ask God to help you trust him enough to do the right thing, even when it's difficult, and to use your life to reveal his kingdom to others.

VERSE 280:
Ephesians 5:21

A LITTLE EXTRA

Read Matthew 26:36-39. How did Jesus submit to God?

And further, submit to one another out of reverence for Christ. Ephesians 5:21

What's the first word that comes to your mind when you hear the word *submission*? Maybe you immediately think of some professional wrestler cranking on some poor guy's neck until he has to "tap out" in total submission, or an older brother sitting on your chest yelling at you to say "Uncle." So why would God want us to submit to one another?

The problem we have with understanding this verse today is that our culture has totally messed up our understanding of the word *submit*. Here are a few things submitting *doesn't* mean:

1. Putting yourself in a harmful situation or allowing yourself to remain in a harmful situation.
2. Being treated as not equal to someone else.
3. Seeing yourself as weak or lost.
4. Being forced to do something.

Here are a few truths about the biblical meaning of submission. It's **voluntary**. It's not something that's forced upon you. Submitting is **mutual**. Submit to one another. Submission is fulfilled when it's a two-way street because both parties love Jesus and want the best for each other. Submitting leads to **serving**, which is one of the major components of healthy relationships and changed hearts. Submitting takes tremendous **inner strength** and **maturity**.

God wants us to submit to one another and to him, because God desires beautiful, healthy, eternal relationships. Are you strong enough to submit?

TALKING WITH GOD
Think about someone you'd like to have a better relationship with: your mom, dad, brother or sister, a friend. Ask God to open the door for you to submit and serve that person in some way today. Ask God for the strength and maturity to submit.

And whatever you do or say, do it as a representative of the Lord Jesus, giving thanks through him to God the Father. Colossians 3:17

Some company names represent a standard of high quality. It's bigger than a logo; it's about the relationship a company has with its customers. Loyalty is the goal, so if the product meets the highest standards, the name makes all the difference.

Being a Christ-follower means that the name of Jesus makes all the difference. He is the high standard by which we measure our lives. His name stands for integrity, quality, perfection, and honesty. If we choose to follow Jesus and be more like him, we carry his name on our lives.

Everything matters to God. The smallest act has significance as a believer in Jesus. Nothing is too ordinary when you work for Jesus.

As representatives of Jesus, everything we say and do reflects back on him. So how's your reflection right now? If you were to get a grade or report on how well you represent the name of Jesus in your actions and words, what grade or score would you get?

TALKING WITH GOD

If you purposely do something today as if you were doing it for Jesus, how would that make it different? How does looking at more things and thinking about them as a representative of Jesus change how you conduct your life? Pray for God's help in this area.

VERSE 281:
Colossians 3:17

A LITTLE EXTRA

Does a song remind you of this verse or the truth it reveals? Find one, and then set it as your morning alarm song. Start your day with a quick reminder of God's standard for every day. Be encouraged by it, and meet it with joy instead of stress. You're working for the absolute best.

GOD HEARS & RESTORES

A LITTLE EXTRA

Read what Paul wrote about groaning for the Lord's return in Romans 8:18-25.

God will do this, for he is faithful to do what he says, and he has invited you into partnership with his Son, Jesus Christ our Lord. 1 Corinthians 1:9

Have you ever been so hungry or in such need of something that you couldn't use words to describe your need? Sometimes a groan from deep within is the best way to communicate the deepest want of something.

This groaning or need for the Lord to return is exactly what God inspired Paul to write this chapter of Scripture. God was changing the Corinthian Christ-followers in speech and knowledge, and that led to great testimony to others about who Jesus was. Then Paul pointed out that God had given them spiritual gifts to help them as they waited on Jesus to return. As they waited then and as we wait now, Jesus himself is sustaining us through our relationship with God.

All of this encouragement explodes into the final two points found in this verse to give us hope: a call to remember that our God has always been and will always be faithful, and our partnership with the Son of God. Not only does God increase oneness with us by sustaining us until the final return of Jesus in his full glory, but we also enjoy the guarantee of joining him then because of a partnership with Jesus living in us now. We can be confident of our future.

TALKING WITH GOD

Thank God for these words today that remind you of all the things he is doing to help you as you wait for Jesus to return.

Fear of the Lord is the foundation of true knowledge, but fools despise wisdom and discipline.
Proverbs 1:7

SIN & SEPARATION

What does it mean to fear the Lord? For the Hebrew readers of Proverbs it didn't mean they were horrified and petrified of God; it meant something quite different. In their world, it meant recognizing God's great character and responding to God by trusting, worshipping, obeying, and serving him.

You probably realize that you often listen to and follow instructions from people you respect and trust. But is this true for God? Is God your source for truth and wisdom? More than that, even if you know his truth and wisdom, do you follow through with living out his truth in your life? In this passage, there is a stark contrast between those who fear God and those who reject his wisdom and call to a disciplined life. It's one thing to respect God's instruction, but it's another thing to put his instructions into practice.

If you are struggling in this area, perhaps you have an inaccurate view of who God is and what he means to you. When you have a "fear of the Lord" and respect and trust him completely, you're more likely to listen to him.

TALKING WITH GOD

Ask God to help you trust him as the source of true knowledge and wisdom. Confess the times you've resisted God's discipline, and ask him to discipline you like a loving father disciplines his children. Ask God to help you become more open to his leadership in your life as you seek to live and reveal his kingdom.

VERSE 283:
Proverbs 1:7

A LITTLE EXTRA

This week, read Proverbs 1–3. As you read through these chapters, write down all the benefits of following God's wisdom. How can seeing God as all-knowing and wise help you?

SIN &
SEPARATION

VERSE 284:
Mark 14:72

A LITTLE EXTRA

Thankfully, Peter's story didn't end here. He would see Jesus again, Jesus would forgive him, and Peter would not deny Jesus again, even if he cost him his life. Read Acts 2 to see one example of how God used Peter to live and reveal the kingdom of God.

And immediately the rooster crowed the second time. Suddenly, Jesus' words flashed through Peter's mind: "Before the rooster crows twice, you will deny three times that you even know me." And he broke down and wept. Mark 14:72

Man, that's heavy stuff. Peter, one of Jesus' closest friends, denied knowing Jesus when he needed him the most. Can you imagine if someone did that to you—how badly that betrayal would hurt? Can you imagine doing that to someone else?

If we were to be honest, we probably could all admit that we've denied knowing Jesus at some point. Perhaps you've never denied Jesus with your words, but what about your actions? Or your attitude? If so, you probably know how Peter felt: wrecked.

Because we serve a God who forgives us, we don't like to think about our failures too long. But it's helpful to remember how sinful we are, because it leads us to a place of gratitude for God's gift of forgiveness.

TALKING WITH GOD

Spend a few moments confessing the times you've denied Jesus by your words, actions, or attitudes. Let yourself feel the weight of your sin. Remember what it feels like. Ask God to forgive you for all of the times you denied him, naming them as specifically as you can remember. Accept God's forgiveness, and let yourself feel the weight of your sin lift away. Ask God to help you trust him more and live in forgiveness.

"Yes, I am the gate. Those who come in through me will be saved. They will come and go freely and will find good pastures." John 10:9

Ever watched the TV game show *Let's Make a Deal*? Contestants choose to receive a prize hidden behind one of several doors, and their decisions determine what prizes they receive. Similarly, the choices we make shape our lives.

In today's passage, Jesus uses a scene familiar to his listeners: sheep passing through a gate and entering a pasture. "Good pasture" represents a relationship with God and life in God's kingdom, the sheep represent all people, and the gate represents Jesus. He is the gate, the doorway to God. Not just one of many ways to God—the only way. Jesus says if we trust him, we will be saved, and we will have free and open access to God any time we want.

Have you taken the step through the gate and begun a relationship with God?

TALKING WITH GOD

If you haven't trusted Jesus for yourself, do it now. Tell God you're sorry for your sin, ask him to forgive you and tell him you trust Jesus to do it, and invite him to lead your life. If you prayed something like that for the first time, tell somebody! And turn to pp. 180-181 for a little more detail. If you've already prayed something like this, thank God for the gift of forgiveness, and look for an opportunity to tell someone else about your relationship with Jesus

A LITTLE EXTRA

Turn on *Let's Make a Deal* and watch the silliness. Contestants never know what's behind each door; they take a guess and hope for the best. But with Jesus, choosing to trust him always leads to the kind of life we desperately want. And every time you walk through a doorway, remember that Jesus is your doorway to God.

CONSEQUENCES & CRYING OUT

VERSE 286:
Psalm 51:17

A LITTLE EXTRA

With your parents' permission, skip one meal today—this is called fasting. (It's OK if it can't be today—pick another day!) During the time you would normally eat, spend time reading the Bible and praying. In other words, substitute physical food with spiritual food! Ask God to help your sacrifice of fasting a meal shape your heart to be fully surrendered to him. Ask God to help you be a living sacrifice, revealing his kingdom to the people in your life.

The sacrifice you desire is a broken spirit. You will not reject a broken and repentant heart, O God.
Psalm 51:17

Psalm 51 records David's response after the prophet Nathan confronted him about his sin of committing adultery and arranging a murder. David knew that one way the people honored their relationship with God was by making appropriate sacrifices for their actions. Sacrifices in the Old Testament ranged from grain and peace offerings to sin and guilt offerings. The purpose of each was to remind God's people of his goodness and their dependency on him. The sacrifice reflected the people's trust in God. David's words in today's passage indicate a deeper understanding of God's desire: a heart that's fully surrendered to God.

TALKING WITH GOD

Pray this prayer or one with a similar theme: *God, sometimes I feel like a pretender who is not fully committed and not fully surrendered to you. But I want to be the kind of person you want me to be, because I trust you. Help me trust you more, so that I can share everything with you and know that you will accept me. I give you my heart today. Use my life to reveal your kingdom today.*

What's your favorite time of year? Spring has many fans: the renewal, and the way the ugliness and death of winter are undone as the flowers break through the dead ground. Life triumphs.

In today's verse, John sees God on the throne, and he has something amazing to say:

And the one sitting on the throne said, "Look, I am making everything new!" And then he said to me, "Write this down, for what I tell you is trustworthy and true." Revelation 21:5

The world around us is full of death, and evil, and hardships, and pain. But spring is coming. The Son is coming out, and the winter of Satan's reign will be over, and everything will be new.

It's more than the change that happens when people put their faith in Jesus. It's the experience of everything being made new. Perfect. Shining. Glorious. What a day that will be.

TALKING WITH GOD

Talk to God about the things in life that bother you. Maybe they're specific things such as bullies, money concerns, grades, or broken relationships. Maybe they're broader concerns, such as wars, murder, or disease. Now thank God for his promise of renewal—that all of those things will be gone when he makes everything new. Ask him to help you trust him and his promise more.

GOD HEARS & RESTORES

VERSE 287:
Revelation 21:5

A LITTLE EXTRA

Go plant something. Seriously! Get some seeds and plant something. If it's spring or summer, you have plenty of options. If it's fall, plant some bulbs that will pop in the spring. If it's winter, you might be able to start some seeds inside so they're ready to go in the spring. When you see them start to bud and grow—even on something you didn't plant—think about the amazing renewal God has promised.

VERSE 288:
1 John 5:4

A LITTLE EXTRA

What are some evil things that you see in the world around you? What are some things that really bother you? Did you realize that one of the most powerful things we can do is talk to God and ask him to fight for these things? Take some extra time today to ask the Lord to take care of the injustices you see.

For every child of God defeats this evil world, and we achieve this victory through our faith.
1 John 5:4

Becoming followers of Christ helps us understand that we belong to him. When we know we are his, we can overcome the evil that Satan sends our way. No, we can't do this on our own, in our own human strength. But what we have is better: God's strength. God is on our side, and God is the one who leads us to victory.

At the heart of true wickedness is a lack of hope. But we find hope and confidence in our faith in who Christ is. Showing others this truth knocks down even the worst evil in our world. When you hold on to a relationship with Jesus, you understand you belong to him. This is what enables us to defeat the enemy and bring a light into the world. Armed as children of God, we can bring down the worst of the worst, knowing it's really the Lord who wins the victory.

TALKING WITH GOD

Ask God to show you some things you can do, in his strength, to take on the evil in the world—at school, on your sports team or band or club, in your neighborhood, at your job, in your youth group, or anywhere else it might be found.

Has someone ever asked you a question that seemed logical and well-intentioned, yet also seemed just way off? Maybe you've trained to run a marathon and a friend asked, "Do you think you'll win?" Probably not. It was a logical question, because your friend knew you had been working really hard. It was a well-intentioned question, because your friend really wanted you to win. But your friend just didn't have the perspective on what it takes to accomplish something like that. Something similar happens between Jesus and a guy named Nicodemus:

Jesus replied, "I tell you the truth, unless you are born again, you cannot see the Kingdom of God."
John 3:3

Jesus is telling Nicodemus that he must be born into a new understanding, a new kingdom; he must become a new person. Jesus is saying that until people believe who he is (the Son of God) and trust what he has come to do (die as a sacrifice for our sins), they can't possibly understand what Jesus is talking about or what he's pointing to. He's basically saying, "Nicodemus, until you fully trust me, it's impossible for you to understand what I'm saying."

What do you understand about Jesus and what he's done for you? Do you fully trust him in the big and small things of life?

TALKING WITH GOD

Ask God to forgive you, and thank him for paying the price for your sin. Ask him to give you a deeper understanding of his plan for your life. Ask God to help you trust him more in the big and small things of life.

GOD HEARS & RESTORES

VERSE 289:
John 3:3

A LITTLE EXTRA

Reach out to family members or friends who have helped you on your spiritual journey. Thank them for helping you understand and trust Jesus more.

GOD HEARS & RESTORES

A LITTLE EXTRA

Write down 10 things that create noise and distraction in your life. Set aside 30 minutes to get away from all of those things at least once this week, and listen to the words of God.

We miss things all the time: a shooting star that flies across the night sky, a stop sign near your school, or the time at your favorite restaurant when your friends got free stuff and you weren't there. Life moves pretty fast, and there's no way we can catch everything.

Do you ever wonder if you miss Jesus?

There's a story in Luke about two people who were followers of Jesus. They'd been in Jerusalem celebrating with him until the last few days of his life. They watched him ride into town like a king and walk out and die like a criminal. They heard that he was alive, but they weren't sure if the stories were true. Today's passage records what happens as they walk down the road out of Jerusalem toward home.

As they talked and discussed these things, Jesus himself suddenly came and began walking with them. But God kept them from recognizing him. Luke 24:15-16

While these two friends are walking down the road, the very person they were talking about joins them. And though Jesus is right in front of their faces, they miss him. How can that be possible?

Are there things in your life that distract you from seeing Jesus? Do these things make you forget that Jesus is walking through life with you? Before you focus on the busyness of your day, enjoy a few moments with Jesus. He promises that he will never leave you or abandon you.

TALKING WITH GOD

Find a quiet place and think about who Jesus is. Sit quietly and enjoy being in God's presence.

And I am certain that God, who began the good work within you, will continue his work until it is finally finished on the day when Christ Jesus returns. Philippians 1:6

ONENESS
WITH GOD

Paul is writing this letter to the church in Philippi. It's a good church. The people have been faithful to proclaim the message of Jesus to their city. And what's more, they started doing that from the moment they trusted in Jesus.

Paul's encouragement in this verse is that it has always been up to God to do the work of drawing people to himself. We need to be faithful to share the gospel (the good news of Jesus' love for us), but God will be faithful to complete it. We receive joy and salvation from Jesus—he nurtures that in us as we share it with others—and he brings it to completion as others embrace the message of Jesus and relationship with him. And no matter how long we live or how many people we share the good news of Jesus with, it won't be over until Jesus returns.

TALKING WITH GOD

Thank God for the day when he began his good work in your life. Ask God to show you the friends in your life who need to hear the message of Jesus.

A LITTLE EXTRA

Use your phone to snap photos of three people in your sphere of influence who need the good news of Jesus. Sync their image with their phone number so that when they call or text, you see their face. Before you answer, say a simple prayer. "God, complete your good work in _____'s life just like you did in mine." Then look for opportunities to share that good news.

VERSE 292:
Matthew 5:3

A LITTLE EXTRA

Is someone in your life going through a rough time? Buy them a card and write an encouraging note telling them you're there for them and praying for them. You might want to include today's verse in the card. Give it to them as soon as you can— and remember to pray for them.

"God blesses those who are poor and realize their need for him, for the Kingdom of Heaven is theirs."
Matthew 5:3

When we hear the word *poor*, we often think of someone who doesn't have any money. But that's not the only definition of *poor*, and Jesus' words in today's passage are not just about someone who doesn't have money, but also about people facing hardships in life.

When you're down, the world will tell you to pick yourself up and try harder. Jesus says that when you feel like life just couldn't get any lower, turn to God and put your faith and hope in him. This goes against everything the world tells you to do.

Jesus then talks about the kingdom of heaven. Throughout the first verses in Matthew 5, Jesus is turning what we know and believe about the world upside-down. He's introducing us to a new way to live and something different to live for—something completely different from what the world offers. The kingdom of heaven is life as God intended, and it lasts forever.

TALKING WITH GOD

Many of us have experienced times "at the bottom of the pit." Think about a time when you felt like there was nowhere else to go, and you couldn't see past the next hour. Thank God for helping you through that time, and ask him to help you think of ways that you can rely on him in the future during life's low moments.

In this section of his letter, the Apostle Peter is discussing when Jesus will return. Many people try to guess or predict exactly when Jesus will return. The Bible warns us not to do that, but to instead be ready for his return whenever it happens. Many other people wonder why he is taking so long to return. This verse explains why he waits:

The Lord isn't really being slow about his promise, as some people think. No, he is being patient for your sake. He does not want anyone to be destroyed, but wants everyone to repent. 2 Peter 3:9

Jesus will return, just as he promised, but every day he waits is an act of grace to people who have not yet chosen to follow him. As Christ-followers, our concern should not be, "Why does Jesus wait so long to return?" Our concern should be, "Every day Jesus waits to return is another day for those I love to trust their lives to Jesus—what can I do to tell my story?"

TALKING WITH GOD

Thank God for having patience and for giving another day for people to have the opportunity to follow him. Take time today to whisper to Jesus the names of the people in your life that you love who do not yet have a relationship with Jesus. Jesus knows their names, but praying for them is powerful.

GOD HEARS & RESTORES

VERSE 293:
2 Peter 3:9

A LITTLE EXTRA

Do you want to know one prayer that is always answered? "Jesus, please give me the opportunity to share your love with someone I talk with today." If you have the courage to pray that prayer today, it will be answered.

GOD HEARS
& RESTORES

"You intended to harm me, but God intended it all for good. He brought me to this position so I could save the lives of many people." Genesis 50:20

One of the most difficult things about trusting God is that we don't have the full picture. When you were a little kid perhaps you wanted to play with an electrical socket and someone was there to tell you no. You had no idea that it would bring pain to you. All you knew was that you wanted to touch it so you cried, pouted, and perhaps even tried to touch it anyway. Whoever stopped you knew more than you about electricity!

This is how it is with God. He knows more. We see pain, uncomfortable situations, or impossible odds. But God sees down the road. He is patient and kind. Whatever mess we find ourselves in, we can look at the lives of people such as Joseph to remember that we serve a God who is in the business of hearing us and restoring our lives.

TALKING WITH GOD

Pray this prayer or one with a similar theme: *God, thank you for the accounts in Scripture that show us how you listen and work to restore broken things in our lives. Help me trust that you see the things might harm me. Help me trust that you are working to save me from those things so that many people may come to know you.*

A LITTLE EXTRA

Declare a day of praise to acknowledge the good things that God has done. Keep a list of good things that came from situations you surely thought would be bad. You will be surprised how you keep thinking of things to add to your list. Keep your list private between you and God. It can be a prayer of thankfulness that lasts all day long.

"I tell you the truth, unless a kernel of wheat is planted in the soil and dies, it remains alone. But its death will produce many new kernels—a plentiful harvest of new lives." John 12:24

Have you ever been to a sports event where the crowd did the wave? It typically starts when one person gets the idea and tries to convince a few people in the area to join in. It's amazing to see and hear the roar of the crowd once it really starts moving. It's cool to be part of something bigger than yourself.

VERSE 295:
John 12:24

In this passage, we see that Jesus understood this concept about God's plan for us. Yes, Jesus is the key component for salvation coming to all of humanity, but he knew that God would use all of his followers to spread the message. Others would rise to spread the good news of Jesus to people around the globe for generations to come.

A LITTLE EXTRA

Choose an area of your life—such as your family, school, neighborhood, team— and think of one thing you can do today to live and reveal God's kingdom in that area.

We each play a role in seeing the work of Jesus fulfilled in the hearts of people, but it requires us being willing to serve others, dying to ourselves, and asking God to help us grow where we're planted and to produce a plentiful harvest.

TALKING WITH GOD

Ask God to open your eyes to the opportunities around you: your family, neighborhood, band, sports teams, school clubs, homeroom, and other places that are part of your life. Ask God to help you see the opportunity the same way he does, and ask God to use you to produce a plentiful harvest.

GOD HEARS
& RESTORES

VERSE 296:
John 6:35

A LITTLE EXTRA

There are a lot of relationships that promise to fulfill your every need, yet they will all fail in the end. Write down the things you're spiritually hungry for, and remember that Jesus is your nourishment for those things. Then write down the things you need to be refreshed in, and remember that he is your water. He is here to sustain you and help you to grow.

Have you ever thought what it would look like if you were dropped off on a deserted island and had to fend for yourself? How would you survive if everything you owned were washed away in a natural disaster? If we were to take away all of the comforts of life and only live on the bare essentials, what would that leave us with? Could you narrow it down to two or three items? Look at what Jesus has to say:

Jesus replied, "I am the bread of life. Whoever comes to me will never be hungry again. Whoever believes in me will never be thirsty." John 6:35

It's interesting how Jesus describes himself in this passage: bread and water. There you have it. The two most essential needs a human has are food and water, and we can only make it a couple of weeks without them.

Imagine what it must be like for our spiritual health. Jesus establishes that everything we need is found in him and that he will never leave us feeling unsatisfied.

TALKING WITH GOD

What is it that you need God to provide today? Is it encouragement or direction? Whatever it may be, allow God to fill you, and resist the urge to seek that in someone or something else.

"But many who are the greatest now will be least important then, and those who seem least important now will be the greatest then."
Mark 10:31

Who do you think is the most influential person in your school? What are some of the characteristics that make this person important? Make a list of those characteristics.

If Jesus is the most influential person who has ever lived, what characteristics make him so important? Make a list of these characteristics, too.

Now compare the two lists. Do the characteristics of Jesus match up with the characteristics of the person you picked as most influential from your school? How similar or different are the lists?

What kinds of traits does our culture value? Do you think that these are traits that would impress God?

TALKING WITH GOD

When you think about your life, which list best describes you? Are you living your life in a way that imitates the traits of Jesus? Create a picture of yourself—it's totally OK if all you can draw is a stick figure. Label the picture with the traits that you know will help you become the person God wants you to become. Pray for each of these traits and ask God to help you develop them in your life. Ask God to bring to light any areas of your life that you should be less concerned with because they will only make you great before other people—areas that ultimately don't matter much to God.

ONENESS
WITH GOD

VERSE 297:
Mark 10:31

A LITTLE EXTRA

To remind you to focus on character traits that are important to God, take a picture of Galatians 5:22-23 in your Bible. Make this your screen saver until you have it memorized.

GOD HEARS & RESTORES

A LITTLE EXTRA

Many songs have been written about the way God will love his people forever. Check out one of the most famous passages of Scripture with this theme: Psalm 136.

The Lord says, "Then I will heal you of your faithlessness; my love will know no bounds, for my anger will be gone forever." Hosea 14:4

Israel was a faithless nation. The people's faithlessness was evident as they turned to other gods and ignored God's commands and even his messengers. The whole Old Testament seems to be like a yo-yo relationship between God and his people. They win wars when they faithfully follow him, but then they are conquered by their enemies when they ignore him.

Verses that talk about God's anger being gone forever and his love knowing no bounds sound like a love letter between two people. God loves his people and wants close relationship, but he cannot be in relationship with anyone tainted by sin. We must call out to God for the healing he talks about in this verse. The healing power of Christ's perfection covers our faithlessness. Only then can God restore and put his anger toward our sinful nature away forever.

There is no in between with God. We are either his enemy or his friend. We're either opposing God or following him. His justice won't allow us to be neutral because we have the sin of faithlessness on us. We must call out to God so that he hears and restores us.

TALKING WITH GOD

Pray this kind of prayer: *God, forgive me for the times that I have been faithless. I want to experience the love you have for me that knows no bounds. I want your anger toward my sin to be gone forever. Cover me in the perfection of your son, Jesus, so our relationship can be restored.*

Jesus called his disciples to him and said, "I tell you the truth, this poor widow has given more than all the others who are making contributions. For they gave a tiny part of their surplus, but she, poor as she is, has given everything she had to live on."
Mark 12:43–44

Many things about worship in Jesus' day looked different from how we worship today. He went to a Jewish temple, and one big difference you would have noticed right away was the way they received the offering. People would wait in line and bring up their offering into a golden container while the rest of the congregation watched.

This was convenient for people who wanted to show off spiritually by letting everyone know how big their offering was. They could take their coins and loudly throw their offering into the containers for everyone to see and hear.

This is why Jesus bragged on the widow who quietly slipped in her last penny.

TALKING WITH GOD

Jesus wasn't impressed by what people gave; he was impressed by their attitude as they gave. He was impressed with the poor widow, because she gave with hope and trust. Jesus focused on the motive of her heart more than her money. In your conversation with God today, ask God to show you anywhere in your life where your motives don't match your actions. It's a dangerous prayer, but you can trust God to gently guide you to a deeper relationship with him.

VERSE 299:
Mark 12:43–44

A LITTLE EXTRA

When was the last time you served God because you wanted to, not because you felt like you had to? Ask God today to change your "have to" into a "want to." Write down any ideas God might bring to mind after you pray that prayer.

GOD HEARS & RESTORES

A LITTLE EXTRA

Is someone in your life experiencing a storm? Write a note of encouragement right now, and deliver it with a favorite cup of coffee or a snack. Share what God is teaching you through this passage, and pray with this person.

Jesus responded, "Why are you afraid? You have so little faith!" Then he got up and rebuked the wind and waves, and suddenly there was a great calm.
Matthew 8:26

Jesus could have prevented this storm. But he didn't. He allowed the whole scene to unfold. He and the disciples got into the boat, Jesus went to sleep, and the storm began to rage. **And the disciples were afraid.**

How could this happen? Jesus was in control, right? Why would he bring the disciples out on the water just so they could be killed in the storm? Should the disciples have done more research to find a calmer path on the water? And how could he be sleeping at a time like this? Didn't he care?

Jesus did care, and he still cares today. Rather than preventing the storm, Jesus allowed the storm to show the disciples his power. There's no smooth sailing in life—expect storms. Many of the storms in life are completely out of your control. You don't see them coming, and you have no ability to fix them. In this desperate moment, call out to Jesus. He's been there all along and wants to calm your storm.

TALKING WITH GOD

A preacher once suggested to pray this way: "Lord, I need you to _____. Because if you don't, I'm afraid that _____." Many people pray the first half, but there's such wisdom in getting to the second half. That's where you can get honest and wrestle with God. Trust him. Share your feelings and fears with him. He's not sleeping.

One of the last prayers Jesus prayed before his crucifixion was for you. Seriously. He had you on his mind when he was about to die.

"I am praying not only for these disciples but also for all who will ever believe in me through their message. I pray that they will all be one, just as you and I are one—as you are in me, Father, and I am in you. And may they be in us so that the world will believe you sent me." John 17:20-21

VERSE 301:
John 17:20-21

Did you get that? Jesus prayed for everyone who would ever believe. That includes you. Think about it. If this prayer was one of the last ones he prayed, it must have been a pretty big deal to him. What is he asking of us? He's asking that Christians be unified.

A LITTLE EXTRA

Try this challenge. The next time someone gets on your nerves (and you know it'll happen), instead of reacting to them, let it remind you to pray for your friends who don't know Jesus. Instead of Satan using other people to cause you to struggle, God can use other people to remind you to pray.

Does that mean we have to get along all the time? No. Churches are made up of a diverse group of people, so there are bound to be disagreements once in awhile. That's not the point of Jesus' prayer. He wants us to love one another because it matters to the mission of the church. The best way to demonstrate that Jesus is real is to love one another.

TALKING WITH GOD

Ask God to help you fulfill Jesus' prayer request. Ask for patience and the ability to love other Christ-followers. Pray by name for people you have a hard time loving.

SHARING YOUR GOD-STORY

EVERYONE HAS A STORY TO TELL. If you're a Christ-follower, you have a God-story to tell, too. It's important that you learn to share your God-story, because there are people in your life that won't listen to anyone else. What if God used your God-story to lead a family member or friend to trust Jesus?

Your God-story can include lots of details, but it's helpful to narrow your focus down to three parts:

1. **Your life before Christ.** What were your struggles? How were you trying to live, and what was going wrong? Warning: Don't fall into the temptation of bragging about your past. Spend the LEAST time on this part.

2. **How you trusted Christ.** Who told you about Jesus? What made you say yes? Be as specific as possible in this part.

3. **Your life since you trusted Christ.** How has God been present in your life since you trusted Jesus? How has God used your life to help others? You may not consider this stuff very often, so take your time and think and pray. You should spend the MOST time on this part.

It's important to think carefully about your God-story, because you may only get a few moments to share it. Write and revise and refine until you can tell your story in three minutes or less.

The first time you tell your God-story is the hardest, so practice telling your God-story to someone you care about and who will give you honest, caring feedback.

Your God-story is actually God's story, so be open to his leadership when it's time to tell the story. God is working in people's lives, and your God-story is likely a part of their spiritual journey. Trust God to open the right door at the right time and give you the right words to say. Tell your story!

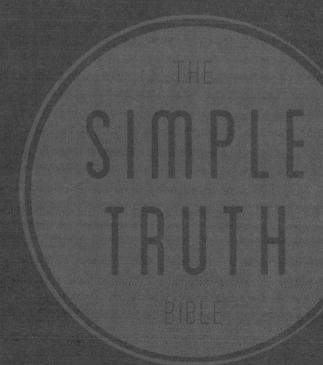

GOD HEARS
& RESTORES

VERSE 302:
2 Samuel 22:4

A LITTLE EXTRA

Read 2 Samuel, and as you look at each of the trials that David went through, write down how God took care of David in each circumstance.

"I called on the Lord, who is worthy of praise, and he saved me from my enemies." 2 Samuel 22:4

From the moment David took down Goliath with one stone, it seems the ranks of his enemies grew bigger and bigger. King Saul grew jealous of David and tried to kill him on several occasions. As king, David was constantly going to war with other countries that wanted to conquer Israel. One of David's own sons even tried to overthrow him as king. David's life was not easy. You would think that David would be angry or frustrated as he looked back on a life spent trying to save his own skin. Instead, after all these struggles, David sings a song of praise to God in today's verse. David recognized that it was God who kept him safe from all of these attackers, and he thanked him for it.

Sometimes life can bring some tough struggles. In those times, remember that God will get you through them. He loves you and has a plan to raise you up and get you to the other side of your problems. This is God's promise. You can praise him for his great works and how he is going to protect you during hard times.

TALKING WITH GOD

In our darkest times, God shines through to give us hope and salvation. Talk to God about some of the problems you are facing today, and ask God to help you trust him to act on your behalf. Then, praise him for loving you enough to come to your rescue.

"For the Son of Man came to seek and save those who are lost." Luke 19:10

Do you want to be like Jesus? Do you really?
If you do, you must be just like Jesus and remain on a constant search-and-rescue mission for people who are spiritually lost.

Seeking and saving people stands at the very center of Jesus' plan and purposes for us. Over and over again in the Scripture, we see him sending his followers out to spread the word about God's outrageous love and amazing grace.

Just think, the very first thing Jesus told his fishermen followers as he was calling them was this: *Jesus called out to them, "Come, follow me, and I will show you how to fish for people!" (Matthew 4:19).* Or consider these words: *"As the Father has sent me, so I am sending you" (John 20:21).* And his parting words before ascending into heaven were, *"And you will be my witnesses, telling people about me everywhere" (Acts 1:8).*

You get the clear picture that from beginning to end, Jesus was calling his followers to get the word out that there is hope for people who are spiritually lost, help for the hurting, and eternal life for those who put their trust in him.

Jesus was all about seeking and saving people. We should be, too. Because what drove Jesus should drive everything we do.

TALKING WITH GOD

Let Jesus know that you want to be more like him. Ask him to give you a heart that burns and breaks for people who are spiritually lost. Pray for your friends who need to hear his message of grace. Then set off on your search-and-rescue mission today.

GOD HEARS & RESTORES

VERSE 303:
Luke 19:10

A LITTLE EXTRA

Read 2 Timothy 1:7-8. Talk to God about how you're feeling about the challenge laid out to you in this passage. Write a four-sentence poem expressing your doubts and fears to God. Then ask him to help you trust him more.

319

SIN &
SEPARATION

VERSE 304:
Proverbs 14:12

A LITTLE EXTRA

Organize a scavenger hunt with your family or some friends. As you search for each item, remember God's words about trusting and following his path. And remember that God doesn't hide from us.

There is a path before each person that seems right, but it ends in death. Proverbs 14:12

Have you ever taken a shortcut, only to find it got you lost? Maybe your dad (or mom) was convinced that Highway 16 really was the fastest way to reach your destination, but it ended up taking you far off course. Or perhaps one of your friends knew the easiest way to get through a new subdivision—but you had to use your phone's GPS to escape the neighborhood's maze.

In life there are many instances where we have the choice to take the path that seems easy and right, yet it only leads to destruction. Many times the paths that seem right are wider, easier, simpler, and more obvious. God's path is often narrower and less obvious, but it leads to life.

As followers of Jesus, we can be sure that there is a great reward waiting for us in heaven when we trust in Christ and follow his path. We can also have confidence that following his path will lead to the best life possible.

TALKING WITH GOD

Ask God to identify the shortcuts you're attempting in your life. Ask God to show you the ways in which you are trying to navigate your own path instead of trusting him and his path. Pray for God's forgiveness for the ways in which your shortcuts are hindering your relationship with him. Seek God's help in getting back on the path of living and revealing his kingdom.

GOD HEARS
& RESTORES

If you confess with your mouth that Jesus is Lord and believe in your heart that God raised him from the dead, you will be saved. For it is by believing in your heart that you are made right with God, and it is by confessing with your mouth that you are saved....For "Everyone who calls on the name of the Lord will be saved." Romans 10:9–10, 13

VERSE 305:
Romans 10:9-10, 13

Today's passage contains two important words: *confessing* and *believing*. Confessing means admitting. Are you ready to admit that Jesus is Lord? He's more than a moral example or a good teacher. He wants to guide your life. Believing means trusting; are you ready to put your trust in the life, death, and resurrection of Jesus? Jesus paid the price for your sins; do you trust him today?

Believing and confessing are the two responses God asks from us as we consider our relationship with Christ. It's a combination of trusting deep in our soul and letting that trust spill out into our lives as we live and reveal God's kingdom. God will save anyone who responds to his invitation.

TALKING WITH GOD

Pray this kind of prayer: *Jesus, you are more than a good guy; you are the only Son of God, Savior of the world. I need you in my life. I need you to do for me what I can't do for myself. Please forgive me when I don't trust you, and help me trust you more today.*

A LITTLE EXTRA

A "trust fall" was an old-school youth ministry game designed to help students learn how to trust their friends. With parental permission, do an online search for videos of "trust falls." After watching a few, try to create a new activity that could help build trust in your youth group or with your friends.

GOD HEARS
& RESTORES

VERSE 306:
2 Timothy 1:7

A LITTLE EXTRA

Write the name of your greatest fear in the middle of a piece of paper. Now cross it out and write 2 Timothy 1:7 underneath. Then write the verse three more times around the paper. Finally, write what that verse means to you in a small paragraph. Fold the paper and keep it somewhere so you can go back and be reminded.

For God has not given us a spirit of fear and timidity, but of power, love, and self-discipline.
2 Timothy 1:7

Ever thought about how much you love to be afraid? There is the heart-pumping speed of a roller coaster. Movies that cause us to bite our nails and hide under our seats grab our attention. There's even a TV show called "Fear Factor," where you could make a lot of money if you would be willing to compete amid some serious terror.

Somehow those spine-tingling experiences are different from moments when you are gripped by true fear. Standing up for what's right when everyone laughs is far more horrifying than any amusement park ride. Fear is a feeling. But it should never define or guide us.

This verse is speaking of the kind of fear that holds us back or stops us in our tracks. God's Spirit lives in us, and he gives us power, love, and self-discipline. He brings order when fear drowns us in chaos. And he gives us strength to live into his story for our lives, even when we're afraid.

TALKING WITH GOD

What's your greatest fear? Tell God about it now. Tell him how you can't just get over it. Ask God to help you trust him and to show you how he conquers even the worst fears.

When you were a kid you probably brought home some blob of art on a paper that made your parents say, "Oh, wow! That is amazing. We have no idea what it is—but it is amazing!" And then they slapped it on the fridge and showed it off to everyone.

Even the smallest amount of faith that we show in God is like refrigerator art to him. God is so excited when we trust him even when we haven't seen him with our eyes. It's what makes God smile. Just listen to what God says about faith:

And it is impossible to please God without faith. Anyone who wants to come to him must believe that God exists and that he rewards those who sincerely seek him. Hebrews 11:6

This verse is nestled in the midst of one of the coolest lists in the Bible: people who displayed faith in their life. It's as if God is a proud parent showing off refrigerator art when he describes their acts of faith. Each person who took God at his word also stole his heart and showed him great love.

TALKING WITH GOD

Take some time to share with God very specifically how you trust him. Let your prayers today be a series of statements to God that start with, "God, I trust you with…." Close by asking God to help you trust him more.

GOD HEARS & RESTORES

VERSE 307:
Hebrews 11:6

A LITTLE EXTRA

Is there any area of your life where you are struggling to trust God? Is it hard for you to trust God with friendships, grades, your parents, your future, or any other worry or fear that runs through your head every day? List the areas where you struggle most to trust God. Then ask God to give you the courage you need to trust him in those areas.

ONENESS
WITH GOD

A LITTLE EXTRA

Ask your youth leader to help you do some research on the kingdom of God. (You can do an online search, but you never know how reliable some websites are!) As your understanding of God's kingdom grows, you'll know better how to live and reveal it to others.

"I no longer call you slaves, because a master doesn't confide in his slaves. Now you are my friends, since I have told you everything the Father told me."
John 15:15

Jesus' ministry was centered on living and revealing the kingdom of God. Part of his mission was to die on the cross to pay the price for our sins, but that's not all he talked about. He preached sermons and told stories about what the kingdom of heaven looked like. Jesus came to live and reveal God's kingdom.

So what happened to the kingdom after Jesus left Earth? To put it simply, it lives on through his followers. You've likely heard the saying, "If you want something done right, you have to do it yourself." But Jesus believed that if you want something done right, you have to involve others.

Jesus invites us to carry out his work on earth. We get to be his partners in living and revealing the kingdom of God! What an honor!

How do we do this? By remembering that Jesus has put us in the right place at the right time to work with him. Your school, your job, and even your team are places that Jesus wants you to live and reveal the kingdom. We have a great friend in Jesus, and he trusts us to continue the mission he started.

TALKING WITH GOD

Ask God to show you specific ways you can live and reveal his kingdom. Thank him for calling you a friend.

The next day there was a wedding celebration in the village of Cana in Galilee. Jesus' mother was there, and Jesus and his disciples were also invited to the celebration. John 2:1-2

When you go to a party, do you keep things exciting, always stirring up something fun? Do you sit off to the side, having a deep conversation with one or two friends? Or are you somewhere in between?

In today's passage, Jesus was at a wedding party, which back then could last for several days. At some point, the host runs out of wine, and Jesus' mom asks him to do something. So Jesus turns water into wine—his first miracle.

But why was he at a wedding in the first place? Didn't he have important, Savior-stuff to do? Wasn't there someone who needed healing, or a demon that needed whooping?

Jesus was at the wedding because celebrations are important. It's important to be a friend who cries when someone else is hurting, but it's equally important to be a friend who celebrates when someone is happy.

TALKING WITH GOD

Pray this kind of prayer: *God, help me find friends that cry with me when I'm hurting and celebrate with me when I'm happy. And help me be this kind of friend, too. I want to live life a rich life, filled with things that matter. Help me trust you to shape my heart to want the things you want and be the kind of person you want me to be.*

ONENESS WITH GOD

A LITTLE EXTRA

Buy or make a party invitation addressed to you from God, inviting you to live a life that reveals his kingdom to others. Post it somewhere you'll see it. If you're really brave, make a few for your friends and commit to living a God-sized life together.

GOD HEARS & RESTORES

A LITTLE EXTRA

Write a letter to yourself to be read 10 years from now. Give yourself some advice. Remind yourself about things that are important to you. Describe who you are today and who you hope to be then. Talk about the hope you have in knowing that God has a plan for your future.

"For I know the plans I have for you," says the Lord. "They are plans for good and not for disaster, to give you a future and a hope." Jeremiah 29:11

One of the most difficult things about being a teenager is enduring the frustration of living in the "not yet." You aren't yet living on your own, living out your dream, or living into your future. Many of your current decisions play into your "not yet," but the reality is, you're still in the "not yet."

The only thing that makes living in the "not yet" bearable is knowing that God has a plan for your future. God knows your past, he's with you right now in your present, and he is preparing the way for you in your future—your "not yet."

Stay present in your today and allow God to take care of your tomorrow.

TALKING WITH GOD

Pray this kind of prayer: *Sometimes I'm so ready to be finished with this whole teenager gig and move on to being on my own. Other times I get completely freaked out by the thought of one day being on my own. God, help me to trust you with my future. Help me trust that your plan is best. I need you every second of my life, Lord. Help me live patiently as I deal with living in the "not yet."*

Then he said to me, "This is what the Lord says to Zerubbabel: It is not by force nor by strength, but by my Spirit, says the Lord of Heaven's Armies."
Zechariah 4:6

Zechariah was pointing the people of Israel back to God as they returned to the Promised Land. The people had been held captive for generations and were no longer a great nation with their own king and army.

Zechariah was telling the people to turn back to a God that they couldn't see. He was telling them about all kinds of visions that promised God hadn't forgotten them and would send a Savior.

This one verse stands out because in the middle of one of Zechariah's visions. God was pointing to a new way. God would not use armies, force, or strength. Instead he would use his Spirit. This would frustrate so many people who wanted to see a king come that would rage war and conquer lands. But how did Jesus come? How did Jesus rule?

We also tend to look for ways that make sense to us because we do not open our eyes to a whole other realm that exists all around us. We are called to acknowledge that God is in control of this physical world and the spiritual world. He has power in both.

TALKING WITH GOD

Pray this kind of prayer: *Open my eyes today to see the power you have in the spiritual world around me. God, forgive me for only looking at things I understand and see. Teach me to trust in you and your ways, which are higher than my ways.*

GOD HEARS & RESTORES

VERSE 311:
Zechariah 4:6

A LITTLE EXTRA

Zechariah describes a new day of power through Jesus in the city of Jerusalem. Read about it in Zechariah 14.

SIN & SEPARATION

A LITTLE EXTRA

Write a letter to the person who's betrayed you most recently or most painfully. "Tell" that person exactly how it made you feel and how it affected your life. And then write that you forgive that person. If you can't bring yourself to write that and believe that, ask God to help you come to a place of forgiveness.

Have you ever been betrayed by a friend? It's painful to discover that someone has been keeping secrets from you or lying to your face about things. When someone you love and trust betrays you, it makes the offense worse.

But even as Jesus said this, a crowd approached, led by Judas, one of the twelve disciples. Judas walked over to Jesus to greet him with a kiss. But Jesus said, "Judas, would you betray the Son of Man with a kiss?" Luke 22:47-48

Imagine how Jesus felt in this moment. He'd spent a great deal of time with Judas. He was one of the 12 who walked with Jesus throughout his ministry. They ate together, ministered together. And then Judas betrayed Jesus—with a kiss!

God wants to walk with you through some healing. In fact, he'd love it if you would give it over to him completely. That means forgiving that person—with God's help. This doesn't mean you have to continue or re-establish a relationship with that person. But you also don't have to hold on to that pain any longer. If you allow someone else's behavior to determine your happiness, you're giving them control in your life. DON'T DO THAT.

TALKING WITH GOD

Talk to God about any betrayal you've experienced. If you're ready, ask God to help you come to a place of forgiveness toward that person. Forgiveness probably won't happen overnight, but it's important to move to a place of being willing to forgive.

GOD HEARS & RESTORES

"For as the waters fill the sea, the earth will be filled with an awareness of the glory of the Lord."
Habakkuk 2:14

The Freedom Tower is a structure built as a replacement, monument, and marker to the World Trade Center towers that were lost in the 9/11 terrorist attacks in 2001. It towers high above any other skyscraper in New York, causing awe to anyone who sees it. How could man make such an awe-inspiring sight? Because God created the hands that formed it, we see him there.

Everywhere you go on Earth, you can be made aware of the glory of the Lord. Take a look around you. What do you see that helps you know how amazing God is? Can you see the vastness of the oceans where you live, or the majesty of the mountains? Yes, even the magnificence of a great structure such as The Freedom Tower makes us aware of God. He is so obviously in everything, it's common sense.

TALKING WITH GOD

Take a look around you. What do you see that makes you aware of God's glory? Be creative! Thank God for being amazing and worthy of all of our attention. Ask him to help you be more aware of his presence in your life today. Ask God for courage to live and reveal his kingdom.

VERSE 313:
Habakkuk 2:14

A LITTLE EXTRA

Find out what time sunrise is tomorrow, and set your clock to see it. Go outside or sit at a window and watch the sun rise. Even if you can't see the sun come over the horizon, notice darkness change to light. While this is happening, ask God to fill you with an awareness of him in a new way.

ONENESS
WITH GOD

A LITTLE EXTRA

In the next week or two, make time to read one of the Gospels (Matthew, Mark, Luke, or John) from beginning to end. Write down all the times Jesus serves someone or helps them in some way. In what ways could your serve others as Jesus did?

You must have the same attitude that Christ Jesus had. Philippians 2:5

Our culture doesn't spend a lot of time talking about humility and selflessness. Even though you'll hear many people talk about the importance of generosity or community, the underlying sentiment is that you need to look out for yourself, you need to protect yourself, and you need to pursue the course that's best for you.

Jesus chose to be humble and selfless. Because he was God, he could have used his power to elevate himself above others, but he chose to be a servant to his people. We cannot possibly be perfect like Jesus, but we can have the same attitude as him. Even though we can't avoid selfishness all the time, we can pursue a servant's attitude that seeks humility and others' best interests first.

If you see selfishness impacting your world negatively, how can a selfless attitude help bring change in your school or community? How can you encourage others to develop a humble and selfless attitude, too?

TALKING WITH GOD

Thank Jesus for his attitude that he displayed while he lived on Earth—his selfless sacrifice for you and his willingness to serve others. Ask him to help you develop this same kind of attitude in your own life. Ask God to help you trust him that his way of living is better than your way.

Here is the background of Matthew 18. Jesus' disciples asked him a question they had been arguing about. "Who is the greatest in the kingdom of heaven?" Translation: "What do I need to do to be the most important person in your group?" Jesus' disciples thought he might become a very important political or war hero, so they expected that being one of his favorites might have its benefits. Jesus shocked them with his declaration:

Then he said, "I tell you the truth, unless you turn from your sins and become like little children, you will never get into the Kingdom of Heaven."
Matthew 18:3

Jesus taught his disciples a lesson we can learn as well. Jesus values people who will depend on him, trust him, and desire to learn from him. That is how children interact with their parents, and it is the same way we ought to interact with Jesus.

TALKING WITH GOD
Make a list of your three biggest worries or concerns on a piece of paper. That's a lot of stress on one piece of paper. Practice the truth you just learned by praying through your list, and at the end of each worry, add this statement: "God, help me trust you to handle this."

CONSEQUENCES & CRYING OUT

VERSE 315:
Matthew 18:3

A LITTLE EXTRA

Go play on a playground with a friend. Or dig out some game you used to play as a child. Or color a picture in a coloring book. Do something that helps you reconnect with the kid inside of you. No matter how old you are, your kid still lives inside of you. God is asking if that kid wants to come out to play—and live and reveal his kingdom.

GOD HEARS & RESTORES

VERSE 316:
Luke 10:21

A LITTLE EXTRA

Find a super challenging Sudoku puzzle and try to solve it all in your head without writing anything down. (Hint: It's pretty much impossible.) Every time you see a word or number puzzle, remember that God never asks you to have everything figured out. He simply invites you to trust him.

Jesus is so backward. Actually, the entire Christian life is backward. God calls us to not only live differently, but also to think differently. We like to think we have everything figured out and under control, but we don't.

Too much of life is a mystery. The moment we think we finally have a grip on something it slips through our fingers. Jesus calls us not to only have a new heart but also a renewing of our mind. The goal, as crazy as it sounds, is to have the mind and faith of a child.

At that same time Jesus was filled with the joy of the Holy Spirit, and he said, "O Father, Lord of heaven and earth, thank you for hiding these things from those who think themselves wise and clever, and for revealing them to the childlike. Yes, Father, it pleased you to do it this way." Luke 10:21

Children don't always like what their parents decide, and they don't always understand the reasoning behind it either. But what they do understand is that the parent knows best and has the best interest of the entire family in mind.

TALKING WITH GOD

Spend a moment confessing to God the times you've been arrogant, thinking you knew everything about everything. Think about something going on in your life right now that you do not know how to handle. Ask God to help you, and trust that he loves you enough to answer your prayer.

This means that anyone who belongs to Christ has become a new person. The old life is gone; a new life has begun! And all of this is a gift from God, who brought us back to himself through Christ. And God has given us this task of reconciling people to him. For God was in Christ, reconciling the world to himself, no longer counting people's sins against them. And he gave us this wonderful message of reconciliation. So we are Christ's ambassadors; God is making his appeal through us. We speak for Christ when we plead, "Come back to God!" For God made Christ, who never sinned, to be the offering for our sin, so that we could be made right with God through Christ. 2 Corinthians 5:17–21

GOD HEARS
& RESTORES

VERSE 317:
2 Corinthians 5:17-21

A LITTLE EXTRA

Read Colossians 1:11-22 and underline the parts that talk about rescue and reconciliation.

Did you catch that? *You* speak for Christ as you share his message—you are his *ambassador*, called by him to live out the incredible privilege and responsibility *of reconciling people to him*!

Your life can be a walking, talking demonstration of Jesus at work in the world. Is it? Take inventory and ask yourself the following questions:

1. Is Jesus your first love? Do you trust him in all things?
2. Are you representing him well and living as a new person in Christ?
3. Is sharing his message a priority?
4. Who could you share Jesus with today?

TALKING WITH GOD

Did you notice the word *plead* in this passage? Think of a time when you "pleaded" for something you really, really cared about. Do you bring that same passion to sharing Jesus with others? Plead with God for your friends who don't know Christ. Then step out today and plead with your friends to *"Come back to God!"*

VERSE 318:
Genesis 12:2-3

A LITTLE EXTRA

Take out a sheet of paper or turn to a new page in your journal. Create a bucket list— that's right, a list of 10 things you want to accomplish before you die. Don't worry; you don't have to be super spiritual here. What do you want to experience in this adventure of life?

What do you think you'll be doing next year? How different will your life be in five years? Ten years from now, what do you hope you have accomplished?

"I will make you into a great nation. I will bless you and make you famous, and you will be a blessing to others. I will bless those who bless you and curse those who treat you with contempt. All the families on earth will be blessed through you."
Genesis 12:2-3

God's promises for your future are grand, incredible, and beyond belief. God knows you better than you know yourself. God knows what's best for you and wants what's best for you. God wants to write a beautiful story in and through your life.

This is exciting stuff! Rather than worrying about the future, take hold of opportunities with the confidence God gives you. Let him lead.

You can start by blessing others. God has placed people in your life—your family, your friends, and those you see around you. You don't need to have a detailed plan, but be open to how you can be an encouragement to others. Followers of Jesus should be in the business of making people's days.

TALKING WITH GOD

Commit your dreams to God. Ask God to make clear to you what things are simply your own dreams and what things he's leading you to do. Do you need to make changes in your life today so you can follow these dreams?

You're not alone. Even when you feel like no one gets you, no one appreciates you, or no one respects you, God is here.

"God blesses you when people mock you and persecute you and lie about you and say all sorts of evil things against you because you are my followers. Be happy about it! Be very glad! For a great reward awaits you in heaven. And remember, the ancient prophets were persecuted in the same way." Matthew 5:11-12

The ancient prophets were persecuted, falsely accused, unnoticed, cast out of society, unhappy, and even betrayed by their own friends and families—all for standing up for God. You even hear tragic stories today of missionaries around the world being hurt or killed because of their devotion to God.

So is it worth it? Does God really want you to follow him, no matter what?

Yes! Even in the midst of persecution, God is with you; he blesses you, strengthens you, and gives you hope. If you feel alone in your walk with Christ, find someone you can talk to (at church, at home, at school, at work). You can encourage one another to remain strong and anticipate God's blessings.

TALKING WITH GOD

Share with God how you're feeling persecuted as a Christ-follower. It could be in the form of a little embarrassment or something much bigger. Tell God how much it hurts, and admit to God how you've wanted to give up. (God already knows.)

GOD HEARS & RESTORES

VERSE 319:
Matthew 5:11-12

A LITTLE EXTRA

Make sure it's OK with your parents, and then visit persecution.com to be inspired and encouraged to pray for Christ-followers around the world who are persecuted for their faith. Let their stories inspire you to deepen your trust in Jesus in the midst of your own persecution.

ONENESS WITH GOD

A LITTLE EXTRA

Read Psalm 42:1-2 and journal your thoughts on these questions.

- Consider the last time you were thirsty—really thirsty. What did you think about before you could get some water?

- What consumes your thoughts each day? Is there just one thing or a group of things?

- How might your life look different if you thirsted for the living God?

Cravings. Everyone craves something sometime. It might be the same thing over and over, or a series of different yearnings—the first pumpkin-spiced latte of the season, or a late-night run for tacos. What about yearning for some downtime to play video games or hang out with friends?

And the people of Berea were more open-minded than those in Thessalonica, and they listened eagerly to Paul's message. They searched the Scriptures day after day to see if Paul and Silas were teaching the truth. Acts 17:11

Consider the things you crave each day. God desires that we crave him and his Word each day. He wants to be at the top of your list in good times and in bad—to infuse your life with his plan.

When you crave things ahead of God, you can waste your time. Those things will never fill the void, the hunger, the desire you have for what God can provide. God wants to be your rescuer, your adviser, and your friend. God knows what's best and wants you to crave his best.

TALKING WITH GOD

Ask God to give you a desire—an eager craving—for him and for Scripture. It's OK if it doesn't come naturally for you. It doesn't come naturally for many people. This isn't a one-time ask. Keep asking God to plant the desire in your heart and help it to grow.

"Look, I am sending you out as sheep among wolves. So be as shrewd as snakes and harmless as doves." Matthew 10:16

Did you realize that nowhere in the Bible does God tell us to stay hidden in the comfort of our youth groups or climb into a bunker with a bunch of other Christ-followers? Not once! Instead, we read in the New Testament about Jesus often sending people out into the world to tell others about him.

In this passage, Jesus sends the disciples out with the instructions to be like snakes and doves. Could Jesus have picked two animals more opposite than these? One slithers; the other flies. One has scales; the other has feathers. One is dangerous; the other is harmless. What does this mean?

Jesus sent the disciples out with a warning that some would find the good news offensive. He likened it to putting sheep in a pasture of wolves. We are the sheep in this story, but Jesus does not want us to sheepishly tell others about him. Jesus wants us to strike the balance between being bold and wise as snakes, and vulnerable and innocent as doves when living sent lives.

VERSE 321:
Matthew 10:16

A LITTLE EXTRA

Draw an animal that is part sheep, part snake, and part dove. (Don't worry; you aren't entering it into an art competition.) Title the sketch, "The Sent One."

TALKING WITH GOD

Pray this kind of prayer: *God, I know I'm a sheep, because often I am afraid. There are wolves all around me. Protect me, and give me the courage to tell others about you. Help me be wise and innocent. Help me get out of my comfort zone and live a sent life.*

ONENESS WITH GOD

A LITTLE EXTRA

Write a "thank you" note to your parents or other adults who have made an effort to teach you about God. Include today's passage in your note, and tell them how you've seen them live out the passage.

"And you must commit yourselves wholeheartedly to these commands that I am giving you today. Repeat them again and again to your children. Talk about them when you are at home and when you are on the road, when you are going to bed and when you are getting up." Deuteronomy 6:6-7

Have you ever been around someone who *really* cares about something? You know you have when the conversation always goes to whatever subject it is they care most about. It doesn't matter where you are or what you are doing; in some way, everything in that person's life relates back to that one single, focused topic. This person is consumed by it!

God wants us to be this way with his commands. God knows that everything we need in life comes from him. If we truly care about him, then everything we do should naturally lead back to God's commands. The path to oneness with God starts with committing yourself to wholeheartedly knowing his commands. You will be able to tell you are on the right track when all the things you do in a day—between getting up and going to bed—remind you of his commands.

TALKING WITH GOD

Pray this kind of prayer: *God, may the words that come out of my mouth be about your commands. I trust you, and I want to repeat your words and talk about them in every situation so I can grow in my oneness with you.*

Then Jesus placed his hands on the man's eyes again, and his eyes were opened. His sight was completely restored, and he could see everything clearly. Mark 8:25

Just one verse earlier Jesus spat in this guy's eyes and asked him if he could see anything. The man replied that he could but it was still "fuzzy."

This exchange seems similar to the conversation you have with your eye doctor as she dials in the lens strength on that submarine periscope-looking thing. Which looks better: one or two? Move the lens a little more—which looks better now? Feels like a guessing game.

Jesus isn't a miracle guesser. In this verse, he wasn't guessing at the blind man's needs. Instead there's a spiritual aspect to this exchange that applies to all of us.

As brand-new followers of Jesus, we begin seeing God's grace for us. We see Scripture, a Savior, creation—but it may be fuzzy at first. Repeatedly experiencing Jesus, repeated time in the Word, repeated conversations with God—we finally start seeing the world, our life, and our need for Jesus much more clearly.

TALKING WITH GOD

Talk to God about what's most "fuzzy" three separate times today. Each time pray in a different way. First, read Mark 8:25 over and over. Second, write down the thing you need clarity about. Third, fall asleep tonight holding on to something that represents where you need clarity. Ask God to open your eyes and make it clearer.

VERSE 323:
Mark 8:25

A LITTLE EXTRA

In this story, the blind man was brought to Jesus by people who wanted to see him healed. It's a good thing to have others praying for you and asking Jesus for clarity on your behalf. So text your prayer request to people you trust, and ask them to prayer about it, too.

SIN & SEPARATION

A LITTLE EXTRA

Check out Job 42 to see how many more sheep God gave Job after this whole ordeal ended. You will be surprised—it's a lot of sheep.

Then the Lord answered Job from the whirlwind: "Who is this that questions my wisdom with such ignorant words? Brace yourself like a man, because I have some questions for you, and you must answer them." Job 38:1-3

Job is one of the most memorable books in the Bible. This poor guy had terrible things happen to him, but he still chose to serve God. His best friends told him to forget God, and his family told him to forget God. But Job didn't. Although Job never doubted God, he questioned God's decisions to let so many bad things happen to him. Some of the sternest words recorded in the Bible to any one man are found in this text.

For four chapters God reminds Job that he is only a man and that God made everything on the earth. God goes into great detail about his power and rightful place to make whatever decisions he wants.

We may not have come right out and shook our fists at heaven asking God what he was thinking, but it's likely we have doubted recently that God really had a purpose or plan in our life. God was forgiving and even generous to Job, but only after Job repented for not trusting God's plan.

TALKING WITH GOD

Pray this prayer, or one with a similar theme: *God, please forgive me for not trusting in you in all situations, whether I can see the outcome or not. You are God, and I'm not. You see and know all things, and I trust that your "better" is better than my better.*

Before you read anything else, watch this:
youtube.com/watch?v=JoC1ec-lYps

God's love for us is indescribable. Even our best attempts at painting a picture of his love fall short. It is all-consuming. It is mighty. It is gentle. It is unlimited. It is powerful. We could literally write all day about it but still not fully describe it.

We love each other because he loved us first.
1 John 4:19

When we begin to experience this great love, we find something happens to our hearts and to the way we see God and see other people.

Our hearts are filled with his love. The natural response is that we love God and others.

How can we love? Why can we love? Because he first loved us!

Our love for God and for others is a response. We love because he first loved us!

When we love someone who is unlovable, it's not something we can own. It's because he first loved us!

When we love someone who is unkind to us, we are reminded that we aren't the first one to love in that way. We are able to love because he first loved us!

TALKING WITH GOD

Take 60 seconds to think about God's love. Now take 60 seconds to think of others in your life that need to experience love so that they might know God's love better. Pray for the courage to give love to the people in your life.

ONENESS

WITH GOD

VERSE 325:
1 John 4:19

A LITTLE EXTRA

Try an experiment today—pay it forward. In other words, do something noticeably nice for someone for no good reason. Then discreetly watch them to see if they pay it forward to someone else. It's amazing what happens when we think about God's love for us and show love for others.

ONENESS
WITH GOD

A LITTLE EXTRA

Look up a game cheat for one of your favorite video games, and follow it step by step as you work to advance to the next level. When you complete the level, think about how following the steps of the video game is a lot like following God's Word.

"Anyone who listens to my teaching and follows it is wise, like a person who builds a house on solid rock." Matthew 7:24

Have you ever needed to go online to find a "cheat" to help you get to the next level on a video game? Funny thing about game cheats—if you don't follow the steps exactly, you won't advance to the next level.

God's Word is a lot like a video game. (No, seriously—it is!) If you hear God's Word but fail to put it into practice, then you won't advance to the next level. To mature spiritually, you need to follow God's instructions or you will deny yourself of the life he has in store for you.

One of the best things about God is that he is a God of second chances. That's right! There's no GAME OVER with God. So if you miss a step or two along the way, try again. Let God be your guide.

Take a risk. Give it a try. Spend a day living out God's Word.

TALKING WITH GOD

Pray this prayer, or one with a similar theme: *God, help me hear you, and give me the courage to follow your truths, step by step. I want to trust your plans, your instructions, and your ways, and I want to deny mine. Thank you for never declaring GAME OVER when I mess up.*

"You are the salt of the earth. But what good is salt if it has lost its flavor? Can you make it salty again? It will be thrown out and trampled underfoot as worthless. You are the light of the world—like a city on a hilltop that cannot be hidden." Matthew 5:13–14

GOD HEARS & RESTORES

Jesus' message and his work in your life ought to be on vibrant, vivid display for all to see. But it's so easy to duck behind the excuse of "I don't want to offend people," causing your "salt" to be in danger of losing its flavor and your "light" to become dim, at best.

Time for an honest reality check: Is your faith virtually invisible to those around you, or are you a walking, talking "Exhibit A" for how God is at work in the world making his kingdom come and his will be done? Does your trust in Jesus overflow into everything you say and do?

Don't lose your enthusiasm and passion for God or let Jesus' work in your life get watered down into a bland, neutralized, nebulous blob of vague "spirituality" that's lost its dynamic, life-transforming power. Your relationship with Jesus is not something to keep hidden or secret; your friends desperately need you to shine for him and share his life-giving message with them.

Don't ever leave people in the dark. Be salt and light to those around you!

A LITTLE EXTRA

Invite a Christ-following friend from your school to join you in your efforts to be salt and light on your campus. Go to everyschool.com and "Adopt" your school— and start praying together with your friend one day a week before school starts.

TALKING WITH GOD

Ask God to show you one way you could be bold today and step out to be salt and light for him. Ask God to guide you and empower you as you shine for him and share his message. Then go do it.

343

GOD HEARS & RESTORES

"I am the Lord, and I do not change. That is why you descendants of Jacob are not already destroyed."
Malachi 3:6

Why is it important that God doesn't change? God is a true constant in your life. Circumstances change. Friends change. Family members change. Where you live changes. What you do each day changes. Why do you need something constant?

An anchor	A compass
A lighthouse	A map
A photograph	The printed word
A rock	A security blanket

VERSE 328:
Malachi 3:6

A LITTLE EXTRA

Go outside and find a small rock. Place the rock on your nightstand or somewhere you'll see it often. Remember that God is your rock—your never-changing presence and Savior.

Review the list above of things that don't change, and answer these questions:

- What would you add to the list?
- Of the items on the list, what is God most like?
- Why doesn't God change?

Think of the early explorers trying to chart new territory without a compass; they'd get lost. Think of a ship, in the middle of a storm, trying to navigate around the shore without a lighthouse; the ship would probably crash. How is it in your own life? How do you find true and constant direction?

It is a true blessing and comfort to know that God doesn't change. Because God doesn't change, you can depend on him. You can trust him. You can believe God's words today and for the rest of your life.

TALKING WITH GOD
Thank God for never changing. Share with God the item you selected from the list above, and thank him for the ways he's been a constant in your life. Ask God to lead in the other areas of your life that are constantly changing.

GOD HEARS & RESTORES

"If you love me, obey my commandments. And I will ask the Father, and he will give you another Advocate, who will never leave you."
John 14:15-16

How do you show people that you love them? Do you give gifts, send texts, write notes, buy dinner, sing songs, or just hang out? When we are captivated by someone or deeply respect someone, it's natural to express how we feel.

Jesus reminds his disciples that if we want to express our love for him, we will obey his commandments. Wouldn't it be easier if we were to just meet with our church, sing worship songs, or even help other people?

Make no mistake about it, Jesus loves you with all of his heart and wants you to love him back. As you read through the stories and teachings of Jesus, you will notice that his commands talk about all different aspects of our lives. He teaches about how to treat others, how to use our money, who we should forgive, how our lives can be the best, and many other important truths. Those teachings are not there to make us feel bad about ourselves, but to help us know how to show him how we love him. And the coolest part is that obeying Jesus' commands is best for us and for everyone around us!

TALKING WITH GOD

Reflect on the love of Jesus. Think about what he's done for you and how that has impacted your life. Ask him for the strength to obey his commands today.

VERSE 329:
John 14:15-16

A LITTLE EXTRA

Do an online search for "the five love languages." How do you show love? How do you receive love? Thank Jesus for making you the way he did. And commit to showing him love the way he asks: by following what he said.

345

ONENESS
WITH GOD

A LITTLE EXTRA

Keep a list every day of all the reasons you're thankful. Each night before you go to bed, write a "thank you" note to God, thanking him for specific things he did that day—and for all the other things he has done for you.

Has anyone recently thanked you for something you have done?

Give thanks to the Lord and proclaim his greatness. Let the whole world know what he has done.
Psalm 105:1

Everyone likes a little thanks from time to time for the things they have done—even God! When was the last time you said "Thank you" to your family, friends, classmates, neighbors, or even a stranger? Has there been a time recently when God did something great in your life, and you ought to tell others about it? Have you thanked God for your family, your home, the beautiful sunset, or even for your little brother or sister?

It's easy to breeze through life without giving thanks. Giving thanks requires effort, intention, and energy. Sometimes it even requires a little dose of humility. But as a Christ-follower, you have the opportunity to turn your thankfulness into a declaration of God's amazing power and grace.

TALKING WITH GOD

Take a moment and think about some of the things you are thankful for: people, blessings, skills, opportunities, freedoms. Why are you thankful for these things? Pray and thank God for all these things in your life.

"If you are faithful in little things, you will be faithful in large ones. But if you are dishonest in little things, you won't be honest with greater responsibilities." Luke 16:10

No one likes to clean toilets. OK, we take that back: There are *some* people who enjoy cleaning toilets, but they're few and far between. And we doubt many of them are teenagers! But cleaning a toilet—or doing anything else that's equally unglamorous—reveals an important truth about God's kingdom.

Jesus spoke the words of today's verse to his disciples as part of a teaching about money and worldly resources, but the underlying truth relates to many areas of life. How you handle *small* responsibilities reveals what you'll do with *big* ones. Being faithful in small things gives you a track record. It proves that you care more about serving than being served. It helps you become a person of trustworthy character—and that's a really great thing!

TALKING WITH GOD

If it seems like your life is filled with small responsibilities and nothing major or meaningful, ask God to give you his perspective and patience. Ask for the strength to faithfully fulfill these tasks so that someday—whether it's next week, a year from now, or further down the road—you'll be a person of character who can be trusted by God and other people, too.

VERSE 331:
Luke 16:10

A LITTLE EXTRA

Go clean a toilet today. Or pick up some trash. Or creatively give a small amount of money. Or serve someone in need. Do something little, something that won't earn you praise or thanks or attention. Do it as a way of saying, "God, help me be faithful in these little things so you can entrust me with greater responsibilities that will honor you and reveal your kingdom."

ONENESS
WITH GOD

A LITTLE EXTRA

Think of one thing in your life that is true, honorable, right, pure, lovely, or admirable. Maybe it's running, or playing music, or something active. Maybe it's a tire swing, or a park bench, or a comfortable place. Once you figure out what your thing is, keep going back to it when life gets tough, and see how God can help your focus.

There's a rule that all oval-track racecar drivers live by: When you are taking a corner and you feel like the car is losing control, don't look at the wall on the outside of the track. Instead pick a point in the track where you want to get to, take your foot off the gas, and you will get around safely.

In life, we can be sure that there will be many "corners" that turn, many "walls" we might hit, and many challenges to face. When we read the Apostle Paul's letter to Philippians, we see that they, too, were facing many challenges and trials. As Paul writes to them, he gives them some life-saving advice that would help them avoid crashing into the walls of life:

And now, dear brothers and sisters, one final thing. Fix your thoughts on what is true, and honorable, and right, and pure, and lovely, and admirable. Think about things that are excellent and worthy of praise. Philippians 4:8

When we face challenges in our lives, we have two choices: focus on the negative and end up crashing, or fix our thoughts on Jesus and all the things Paul mentions in today's passage.

TALKING WITH GOD

Think about some of the challenges you are facing today. Now reflect on the things in your life that are true, honorable, right, pure, lovely, and admirable. Thank God for each of these things.

The Lord says, "I will guide you along the best pathway for your life. I will advise you and watch over you." Psalm 32:8

Have you ever gotten lost? Did you look at a map, or stop and ask for directions? Did you use your GPS or smartphone to determine where to go? Or did you just try to figure out where you were going on your own?

We can easily get lost in life. We get lost in our problems, and we forget we can go to God for directions. God has given us a roadmap in the Bible and in prayer. God has given us spiritual mentors including pastors, youth ministers, small group leaders, Sunday school teachers, our parents, and our friends to help us in our spiritual journey.

When you are lost, you can turn to God, who promises to instruct you and teach you in the way you should go. God's guidance and direction are there when you need them. God is working with you, whether you're waking or sleeping, all the time, every day. It is our job, as followers of Christ, to have obedient hearts and to actively seek God's will in everything we do.

TALKING WITH GOD

Ask God to guide you in your life. Pray that God will continue to watch over you and give you wisdom and direction each day.

ONENESS WITH GOD

VERSE 333:
Psalm 32:8

A LITTLE EXTRA

Make a list of three to five things for which you need God's guidance. Then make a list of ways you have seen God's guidance in your life lately. Keep this list nearby as a frequent reminder of how God is leading you along the best pathway for your life.

ONENESS WITH GOD

A LITTLE EXTRA

Get your church directory and look at all the ministries in the church. Spend some time praying for each ministry in your church. Pray for the other Christian churches in your town. Pray for other ministries that are reaching out to teenagers in your community. God uses us all to accomplish his mission in the world.

Take a moment and examine your fingers and toes. Now go find a mirror and take a look at yourself. Look at your hair, your eyes, every detail of you!

The human body has many parts, but the many parts make up one whole body. So it is with the body of Christ. 1 Corinthians 12:12

Our body is made up of many parts that make it function and keep us alive. Likewise, the body of Christ consists of parts of different sizes and functions. Look at all the different churches in your hometown—different sizes, different styles, different personalities. Think about your own church and all of its different ministries. Then consider all the members of each ministry. As you can see, everyone has an important task in the body of Christ to make it alive and functional.

TALKING WITH GOD

Think about how important your walk with God is to the entire body. Ask God for strength to either remain or become a strong part of the body, so you can do your part.

Do you ever need a do-over? Maybe you did something that seemed like a good idea at the time, but now you regret it. Reset. Or maybe you said something that was ugly, and now you feel bad. Reset. Or maybe worst of all, you hurt someone that you really care about, and you're miserable about it. Reset.

Sometimes we fail to do something good. Have you ever intended to do your devotions every day, and three days later, you're wondering how you messed up already? Have you ever felt a God-nudge to do something nice for someone but ignored it? Have you ever forgotten to follow through on something you said you'd do?

The faithful love of the Lord never ends! His mercies never cease. Great is his faithfulness; his mercies begin afresh each morning.
Lamentations 3:22–23

You can't turn back the clock, but God gives you a fresh supply of mercy every time you ask. He never runs out of grace. God's love never fails. We all get stuck, but don't stay stuck. Accept God's invitation to restoration, and start a new day living into his plan for your life.

TALKING WITH GOD

Pray this kind of prayer: *God, I need a new serving of mercy today. Help me be faithful with the grace you've given me—not keeping it all to myself, but spilling it messily into the world around me. Remind me that your love never fails.*

GOD HEARS
& RESTORES

VERSE 335:
Lamentations 3:22–23

A LITTLE EXTRA

With parental permission, watch the video "Othello: Isaiah 53" (youtu.be/klAw_XiWAQA). Then read Isaiah 53 in your Bible. This describes who Jesus was to be, before he ever came to earth. When we learn more about who he is and how he was promised, we see that his love is faithful and never-ending.

CONSEQUENCES & CRYING OUT

A LITTLE EXTRA

With a cleaned-out heart, fill it with something good. Memorize today's verse on humility as a short rap or song to remind you of what God promises. Allow God's words to be a beautiful challenge to you as you pursue a Jesus-centered life.

"For those who exalt themselves will be humbled, and those who humble themselves will be exalted."
Luke 14:11

Humble? You probably don't hear that word every day at school or when watching TV or when hanging out with your friends. Aren't we supposed to look out for number one, develop a healthy self-esteem, and live by the motto "It's my way or the highway"? In our me-focused culture, *humility* is a word that doesn't get nearly enough exercise!

But this is what God wants from us. Jesus' life and ministry were filled with humility, as he reached out to society's outcasts, washed the feet of his disciples, and ultimately went to the cross to pay the price for our sins—the greatest act of humility possible.

So how do we humble ourselves? We begin the journey by getting rid of humility's greatest enemy: pride. Pride is an unhealthy focus on us—and a lack of proper focus on God. Pride is sneaky and deceitful. It feeds that me-focused attitude, at the expense of everyone around us. It's a destroyer, and before you know it, it'll trap you in a life of bondage.

TALKING WITH GOD

Find a position of humility: kneeling, sitting quietly in a corner, or lying face down on the carpet. Confess your pride. Talk with God about your human tendency to think too highly of yourself, and ask for forgiveness and the ability to see yourself as God does.

The Son radiates God's own glory and expresses the very character of God, and he sustains everything by the mighty power of his command. When he had cleansed us from our sins, he sat down in the place of honor at the right hand of the majestic God in heaven. Hebrews 1:3

That's the Jesus we serve. He's big and powerful. He has a place of honor before God in heaven, and he radiates God's glory. He uses his authority to forgive our sins even though we don't deserve it. He's more than a friend and confidant. He deserves our respect and adoration.

Read today's verse again. Picture what this Scripture describes. What image comes to mind when you read these words? Do your best to sketch out the image on a piece of paper. If you were in the scene, what would you look like in comparison to Jesus?

TALKING WITH GOD

Spend time thinking about how awesome Jesus is. How many adjectives—descriptive words—can you think of to describe him? See if you can create a list of at least 20. Then use these words in your prayer—thanking, praising, and honoring him for all these amazing attributes and qualities.

VERSE 337:
Hebrews 1:3

A LITTLE EXTRA

Another way to show honor to God is to *prostrate* yourself before him. The word *prostrate* means to "lay flat" or "to put yourself face down on the ground." This isn't how most of us pray, but it can help us honor God in a unique way. While in this position, pray words of thanks out loud to him as if he was on his throne right in front of you.

VERSE 338:
Psalm 73:26

A LITTLE EXTRA

Read the story of humanity's fall in Genesis 3. Also read a special promise about oneness with God in James 4:4.

My health may fail, and my spirit may grow weak, but God remains the strength of my heart; he is mine forever. Psalm 73:26

When we come into a relationship with Jesus Christ, he makes many things right simply by living inside of us. But other things take time to heal—and some of those things seem to take way too long. When we face such challenges as failing health or situations that make a person's spirit weak, we can't help but cry out to God and wonder what he is up to! How can bad things happen to good people who are supposed to be sons and daughters of the Creator of the universe? This question can be difficult to understand no matter what age you are or how much you know.

In Genesis 3, humanity sinned against God, and that broken part of our story is not yet made fully new yet. We still live in the brokenness of that first sin in the world. The work has been finished to make all things right, perfect, and new—but won't be finalized until the return of Jesus. Until that time there will be things that happen that make us feel exactly like this verse— failing health and a weakening Spirit.

Until the brokenness of Genesis 3 is finally set right by Jesus, we rely on the strength of the Lord. More pain may even come in this life, but the Lord is ours forever.

TALKING WITH GOD

Pray to God about things that make your spirit grow weak when you think about them. Ask for strength to trust that God's version of "better" is better than yours.

What does it mean to be a rebel? Maybe you've seen movies that portray rebels battling against an oppressive ruler. Or perhaps you've read a book that portrays a group of students rebelling against a corrupt and unfair system. The descriptions don't always portray a person in a terrible light. In fact we often look up to rebels, don't we?

In this passage, James refers to a different kind of rebel who is sinister, calculating, and dangerous. James appeals to his readers to flee from the leader of the ultimate rebellion against God. The devil began a rebellion against God a long time ago, and his ultimate goal is to recruit people to join him in his rebellion. Here's what James has to say about this:

VERSE 339:
James 4:7

So humble yourselves before God. Resist the devil, and he will flee from you. James 4:7

James' audience was getting caught up in following the devil's sin and rebellion. As a result, their lives were impacted in negative ways. It's true for us today, too. We can choose to join the sin rebellion. Or we can choose to humble ourselves (truly see our lives in light of God's greatness), join God's uprising against sin, and flee from the devil. It's a decision we each must make. What do you choose today?

A LITTLE EXTRA

Say the name "Jesus" aloud. Seriously, say it out loud. Say it again. How does that feel? For one day, try this experiment: Whenever you feel tempted, say aloud, "Jesus, I need your help." Jesus' name isn't magic, but it is full of power.

TALKING WITH GOD

Confess to God the times over the past week that you chose rebellion over God's leading in your life. As you pray, intentionally commit your day to God and actively choose to follow him and flee the devil.

ONENESS WITH GOD

By his divine power, God has given us everything we need for living a godly life. We have received all of this by coming to know him, the one who called us to himself by means of his marvelous glory and excellence. 2 Peter 1:3

When you were younger did you ever assemble a model? The first page of the instructions always included a picture of each piece in the box. What would your model have looked like if you had refused to use all of the red pieces? Probably nothing like the picture on the box!

God has given us everything we need to live a godly life—all of the pieces are there. When we came to know him, he placed them all out for us to use. But some people's faith walk doesn't look like the image of Jesus because they only used the pieces they wanted to use instead of everything that's available to them.

TALKING WITH GOD

Are you using all that God has given you to grow in godliness? Ask God to show you what you might be missing or ignoring as you follow him.

A LITTLE EXTRA

If you have some Lego® pieces at home, take a permanent marker and, on a few pieces, write down areas of godliness you are missing or ignoring. Put your Lego reminder in a place that you will see it on a regular basis. If you don't have any Lego pieces in your home, go to Lego.com. Click on "Games." Pick the "Creative" tab and choose one of the "Building" games. Each time you click on a building piece, pray for a specific area where you need God's help. When your project is done, ask God to remind you that you have all you need to live a Christ-like life every day.

They are like trees planted along the riverbank, bearing fruit each season. Their leaves never wither, and they prosper in all they do. Psalm 1:3

Consider the picture that the psalmist creates in this verse. Can you imagine that tree right next to the riverbank and the incredible green leaves and amazing fruit hanging from its branches?

Now imagine that you can see the tree's roots underground. Can you see the large roots that go down deep into the soil of the riverbank and are soaking up the water? Can you see the water as it goes up into the roots and makes its way around the tree, bringing life and vitality?

This picture mirrors our lives when we choose to stand firm on the truth of God and to live by his good commands. Our lives will bear fruit when we stay closely connected to God and are fed by his living water of truth. Even when we have seasons that feel cold and harsh, we can trust that God will still help our lives bear good fruit. How are your "faith roots" today?

TALKING WITH GOD

Be quiet for a few moments and ask God to show you the areas in your life where you are planted well and growing strong. Then ask God to show you areas where you are moving away from him and struggling to stay healthy. Ask God to show you what daily habits can help you stay rooted and connected with him.

ONENESS
WITH GOD

VERSE 341:
Psalm 1:3

A LITTLE EXTRA

Do some research on roots, either online or at the library. Compare the pictures of healthy roots and dying roots. Then, every time you see a healthy tree, ask God to plant the roots of your faith in good soil.

ONENESS WITH GOD

VERSE 342:
Romans 10:17

A LITTLE EXTRA

Look up Hebrews 11:1-3, 6. Write these verses— as well as Romans 10:17—on a piece of paper and look at them every day for the next week.

What is your favorite sound in the entire world? Is it the sound of your cell phone, your grandmother's voice, or maybe the sound of the ocean? Why is it your favorite sound?

So faith comes from hearing, that is, hearing the Good News about Christ. Romans 10:17

As we grow in our relationship with God, we learn to hear God more clearly. We hear God through such habits as prayer, reading our Bible, and worship. Through the Bible we discover how great God is and the plans he has for us. As we continue to grow through prayer, reading and studying Scripture, and worship, we grow in our faith and can hear God's voice more clearly. Faith is not something we can make up. It is the result of getting to know God, trusting him more, and listening to him, instead of always just talking to God and giving him our requests. Faith is about believing and trusting God with absolute certainty. It's about being convinced that God is always present and takes care of us, even if we can't see or feel him.

TALKING WITH GOD

Stop for a few minutes and find a quiet place. Take time to listen to what God is saying to you today.

"So don't worry about tomorrow, for tomorrow will bring its own worries. Today's trouble is enough for today." Matthew 6:34

Are you a procrastinator? Sometimes we read this verse and think it means we can put off work and not worry about the stress of finishing it until another day. As much as we may like, that is not what God is telling us in this verse. Jesus is saying that he wants us to let go of our anxieties and fears and worries, and live in the confidence of knowing God has everything under control.

God may be planning a great opportunity for us today, but we might miss out if we are too focused on the troubles of tomorrow. Tomorrow is in the hands of God, so rest in his grace and seek him today!

TALKING WITH GOD

Thank God for the things he is doing in your life today. Confess all of your struggles to him, and ask him to help you keep things in the proper perspective. Pray for each worry individually, and find peace in knowing that God will walk with you through every struggle you face.

VERSE 343:
Matthew 6:34

A LITTLE EXTRA

Look at what Psalm 55:22 tells us: *Give your burdens to the Lord, and he will take care of you. He will not permit the godly to slip and fall.* Doesn't that make you feel better already? God will not give us more than we can handle, and he will not cause us to "slip and fall." Each time today that you walk up or down a set of stairs, offer a quick prayer of thanks for God's promise to keep you from spiritually slipping and falling.

GOD HEARS & RESTORES

A LITTLE EXTRA

Memorize today's passage. Write it in pencil on a note card. Erase one word at a time as you memorize it. When you have it memorized, write it out again and pass it on to a friend.

And so, dear brothers and sisters, I plead with you to give your bodies to God because of all he has done for you. Let them be a living and holy sacrifice—the kind he will find acceptable. This is truly the way to worship him. Don't copy the behavior and customs of this world, but let God transform you into a new person by changing the way you think. Then you will learn to know God's will for you, which is good and pleasing and perfect.
Romans 12:1-2

When you study for a test and put time into your schoolwork, your parents are usually pretty proud of you. When you watch TV or hang out with friends instead of doing your schoolwork, they probably aren't so proud—especially if you end up failing that test. Yikes!

Similarly, God is incredibly proud of us when we follow his path and choose to do what is right instead of following the path of the world and going along with the crowd. If we don't *want* to do things God's way, we ask God to help us by changing the way we think through prayer and Bible study. We show our love for God and honor him when we make sacrifices and do what is right.

TALKING WITH GOD

Do you want to live your way or God's way? Do you need God to change your mind? Commit to spending more time with God today, to give him space to transform you.

GOD HEARS
& RESTORES

Then God gave the people all these instructions: "I am the Lord your God, who rescued you from the land of Egypt, the place of your slavery."
Exodus 20:1-2

Here's the deal, God is about to give the Ten Commandments to the Israelites. This is serious. The big 10. Before he starts, he makes two statements:

I am God.
And I saved you from slavery.

Essentially, he is declaring who he is and what he had done for them.

Understanding who God is and what he has done is foundational in determining our response to what he will ask of us. The Ten Commandments are not extremely hard, especially when you consider who is asking and what he had done for the Israelites—and what he has done for us.

God is still God, on the throne and over the entire world. And God has rescued us and is always rescuing us.

When we begin to understand those things, we become more willing and more available to do exactly what he is calling us to do each day: to follow him in a radical journey of loving him and loving others.

TALKING WITH GOD

Spend time reflecting on who God is in your life and on the many things God has done for you. Offer a prayer of thankfulness followed by a prayer of submission to whatever God may ask of you today.

VERSE 345:
Exodus 20:1-2

A LITTLE EXTRA

Draw a picture of one way God has rescued you. Explain it to your family, and then hang it on your refrigerator as a family reminder of God's goodness in your lives. Encourage other family members to draw their own pictures and hang them next to yours.

VERSE 346:
Ephesians 6:13

A LITTLE EXTRA

Read Ephesians 6:10-13. Draw a picture of a superhero wearing each piece of God's armor. Put it someone as a reminder of God's power in your life.

Are you a fan of *The Lord of the Rings*? Or maybe you prefer Thor? Perhaps you're a fan of Harry Potter?

What do these stories have in common? Each one has an enemy and a great battle—or multiple great battles! What do these things have in common with our lives? There is a real enemy and you are in a real battle. Think about a great battle scene from one of those movies. Now, accept that in some ways, your life is exactly like that scene.

Therefore, put on every piece of God's armor so you will be able to resist the enemy in the time of evil. Then after the battle you will still be standing firm. Ephesians 6:13

The Apostle Paul, who wrote today's verse, wants you to be prepared for this great battle called everyday life. And he wants you to be prepared to stand against the great enemy known as Satan.

If you are prepared, you will stand firm. If you are prepared, you will not be destroyed by the devil. If you are prepared, you will not falter in your faith when the battle gets tough.

What do you need to do? Be prepared! Put on every piece of God's armor today!

TALKING WITH GOD

Pray this prayer: *Jesus, I realize that each day is a battle not against other people but against an enemy who wants to destroy my life and the lives of those around me. Thank you for your Spirit and for your armor that keeps and protects me from the attacks of the enemy. Help me stand firm and live and reveal your kingdom.*

"I am the good shepherd. The good shepherd sacrifices his life for the sheep." John 10:11

In Bible times, shepherds were much more common than they are in most parts of the world today. In fact, you've probably never seen someone crossing the street with a flock of sheep. However, if you had been alive during the time that Jesus lived on Earth, this passage would be much easier to understand!

Shepherds take their jobs very seriously. They count their sheep constantly to make sure one hasn't wandered off. If a bear or wolf comes to hunt their sheep, the shepherd does all that he can to fight it off, even if that means giving up his life. How crazy is that?

It may sound a little ridiculous to sacrifice your life for something as small and insignificant as a sheep, but that is exactly what Jesus did for us! To someone as huge and powerful as he is, you would think that we tiny humans would never be worth dying for, but Jesus thought otherwise. He truly is the good shepherd, and he willingly sacrificed his life for us.

TALKING WITH GOD

Let the image of the shepherd giving up the life for his sheep sink in. What would it take for you to sacrifice your own safety to protect someone else? Thank God that Jesus loved us all enough to pay the price of our sin with his own life.

GOD HEARS & RESTORES

VERSE 347:
John 10:11

A LITTLE EXTRA

Next time you are lying in bed and can't fall asleep, try counting sheep! It is an old trick that doesn't always work well, but while you're counting, think of the courage Jesus needed in order to die for us, insignificant little sheep. Sleep will come much easier to you with that peace in your mind!

GOD HEARS & RESTORES

A LITTLE EXTRA

Find something to plug your ears with. You can just press on the "nubs" of your ears if you can't find anything else. Spend a couple of minutes and listen to yourself breathe. Listen to the beating of your heart. Someday death will steal away the beat of your heart and the breaths you take. But it doesn't have to steal your soul.

Jesus' life, death, and resurrection leave us with a choice. If you choose to follow the path Jesus made for us, then spend some time thanking him and asking for guidance on this path. If you're unsure, pray for Jesus to provide you with some clarity, and then read the story that leads into Matthew 27:50.

Then Jesus shouted out again, and he released his spirit. Matthew 27:50

After Jesus prayed all night in a garden, Roman guards captured him, beat him, scourged, spit, and mocked him. Adding to those injuries, they forced a crown of thorns onto his head. Finally he was stripped naked, stretched and nailed to the cross he had carried to the site of execution, and then left to hang for several hours until death.

Bleeding to death and barely able to breathe through the pain, Jesus cried out one last time with a fierce confidence. A cry that made a way to life for all of us. He laid down his own perfect life and offered himself freely as the way to life. Forever.

TALKING WITH GOD

What situations, or people, or issues do you trust God to come through on? Write them down on this page. Then write down something you don't fully trust God with right now. Wrestle with the question of what's preventing you from trusting God with this particular thing. As you move toward trust, read Psalm 56:3-4 as part of your prayer.

For a time is coming when people will no longer listen to sound and wholesome teaching. They will follow their own desires and will look for teachers who will tell them whatever their itching ears want to hear. 2 Timothy 4:3

In today's verse, the Apostle Paul is talking about a time when people everywhere would believe false prophets and turn their backs on Christ. Some people believe Paul is talking about the "End Times" (look up that phrase, if it isn't familiar), and others believe he is talking about the times that we are already living in. Regardless of the time, one thing is certain: It is very easy to fall for the lies of this world.

That's why it's important to know the Bible well and to spend time learning from pastors, teachers, leaders, and friends who understand and obey Scripture. Instead of building our lives around our self-centered desires or what other people claim is truth, we can choose to remain faithful to God's lasting, reliable, dependable truth.

TALKING WITH GOD

Stop whatever else may be distracting you right now. Seriously, turn off your music or TV or whatever. Ask God to help you keep your sights set on him and to only trust in what he says is true. Ask for strength to stand up against people who may be telling you lies, and ask God to help you become a person that speaks truth in love into other people's lives.

VERSE 349:
2 Timothy 4:3

A LITTLE EXTRA

Write the number 1 on your hand as a reminder that there is only ONE person who will always tell you the truth and remain constant in your life when everyone else seems to be falling for the lies of the world: God.

ONENESS WITH GOD

A LITTLE EXTRA

Watch this video: youtube.com/ watch?v=uRUCV78IULQ. Now consider writing or drawing a picture of God's creative goodness found in the Earth. Honor the Creator by being creative!

Sometimes in our minds God is small and little—and not capable of being the all-powerful and all-consuming God he truly is!

O Lord, our Lord, your majestic name fills the earth! Psalm 8:9

Today's verse gives us a glimpse of his power. God's name alone (not him—just his name) is so powerful that it fills the earth! Every corner of the earth is filled with the name of the Lord.

Get to a window or get outside, if you can. No, seriously, do it!

Look at the sky and the clouds, the sun, or the moon. Look at the mountains, the trees, a flower, the ocean, or the face of another person. God's name is written all over them.

Creation is a reflection of God's power. The beauty and the strength of his creation point to his beauty and his strength.

The power to create it all is God's. The power to hold it all to together is God's. He is not small or little. He is MAJESTIC! (Just a fancy word for impressive beauty and dignity!) And we belong to God—he is also our creator. All praise should go to him and to him alone! (Side note, if creation has his name written all over it, then an act of worship would be to care for it! Just saying!)

TALKING WITH GOD

One of the easiest ways to talk with God is by reading Scripture. We read it with agreement and conviction. Pray all of Psalm 8. Read it aloud and pause after each verse to soak in its powerful truth.

For the word of God is alive and powerful. It is sharper than the sharpest two-edged sword, cutting between soul and spirit, between joint and marrow. It exposes our innermost thoughts and desires. Hebrews 4:12

GOD HEARS & RESTORES

God means business. When you are reading the Bible, you never have to doubt what he is telling you. In order to fully believe in the promises he makes us, we must hear his Word and trust in what he says. If we believe what the Bible says, then we can allow those words to completely penetrate our being. Just as a sword can cut through bone, the Word of God fills us and assesses what is happening in our lives and reveals those thoughts and desires deep inside us. That can be a pretty scary thought, but God is good, and we can trust him.

TALKING WITH GOD

God already knows every thought you have, so ask him to show you the sin in your life that you may not even recognize yet! Read over today's verse a few times, and thank him for his Word that is reliable, dependable, and trustworthy. Thank him for his Word that is sharp enough to expose and heal your sin.

VERSE 351:
Hebrews 4:12

A LITTLE EXTRA

God has given you the Bible to comfort you and help you overcome the sin in your life. Do you have a favorite Bible verse? If not, look through the verses in this book—maybe one will grab your attention. Once you find one, write it on several index cards and put them in places where you'll see them throughout the day. Each time you see one, let it remind you that God is trustworthy and that the Bible is your guidebook to life.

ONENESS
WITH GOD

A LITTLE EXTRA

Whether you are artistic or not, grab some colored pencils and paper, and draw an amazing sky. Once you have drawn your creation, write Psalm 19:1 on your picture and hang it somewhere you can see it regularly. Let it remind you to be in awe and wonder of God's incredible handiwork.

The heavens proclaim the glory of God. The skies display his craftsmanship. Psalm 19:1

When was the last time you went out on a clear night and gazed at the stars? When was the last time you sat and looked intently at the clouds in the daytime? Have you ever looked at the shapes of the clouds and imagined them to be objects or people?

Our sky is filled with incredible and unique images. But it's easy to see the sky every day (or night) and forget the incredible and awesome creation around us, isn't it? It's easy to take the beauty and creation around us for granted.

In a similar way, although God is ever present in our lives, it's easy to lose the awe and wonder of God and all that he means to us. What might your life look like today if you were to see God in a new and brilliant way? All around us, nature and creation are declaring the wonder and glory of God, but we can easily miss it. What are you missing out on today?

TALKING WITH GOD

Go outside and look up to the sky as you pray. Even if it's cloudy or dark, take a few moments to let your eyes adjust. As you pray, look for the detail in what God has made. Thank God for his incredible craftsmanship, for being creative, and for inviting us to be co-creators with him. Then go create something!

But as he came closer to Jerusalem and saw the city ahead, he began to weep. Luke 19:41

CONSEQUENCES & CRYING OUT

What breaks your heart? What stirs your emotions and makes you want to do something—*anything*—to create lasting change?

Our world is filled with heartbreaking realities: modern-day slavery, poverty and malnutrition, AIDS and HIV victims, widows and orphans, violence and injustice, abuse and neglect, the hungry and the homeless, and people who don't know the joy of following Jesus.

In today's verse, Jesus' heart was broken because he knew what the future held for Jerusalem: Just a few decades after Jesus walked through its streets, the city would be conquered and destroyed and its residents would suffer tremendously.

Jesus wept because of the heartache and anguish that would come. Jesus wept because of people who would reject him and his gift of forgiveness. Jesus wept because of injustice, pain, hatred, hurts, and violence.

Do you weep, too?

TALKING WITH GOD

If your heart doesn't break because of all the needs, sins, and problems in our world, ask God to give you his insight and perspective, to see the world with compassionate and Christ-like eyes. If your heart is already broken, ask God for direction on how you can live and reveal his kingdom in a way that leads to changed lives.

VERSE 353:
Luke 19:41

A LITTLE EXTRA

Visit a cemetery (in the daytime, not at night!). As you walk along the rows of tombstones and markers, consider what you want people to remember about you after your life has ended, including the impact you had. Pray for clarity and direction from God on leading a life that makes a difference— here in this lifetime and for all of eternity.

VERSE 354:
John 6:66

A LITTLE EXTRA

With parental permission, watch the video "Entitlement" by Beautiful Eulogy (youtube.com/watch?v=nwmDUSGAb5U). Journal what you believe this video is about. What are some ways today you can hold on to grace?

At this point many of his disciples turned away and deserted him. John 6:66

Have you ever been abandoned? Left alone? Completely isolated? Maybe it wasn't physical; maybe friends or family members emotionally deserted you. In today's passage, Jesus was abandoned—physically and emotionally. The saddest part: Jesus was actually trying to help people when they deserted him. He was teaching some hard truths, but these were truths that would help people lead lives that revealed God's kingdom.

Have you ever turned your back on Jesus? Have you ever found God's truth difficult to accept? Maybe you read something in the Bible you didn't agree with, or God's Spirit revealed a sinful attitude that is holding you back from the life of impact that God has called you to lead.

Please understand that the way of Jesus is always for our good, and when we reject Jesus, we are rejecting real life. At some point, we all turn away and desert Jesus, or we are tempted to make that choice. The bigger question is this: When will we turn back to him?

TALKING WITH GOD

Following Jesus comes down to trust. Do we trust that Jesus is who he says he is? Do we trust that his way is best? Do we trust him in the big and small decisions of life? Ask God to help you trust him today. Confess your doubts and struggles, and ask God to help you never turn away from him again.

Have you complained about anything today? What was the focus of your complaint? Who did you complain to—and why did you choose that person?

Do everything without complaining and arguing.
Philippians 2:14

Complaining just seems to be part of life for a lot of people, doesn't it? We complain about friends, school, and our parents. In the church we complain about how long or short the sermon went, or if the worship area was too hot or too cold. We complain all the time without even noticing that we are complaining.

Today's Scripture is a bold and tough statement to read. We are all guilty of complaining many times daily—complaints about being told to do our chores at home or about the amount of schoolwork our teachers assigned. It can be hard not to complain, yet God is telling us to stop.

We can choose to practice the opposite of complaining, which is joy. Joy is the main theme in the book of Philippians and is mentioned 16 times. Being joyful instead of complaining helps us grow in our faith and helps us realize how blessed we truly are.

TALKING WITH GOD

Pray that God would help you to show joy instead of complaining the next time something does not go your way.

SIN &
SEPARATION

VERSE 355:
Philippians 2:14

A LITTLE EXTRA

Write down things you are tired of complaining about. Identify ways to be joyful in these situations instead of complaining. Ask God to help you to be joyful when you want to complain. Tell a friend that you want to stop complaining. As a way to remind you of today's verse, come up with a code word or phrase (such as "green iguana") that your friend can say when you're complaining.

GOD HEARS & RESTORES

A LITTLE EXTRA

Be an encouragement to someone! Write at least one email or letter to a friend or family member who might need to hear today that they are not alone.

Life is hard. Maybe you have already experienced pain. Or maybe you haven't yet; just know that you will. Pain can come in all shapes and sizes. It doesn't have to be big to feel big and to leave us feeling discouraged and alone.

All praise to God, the Father of our Lord Jesus Christ. God is our merciful Father and the source of all comfort. He comforts us in all our troubles so that we can comfort others. When they are troubled, we will be able to give them the same comfort God has given us. *2 Corinthians 1:3-4*

We are not meant to be alone in our pain and our suffering. Our hearts and souls are designed by a compassionate and caring God who knows exactly what we need to endure all that this life hands us.

God is merciful and comforting. He is with us, always offering us comfort. When we suffer and struggle we can be comforted by his Spirit and by his followers.

It is possible for God to comfort us through the arms and words of other people. Each of our experiences with pain can be a tool of encouragement to others around us who are suffering.

TALKING WITH GOD

If you are in pain, ask God to bring you comfort. Invite his Spirit to fill you with peace and comfort. If you are not currently struggling or suffering, pray for those in your community and in your family who might need God's comfort. Ask God to give you an opportunity to live and reveal his kingdom as you comfort others in their suffering.

The Lord is my light and my salvation—so why should I be afraid? The Lord is my fortress, protecting me from danger, so why should I tremble? Psalm 27:1

What are you afraid of? What worries you the most? If you are like most people, fear and worry have a profoundly negative impact on you.

As kids, most of us are afraid of the dark, aren't we? Even when we get older, that doesn't entirely change, does it? When David wrote this psalm, he was all too aware of the negative impact of the dark world he was living in. The darkness at times consumed him with fear and sometimes caused him to sin. It's not too different for us today, is it? As a teenager, you live in a world full of pressures and struggles. Being accepted by friends, making your grades, making the team—there is a lot of pressure to succeed. There's also a lot of temptation to take the easy road of sin, and it's possible that many times you have fallen hard.

David could have been consumed by his fears and eaten away by his sin, but he knew that only God could bring light into his fears and only God's forgiveness could allow him to be renewed. With a God who gives light and forgiveness in our lives, why should we be afraid?

TALKING WITH GOD

In your mind, list fears and sin that you are struggling with. Spend a few minutes asking God to replace your fears with his truth, and confessing your sins to him. Ask God to help you trust him with your fears.

CONSEQUENCES

& CRYING OUT

VERSE 357:
Psalm 27:1

A LITTLE EXTRA

Tonight when it's dark, grab a flashlight and your Bible, and go into a dark room. Using your flashlight, read Psalm 27 all the way through.

GOD HEARS & RESTORES

VERSE 358:
John 5:24

A LITTLE EXTRA

If the school gave out passing grades from now until graduation, you would tell everyone you know. Have you told anyone about Jesus' offer? Write the words "No Fail" on your school notebook. Every time you see these words on your notebook, tell the nearest person what you read in the Bible today.

"I tell you the truth, those who listen to my message and believe in God who sent me have eternal life. They will never be condemned for their sins, but they have already passed from death into life."
John 5:24

Imagine a noisy classroom filled with lots of distractions. (Not hard to imagine, right?) The principal comes over the school's speaker system and says that if you report to the cafeteria right now, failing grades will be bumped up to passing grades. In fact, you will be extended the opportunity to correct all failing grades from now until you graduate. But students must report to the cafeteria immediately.

You look around, but no one seems to be listening. You desperately try to tell your friends what you just heard, but only two classmates believe you and go to the cafeteria with you.

Jesus' message of forgiveness is available to all who will listen and believe. But it requires action. He asks you to have the faith to accept that what he is saying is true.

TALKING WITH GOD

Jesus has gifts to offer you that only he can give. You have the opportunity to not be condemned for your sins and to receive the promise of life with a future in eternity. Tell Jesus you are listening and you believe in God. Accept his gifts of forgiveness and eternal life. (Turn to page pp. 180-181 for help with what to say to God.)

"I tell you the truth, anyone who believes in me will do the same works I have done, and even greater works, because I am going to be with the Father. You can ask for anything in my name, and I will do it, so that the Son can bring glory to the Father. Yes, ask me for anything in my name, and I will do it!" John 14:12-14

Can this really mean what we think it means? Is Jesus saying we will do the very things he did—and greater?

Jesus came to bring God's kingdom to earth. He invites his followers to be a part of living out his kingdom. When we pursue him and the things that matter in the kingdom of heaven, we do find that great works are happening! And as we live out God's kingdom, we begin to reveal it to others. That's great stuff!

So what does kingdom living include? Caring for the poor and outcast. Healing the hearts of the broken. Sharing the good news with those who have no hope. (See p. 271 for more ideas.)

Lives are being transformed. Hearts are being healed. The spiritually sick are finding healing. The kingdom of heaven is growing. And God invites you to be a part of it!

VERSE 359:
John 14:12-14

A LITTLE EXTRA

Start a prayer journal—or use one you already have. Write down a list of people who need help and a list of your prayer requests. When a prayer gets answered, write down the date and how the prayer was answered. You'll find that Jesus was right—great things are happening through and in us!

TALKING WITH GOD

Read and speak this prayer: *Jesus, I want to be a part of your kingdom and the continuation of your kingdom on earth. Use me to live and reveal your kingdom in great and mighty ways.*

GOD HEARS & RESTORES

A LITTLE EXTRA

Make a list of the top 10 things you want. Then create a list of your top 10 needs. Compare the differences. Would you trade to get everything on your "want" list if it meant you would never have anything on your "need" list? What about the other way? Ask Jesus to help you learn the difference between your wants and needs. Ask Jesus to help you learn to trust him to give you what he knows you need.

"What do you want me to do for you?" Jesus asked. "My rabbi," the blind man said, "I want to see!" And Jesus said to him, "Go, for your faith has healed you." Instantly the man could see, and he followed Jesus down the road. Mark 10:51-52

Jesus was a master at asking good questions. But sometimes he asked some really odd questions. How else would you describe asking a blind man what he wanted? What else would a blind man want? C'mon Jesus, isn't it obvious?

Unless Jesus knew there was something powerful in the man speaking his request. Or Jesus knew there was something powerful in the crowd hearing the exchange. Or Jesus knew there was something powerful going on in the man that a conversation could begin to uncover.

What do you need Jesus' help uncovering in your life today? What will you answer when Jesus asks what you want? What will Jesus say about your faith in response?

TALKING WITH GOD

Pray this kind of prayer: *Jesus, thank you for asking me what I want you to do for me. I could give you lots of answers, but I'm not sure what I want is what I need. Please help me trust you enough to give me what I need, not what I want.*

"Who is like you among the gods, O Lord— glorious in holiness, awesome in splendor, performing great wonders?...With your unfailing love you lead the people you have redeemed. In your might, you guide them to your sacred home." Exodus 15:11, 13

Close your eyes and think about something amazing God has done for you. If nothing immediately comes to mind, just think about your birth. Have you ever thought about how every blood vessel, every hair on your head, ever freckle was put in place by him? Does that make you even a little in awe of who God is?

That is exactly what happened to Moses and his sister Miriam. After the nation of Israel left slavery in Egypt, God provided an amazing miracle of protection and deliverance. Moses was so thankful he immediately burst into song.

Sometimes we look at God and understand we must honor him. Other times it is not as obvious. Many times we make a choice to be in awe of God. Read the verse again. Are there more "great wonders" you can recall that God has done for you?

TALKING WITH GOD

Today take a moment to talk with God a little differently. Take a moment and find a favorite song that makes you think about God, and just sing along. If you can't find a song that will work well, take a look at the video for "I Wonder" by the band Leeland (youtube.com/watch?v=y_45BTOcLuE). Think about the words and sing them to God.

VERSE 361:
Exodus 15:11, 13

A LITTLE EXTRA

Think of some ways you're in awe of who God is. Try writing the Lord a song, poem, or letter. To get you started, read the whole song that Moses and Miriam wrote in Exodus 15:1-20. (If you want to see the full reason why they wrote it, also read Exodus 14.)

ONENESS WITH GOD

Jesus entered the Temple and began to drive out all the people buying and selling animals for sacrifice. He knocked over the tables of the money changers and the chairs of those selling doves. He said to them, "The Scriptures declare, 'My Temple will be called a house of prayer,' but you have turned it into a den of thieves!" Matthew 21:12-13

VERSE 362:
Matthew 21:12-13

A LITTLE EXTRA

Evaluate your interests. Is there anything on there that would make Jesus angry because it diminishes God's glory? What about in your favorite music? The game you play the most? How about the conversations you have when it's just you and your buddies? What about the pictures you look at? Would Jesus be turning over tables in your temple?

Have you ever been so angry that you just wanted to break things? Jesus felt that way, too. Does it surprise you that Jesus could be this angry? Take a look back over these verses and see what made him so angry.

When you get angry enough to slam doors and throw things, is it because God is not getting the honor he deserves? Do you get angry because God is dishonored at school, on TV, on the Internet? Does it even get a reaction from you when you see something that is very obviously meant to be an insult to God and his followers?

It's easy to become desensitized to the dishonoring of God. Just like in Jesus' day, we walk through our culture and don't even notice how cluttered with distractions and irreverence our world has become.

TALKING WITH GOD

Pray that God would make you sensitive to the things that anger and dishonor him. Ask God to show you the best way to honor him while the world devalues the things he loves.

Jesus and his disciples were talking about the "End Times", and it was pretty scary stuff. Jesus described war and earthquakes and famine and persecution and other bad news. But in the midst of the destruction of the End Times, Jesus said that his followers would have an opportunity to share their faith.

"For the Good News must first be preached to all nations." Mark 13:10

People hold different views and interpretations of the End Times, but what people do agree on is that Jesus' followers telling their God-story is an important part of those times. Are you ready to share your story of trust in Jesus? Your story may be dramatic, or it may seem ordinary. But God can use your story to draw others to faith in Christ. Simply be willing to share and tell people what God has done in your life.

TALKING WITH GOD

Consider praying a prayer such as this: *Jesus, I don't understand everything about the End Times, but I do understand that you want me to tell everyone I know about your love for them. Help me not get distracted by discussions or debates. Instead, help me stay focused on living and revealing your kingdom. I trust that you will take care of everything else.*

GOD HEARS & RESTORES

VERSE 363:
Mark 13:10

A LITTLE EXTRA

Make a list of 10 people you know you will see today. If you're not sure about their relationship with Jesus, draw a small cross next to that person's name. Ask God to give you an opportunity to talk with at least one of them about your trust in Jesus. And when the time comes, trust God enough to tell your story.

SIN &
SEPARATION

Then Jesus wept. John 11:35

Today's passage is the shortest verse in the Bible, and it's probably the favorite verse for kids to memorize in Sunday school. But don't let its length fool you: The amount of power these few words carry is much more than meets the eye.

Jesus had just witnessed the death of his dear friend Lazarus, and after seeing the pain in the eyes of Lazarus' sisters, Mary and Martha, Jesus wept alongside them. After seeing his reaction to the death of a loved one, Jesus becomes more of our friend. Rather than being the strong, powerful Jesus we always picture, he humbles himself, reveals his humanity, and proves that he could, in fact, be both fully human and fully God. As a good friend would, Jesus shared in the pain of those he loved.

TALKING WITH GOD

Instead of expecting Jesus to know and understand what you are going through, take some time to talk to him as if he were your best friend, sitting in your room with you. Share everything with him. Even though he already knows what is going on in your life, open up to him as you would any of your friends, because he truly can feel your pain and understand your human emotions as if he were going through your problems himself.

A LITTLE EXTRA

Before you go to sleep tonight, write a letter to Jesus as if you were writing a letter to your best friend. Tell him all about your day: who you ate lunch with, what you learned at school, anything! It is important that we see Jesus as our friend, someone who wants to be there for us through everything! Thank him for being someone who you know will always understand you.

The most emotional times when the church gathers, for many people, is when teenagers and adults get baptized. As they watch, they can barely hear the pastor whisper to the follower of Jesus these words: "buried with Christ and raised to walk in new life." Seriously, it gets them every time!

Those powerful words (or similar ideas) are used in many churches, and they come straight from Romans 6:

Since we have been united with him in his death, we will also be raised to life as he was. Romans 6:5

Baptism is an outward symbol of an inward commitment. Christ's death makes this commitment possible. We have been united with Christ by death. His death allowed us to die to our old life and ways.

But he didn't stay dead. Jesus rose again. In the same way, we are given a new life now—and later. You see, physical death is no longer the end for us because with Christ we will live forever.

Following Jesus is both about death and life. We experience both of those just like Jesus experienced both of them thousands of years ago.

Buried with Christ and raised to walk in new life! Amen!

TALKING WITH GOD

Take a minute to reflect on the death and resurrection of Jesus. Take 60 seconds to express your gratefulness. Then take another 60 seconds to commit or recommit to dying to your own desires and embracing new life with Jesus.

GOD HEARS & RESTORES

VERSE 365:
Romans 6:5

A LITTLE EXTRA

Check out 2 Corinthians 4:10 and Philippians 3:10-11. Reflect on what these verses say about Jesus' death and resurrection. The next time you see a baptism when your church gathers, consider the life-changing significance of that event.

GOD HEARS & RESTORES

Then Jesus shouted, "Lazarus, come out!"
John 11:43

In today's passage, Jesus is showing his power by bringing a man named Lazarus back to life. Lazarus and his sisters, Mary and Martha, were three of Jesus' closest friends. They were faithful followers, and Jesus often stayed in their home when he visited Bethany. Read John 11:1-44 to get the full story.

Most of Jesus' miracles were about fixing something that was broken. Every miracle was done to show life the way God wants it and to demonstrate that Jesus has the power and authority to do whatever he wants.

What is broken in your life? Do some parts of your spiritual life feel dead? Where do you need Jesus to show his power? Jesus wants to breathe life into the empty spaces of your life and point you in the right direction. Are you ready?

TALKING WITH GOD

Pray this kind of prayer: *Lord, my life feels broken, and I need you to fix it. Sometimes I get so distracted by my problems that I forget that your plan for my life is amazing. Help me see the life you want me to live. Help me trust you to live a life that reveals your kingdom to those around me.*

A LITTLE EXTRA

Find a seed to carry around today—an acorn, an orange seed, whatever. Put it in your pocket, and every time you see it, think about today's passage. Remember that a seed falls to the ground to die, but with the right environment, it grows into something amazing. Ask God to turn the dead things in your life into something amazing today.

strength one of capabili
if you
too high for
the other

strength
ing the resista
ing out of control
eds—isn't an effective way to t
either. Discovering the balance b
too much and too little resistan
to some experimentation. "A g
thumb is that if you are using
stance your muscles shoul
ed but not straining to com
's says Harris.

MEMBER TO...

One of the el
over other equipme
backward. Stride forv
your hip flexors and
ckward and you
hamstrings. "W
groups not only
enly but
says Harris.

distinguish

INDEX OF VERSES BY THEME

INDEX OF VERSES BY THEME

INDEX OF VERSES BY THEME

INDEX OF
VERSES
BY THEME

KURT JOHNSTON has been in youth ministry since 1988 and currently leads the student ministry team at Saddleback Church in Orange County, California. His ministry of choice is the junior high department, where he tries to spend approximately 87.4% of his time. Kurt and his wife, Rachel, have been married for a long time and have two teenage children, Kayla and Cole.

GREG STIER is president of Dare 2 Share (D2S) and has impacted the lives of hundreds of thousands of teenagers across the United States through D2S evangelism training conferences. Dare 2 Share's mission is to mobilize teenagers to relationally and relentlessly reach their generation for Christ. Greg has written numerous books to help teens share their faith, including *Firestarter*, *Venti Jesus Please*, and *Dare 2 Share: A Field Guide to Sharing Your Faith*. He lives in Arvada, Colorado, with his wife, Debbie, and children, Jeremy and Kailey.

TIM LEVERT has been following Jesus for 25 years, and he's still a major doofus. He's been working with students for 20 years, hoping they learn a little from him, because he learns a TON from them. Tim's life goal is to live and reveal God's kingdom in every part of his life

TASHA LEVERT has worked with youth and college students for over 20 years. She has three amazing daughters, a lazy schnauzer, and she's married to Tim, the hottest youth pastor on the planet.

ELLE LEVERT is a junior high student who enjoys singing, acting, writing, and hanging out with her family and friends. She loves Jesus, is strong in her faith, and hopes everyone she knows will grow to love Jesus, too.

MARK OESTREICHER (Marko) is a veteran youth worker and founding partner in The Youth Cartel, providing resources, training, and coaching for church youth workers. The author of dozens of books, including *Youth Ministry 3.0*, Marko is a sought-after speaker, writer, and consultant. Marko lives in San Diego with his wife, Jeannie, and teenage children, Liesl and Max. Marko's blog: whyismarko.com.

JOHNNY SCOTT has been working in student ministry for over 15 years. From 2001 to 2012, programing the Jr High Believe Tour (a Christ In Youth event) was his main gig. Johnny, his wife, Jen, and their three boys have recently moved back into local ministry in Orlando, Florida, at Harvest Bible Chapel of Orlando.

CHASE ALLCOTT currently serves as program director for Christ In Youth's Move event, a five-day experience designed to help mobilize and equip students for kingdom impact. Chase loves to cheer on the Chicago Cubs and Auburn Tigers from his home in Webb City, Missouri.

JOHN LUZADDER works as the senior director of high school events for Christ In Youth. Since graduating from Lincoln Christian University, John has served 15 years in youth ministries in Illinois and New Hampshire. His passion is to see students meet Jesus and live life following him to the fullest. John and his wife, Michelle, spend their free time playing Legos or Star Wars or any combination of the two with their three sons, Atticus, Silas, and Zeke.

TOBY ROWE has served in junior and senior high ministry since 1990 and has helped lead more than 30 missions experiences throughout the U.S. and Canada. Currently, Toby works for Group Publishing where he oversees the spiritual content and programming of mission trips.

CONTRIBUTORS

MATTY McCAGE convinced Joyce to marry him and a church to hire him. Matty has spent nearly 20 years in youth ministry, teaching the proper wedgie technique and regularly pontificating on MinistryRamblings.com. He and Joyce are living happily ever after with their three offspring: Aeden, Warren, and Emmalicious.

VERONICA PRESTON loves Jesus, design, and coffee. She is an art director for Group and Simply Youth Ministry and has spent several years serving in youth adult ministries and small groups. Her native state is Colorado, where she lives with her handsome husband, Matt Preston, and their super sweet Great Danes, Fletcher and Finley. Follow her on Instagram @veronicalea.

JEFF STORM is the art director for Group Magazine and Unfiltered Magazine. He is also the author of *Stripped Clean: Down to Nothing but the Cross*. Follow him on twitter @zafdaddy.

ROB CUNNINGHAM is the youth ministry editor for Group Publishing and Simply Youth Ministry. A former staff pastor and newspaper editor, he's the kind of guy who notices typos in business signs, bizarre grammar from anchors during the evening news, and poor word choices in song lyrics. Remarkably, he still has friends. Rob and his amazing wife, Trista, live near Denver, Colorado.

PHIL BELL is a youth pastor, writer, and blogger (youthworktalk.com). He is originally from England and now lives in Michigan, where he has been ministering to students and their families since 2000. Phil is passionate about helping students own their faith for the long haul and is deeply committed to leadership development of youth workers in the local church.

JANNA FIRESTONE lives in Colorado with her husband and two energetic boys. She's contributed to numerous books for women in the church, speaks to women's groups across the country, and leads a small group of teen girls in her home church. She's an unapologetic Dallas Cowboys fan, and an even bigger fan of coffee.

SCOTT FIRESTONE IV is an editor for Group Magazine and youthministry.com. He's the author of the book *10-Minute Moments: Parables*, and leads a small group of teenage guys at his church. He and his wife, Janna, live in Colorado with their two sons.

DARREN SUTTON has served in youth ministry for over 20 years. He has a passion for students and the adults who influence them. Darren and his wife, Katie, co-founded Millennial Influence and produce a weekly podcast reaching parents of teenagers. They currently serve a student ministry in Corpus Christi, Texas. Darren is the paid staff youth pastor—Katie is the unpaid, unsung hero of the ministry!

KATIE SUTTON has loved ministering to teenagers and their families for over 20 years. Katie and her husband, Darren, host MiPodcast for parents of teenagers, and she writes a weekly blog for ministry spouses, Glass House Spouse. She also is a contributing author for several books in the Everyday Youth Ministry series and has contributed to youth Bible study curriculum for Lifeway.

JEFFREY WALLACE is the president and CEO of Front Line Urban Resources, Inc, which focuses on training and mentoring other urban youth pastors and leaders and providing life-changing youth ministry resources, and founder of Simply Urban Ministry. He also serves as pastor of youth development at Peace Baptist Church in Decatur, Georgia.

LENEITA FIX recently celebrated her 20th year in ministry. Her passion is multiplying ALL youth workers (full time, paid, unpaid, volunteer, or bivocational) by aiding them to become better trained and equipped. She is honored to be a part of a family that ministers together, with her husband, John, a niece, and three beautiful children.

JOHN FIX is currently the COO for Aslan Youth Ministries in Red Bank, New Jersey. He has been in the youth ministry field for almost two decades, working with both suburban and urban youth. John has three children and a niece at home. He is passionate about Jesus, spending time with his family, running, the great outdoors, and serving in ministry with his beautiful bride of almost 15 years.

KAYLA JOHNSTON is the daughter of a youth pastor...and she lived through the experience! She's a student at Azusa Pacific University in Southern California. When she's not in class, Kayla enjoys reading and taking naps. She also likes to camp with her family and go to Disneyland with her friends.

NEELY MCQUEEN is married to a surfer/pastor and is the mom of three super cool and cute kids. She's been spending her extra time with teenage girls for the past 15 years—at the mall and at church. She thinks they are super fun and, even more, have what it takes to make a huge impact for change in the world.

DUSTIN ICHIDA loves Jesus and students. He is the youth ministry coordinator at his church, and his passion is to show students how cool it is to trust Jesus.

ERIC HENDRICKSON has served in youth ministry since 1997 in the United Methodist Church. Eric graduated from the University of South Carolina with an undergraduate degree in political science and received a master's degree from Pfeiffer University and Wesley Seminary in Christian education with an emphasis in youth ministry. Eric is married to his wife, Jessica. They have two children, Mallory and Hayes.

GREG WILMER has been working with youth for over 20 years. He desires youth to know who Christ is and what he has done for them. Greg and wife, Cindi, have been married for 20 years and have two children of their own. Greg is president and CEO of JumpMind Inc., a software and services company based in Columbus, Ohio.

JOSHUA DORSETT is a fully devoted follower of Jesus Christ. He will be attending Ohio Christian University in the fall of 2013 and majoring in youth ministry. He lives in Reynoldsburg, Ohio, and spreads the gospel to whoever will hear it. He plans to become a youth pastor and spend the rest of his life spreading God's Word to everyone he meets.

JOYANNA THOMPSON has one purpose in life: to glorify God. She is currently studying early childhood education, while also serving as a children's ministry intern at her church. Her life's desire is for everyone to know how much Jesus loves them.

CHRISTINA HESS is a senior, class of 2013, at Reynoldsburg High School in Columbus, Ohio. She has been a Christ-follower since 2009 and plans to go into social work once she graduates from high school.

JEREMY LEE has been a youth worker for 20 years and loves to create cool websites that help parents of teenagers and youth ministers. He helps parents at parentzilla.com, youth ministers at parentministry.net, and middle school ministers at uthmin.net. Jeremy lives in Nashville, Tennessee because if this website thing doesn't work out he is going to be the next Garth Brooks.